Diplomacy, War, and Technology since 1830

MAURICE PEARTON

STUDIES IN
GOVERNMENT AND PUBLIC POLICY

UNIVERSITY PRESS OF KANSAS

For Erhard Tamchina
'. . . und leider auch Strategie'

Published by the University Press of Kansas (Lawrence, Kansas 66045),
which was organized by the Kansas Board of Regents and is operated
and funded by Emporia State University, Fort Hays State University,
Kansas State University, Pittsburg State University, the University
of Kansas, and Wichita State University

Library of Congress Cataloging in Publication Data

Pearton, Maurice.
    Diplomacy, war, and technology since 1830.
    (Studies in government and public policy)
    Reprint. Originally published: The knowledgeable state. London: Burnett
Books: Distributed by Hutchinson, 1982.
    Bibliography: p.
    Includes index.
    1. Military art and science – Europe – History – 19th century. 2. Munitions –
Europe – History – 19th century. 3. Civil-military relations – Europe – History
– 19th century. 4. Europe – History, Military – 19th century. 5. Europe –
Politics and government – 1789-1900. 6. Military art and science – Europe –
History – 20th century. 7. Munitions – Europe – History – 20th century.
8. Civil-military relations – Europe – History – 20th century. 9. Europe –
History, Military – 20th century. 10. Europe – Politics and government –
20th century. I. Title. II. Series.
U43.E95P43   1984   355'.02'094   84-7272
ISBN 0-7006-0254-2 (pbk.)

Printed in the United States of America
10 9 8 7 6 5 4 3 2

Contents

Acknowledgments

This book owes much to my brother, Colin Pearton, and to Daniel Snowman and Philip Windsor, all of whom read the manuscript and made valuable suggestions. It has also considerably benefitted from discussions on particular aspects of its theme with John Bailey, Corelli Barnett, Neil Cockett, the late Stanley Edmund, Richard Gandy and Iain Hamilton. I am indebted to Susan Madden and Helen Powell and to the Bundeswehrarchiv, Düsseldorf for assistance with materials, and to Hilde von Fehlerlesen for her acute comments on presentation.

The book, like the subject it explores, relies on 'what lay to hand' and in respect of the necessary source materials for the argument, I wish to record my gratitude to the archivists and librarians of the following collections for their unfailing and courteous assistance: the Contemporary Scientific Archives Centre, Oxford; Churchill College Archives Centre, Cambridge; the John Rylands Library, Manchester; and in London, the Goethe Institute; the Imperial War Museum; The International Institute for Strategic Studies; The Royal Institute of International Affairs; The Institution of Mechanical Engineers; the Naval Historical Library and the Whitehall Library, both of the Ministry of Defence; the University of London and the London Borough of Sutton.

Finally, I wish to thank Mrs Kay Vincent for typing the original manuscript and Mrs Muriel Hand for tackling the subsequent amendments.

The responsibility for the selection of the materials and the treatment of the topics is entirely my own.

Maurice Pearton

Preface to the Paperback Edition

The appearance of a North American edition of this work has given me the opportunity to make minor corrections to the text – matters of focus rather than of fact – and to add new prefatory material making explicit the particular use of 'the military-industrial complex' in the argument.

Since President Eisenhower, or his speechwriter Dr. Malcom Moos, launched the phrase on its career in January 1961, it has done duty both as description and as explanation, and in both forms is held to be universally applicable. It conveys the notion that the armed forces and their industrial suppliers commit the state to policies determined by their own sectional interests. In this the 'complex' itself is held to be a network of alliances between officers, politicians and business interests, and the dependents of all three. The phenomenon is identified in terms of institutions.

Clearly, if a society wishes to maintain armed forces equipped with advanced weapons, there has to be, in the nature of things, some close relationship between the military, organised science and industry. Inspection of existing relationships shows that 'complex', far from being merely institutional, extends to two kinds of complexity, which are in practice related; the first is the complexity of the task of producing advanced weapons (or indeed any advanced technology); the second is the complexity of the relationships required to initiate and manage such tasks. This remains the case irrespective of the political order in which the tasks are being attempted, and it is in that sense that the phenomenon may be considered universal. The problems resulting from these complexities, whatever they may be, can only be avoided by staying out of the business. However, what precisely the problems are and the forms they take depends upon the political culture in which they are experienced. They work out differently in different societies; and at that point, 'the military-industrial complex' as a universal explanatory concept disintegrates.

The concept is sometimes expanded to include all those who have an interest in production for defence, but in practice the crucial relationship is that between the bureaucracy and industry. That itself is an amalgam of assumptions, received ideas and practices, and the structures to which they are related. In this respect, states differ, but certain broad distinctions can be drawn from the way their political cultures have developed.

7

In Europe, the state was securely entrenched before industrialisation took place; accordingly its consent had to be sought before private initiatives could be taken because the state was the guarantor of internal order and external security. Official policy was articulated through the bureaucracy, which in ethos if not practice was mandarin; capitalist enterprise was subjected to a running critique from the beginning. In our own day these characteristics have been reinforced by putting sections of the economy under state control and management and introducing planning systems which either direct or set guidelines for private corporate business.

This has not been the experience of the United States. Since, say, the 1840s, there has been only one power in the Western Hemisphere. America, therefore, during its period of industrialisation was not seriously bothered by questions of fundamental security and could devote itself to one question of public policy; namely, the terms on which the cornucopia of America's resources could be opened up. Uniquely in modern experience, business has become central to the culture. The United States has evolved procedures and practices which are not duplicated anywhere else. The institutional framework within which power is broken down; the relative ineffectiveness of the bureaucracy as the regulator; the social approval and political necessity of 'pork barrelling'; the timidity of legislators in relation to their constituents are all, either individually in degree or in their totality as a political culture without parallel in any other country in the world. These characteristics represent a particular way of doing things, buttressed by a particular structure of values, which Americans show no desire, overall, to change. They make the United States, as state and as society, *sui generis*.

Now 'the military-industrial complex' was minted in the United States and at a time when rising and apparently unrestrainable expenditures for military purposes were the main element in upsetting a balanced budget. They were taken as evidence of the 'disastrous rise of misplaced power' and as such an aberration, blurring distinctions which necessarily had to be maintained for the health of the body politic. Hence the note of alarm sounded by President Eisenhower.

But the distinctions which were being blurred were specifically those of *the United States*, which has its own particular ways of registering authority and accountability: they either are not shared by any other polity or are worked out through a different pattern of relationships. Thus, the 'military-industrial complex' as a phenomenon is the result of devising military products requiring basic theoretical research and advanced technology in a polity with the values and practices of the United States. The term fails to explain with any degree of precision what takes place elsewhere, where values and practices differ. Hence, as stated in the Preface, the United States rounds off the argument of the book: in an account beginning in 1945 it would, of course, be central.

This points to a second ground for the late introduction of the concept. The account given here demonstrates the coming together of knowledge (construed either as pure or applied science, or as industrial networks, or as the content of education) on the one hand, and the traditional power of the state for war or peace on the other. Historically, these two elements have been separate and remained so, though with diminishing force, till the middle of this century. In the beginning, the only interest of the state, represented by officers of the army or navy, was in performance; then the state moved to concern itself in the kind of industrial development and configuration which could secure that performance; it then found itself underwriting the enterprises, either by profit guarantees, subsidies and bounties, or tariffs and similar traditional instruments. As long as these conditions obtained, the relationship could be, basically, at 'arm's length'. But as soon as the state found itself having to interest itself in the process to the extent of financing research into unknowns in order to arrive at results which might conceivably be of use in designing a weapons system – and all that in peacetime – then the 'arm' disappeared and 'complex' became the appropriate term. It is not, simply, descriptive of the arrangements governments have made with manufacture over the centuries to procure weapons: it is the end result of a process analysed in this book, and for that reason properly appears in its concluding pages. It follows that attempts to use 'the military-industrial complex' to account for what took place before our own day, in, eg, the France of Louis XIV, or even Prussia in the nineteenth century may be a convenient verbal shorthand but are, strictly, anachronistic and misleading.

The argument itself, however, remains; it is designed to show the relationships which, in the industrial age, have developed between knowledge – construed as theoretical science, industrial systems and the content of education – and action, that is, the foreign and military policies of the state. This development has proceeded in response to immediate needs, but the successive applications of knowledge for short-term ends have, in the longer perspective, induced us to revise the conceptual framework within which 'war' and 'peace' are analysed and justified.

I am grateful to Russell Weigley for his comment.

Preface

The traditional view of peace and war holds that irrespective of how they may be defined and justified, they represent opposite poles of experience. The transition from one to the other, though often readily accomplished, nevertheless entails going through some basic change, signalled by some kind of ritual, if only by making a proclamation or banging a drum. By the nineteenth century, the notion that 'peace' was 'peace' and 'war' was 'war' hardened into an accepted doctrine of international political behaviour, with the rider that 'peace' was the norm, from which 'war' was a departure. Politics and diplomacy rested on the assumption that war, though the antithesis of peace, was a dread, but legitimate and honourable, option open to governments in the settling of differences which diplomacy had failed to resolve. In our own day, however, the polarity of 'peace' and 'war' has ceased to be axiomatic. Preparedness for war is no longer a matter of keeping barracks manned and powder dry. It is a continuous activity, reaching into all aspects of society and eroding, even nullifying, conventional distinctions about the 'civil' and the 'military' spheres of life. The reasons are mainly to be found in men's response to the opportunities offered by technology in the industrial age.

Technology has enlarged the options open to policy-makers in their pursuit of the aims of the state, either 'offensive' or 'defensive' (another pair of terms which in practice are far from opposed). It has also made the problems and costs of choosing more onerous. But technology has not been applied once-and-for-all: the process has been continuous, gathering momentum and complexity with the passage of time, and has come to affect the choice of aims. Military high commands and diplomats found they could transcend the restrictions on the exercise of power which nature and custom had imposed. Systematic recourse to technology ensured – when men realised it – that the traditional structures of power could be permanently altered; a rival could not merely be held in check but could be eliminated from the international competition. Makers of policy, therefore, could, if they wished, aim at decisive, 'ultimate' victory. Reasoning based on these expectations, and the practice which followed, upset the European order which for centuries had assumed that the ultimate was not desirable. Even the Napoleonic flood had receded, leaving intact the powers whose interactions constituted European diplomacy. A century later the disappearance of Tsarist Russia, Imperial Germany, Austria–Hungary and the Ottoman Empire represented (among other factors) technological failures. Their rulers found that the obverse of total victory was total defeat. Policies intimately related to complex technologies were harder to stop.

The possibility of totally realising political aims has also affected the framework of ideas within which war is regarded as legitimate. The traditional view was that war was an awful arbitrament, to be enterprised only under God and as the last resort in a just cause. During this century, we have seen emerge ideologies which suggest that war, so far from being an aberration, is the necessary state of man until some fundamental transformation of society allows peace to begin. 'Peace' and 'war' are opposites only on an epochal scale, revealed in the processes of History. Until their culmination – and as the necessary means of bringing it about – war is not only necessary but laudable. Killing, so far from being morally regrettable even when accepted as necessary, is commended as therapeutic for society and for the individual, and neutrality, defined as a recognised right to stay out of the conflict, is inadmissible. The operative categories are no longer 'combatant' and 'neutral' (which can be defined with some objectivity) but 'guilty' and 'innocent' (which, in politics, cannot). On this view, terrorists, who from the standpoint of tradition are, at best, licensed psychopaths, become 'freedom fighters', justified because war is natural and inevitable, and, pending the ultimate metamorphosis of society, permanent.

The origins and consequences of this fundamental change in attitude have been analysed elsewhere: what has been less discussed is the transformation of the concepts of 'peace' and 'war' in societies which would regard themselves as adhering to the traditional distinctions and as being currently in a state of peace. This book attempts to sketch how this transformation has come about, by propounding an argument in Part I on evidence which is elaborated in the rest of the book. The cases in point are selected largely from Western Europe, since industrialisation originated in that area within a political system of sovereign states for the rulers of which foreign policy was paramount. Western Europe is therefore a convenient matrix in which to examine the interaction between the authority of the state, as expressed in its foreign policy and military objectives, and the characteristics and requirements of science-based industry. We can then define and demonstrate the difference industrialisation has made to our ideas of war and peace, and to show how that difference has affected the making and carrying out of policy. In short, this essay explores relationships between certain kinds of knowledge and certain modes of action. It seeks to show how changes in these relationships over time have brought us to the point at which the ability of states to contemplate a particular mode of action – advanced war – depends on the prior ability systematically to explore and exploit particular theories in the natural sciences; states which cannot consciously create and use that dependence have to take their cue in world politics from those which can. The cases relied upon are intended only to exemplify this theme; they are not intended to constitute a history of technology or of the mechanisation of war or of the impact of war on society – all of which are covered in the specialist literature.

The text proceeds within other formal limits. It assumes that war is a form of behaviour between states, or alternately, that the state is the recognised war-making agency. On this view, the more states, the greater the possibility of war, at least in theory. Further, guerilla warfare implies operations either augmenting those of regular forces or as an alternative to them, as in Spain where the term was originally coined. Much of our contemporary guerilla warfare should be differentiated as guerilla violence since it proceeds from the unilateral decisions of individuals to take up arms to rectify grievances, real or imaginary. In this essay, however, war connotes the application of force – that is of violent action in some way formally legitimated. Recent debates in Geneva on the treatment of guerillas testify to the continuing demand for legitimacy, even at the cost of fudging the distinction between a soldier and a murderer.[1]*

'Diplomacy' is, likewise, considered in a particular sense, namely as the continuous attempt to define and settle the problems arising between states by rational negotiation within agreed rules. It therefore aims at creating and sustaining confidence and resorts to compromise. I am aware that there have been and are currently used other modes of conducting business between states, with other aims and methods, and that even within the definition adopted here, widely differing practices are followed – in particular the traditional British reluctance to assume anything like a specific commitment defined under a general principle, in contrast to the French preference, amounting at times to a passion, for precise statements translating a general principle into specific guarantees of future action. These practical preferences notwithstanding, the overall concept that diplomacy rested on rational negotiation in an atmosphere of confidence was accepted by the governments of the industrialising states with which this argument is concerned.

'Industrialisation' is used to mean both a condition and a process. In either case, it connotes the displacement of 'an agrarian, handicraft economy' in favour of one 'dominated by industry and machine manufacture', through technological innovations, as analysed by David Landes in *The Unbound Prometheus.*[2] It stems from the Industrial Revolution, regarded as a phenomenon beginning in the late eighteenth-century. Again, I am aware that other definitions exist, and that economic historians have challenged, antedated or subdivided the concept of 'industrial revolution' in the course

---

*References identified by numbers are listed on page 259ff.

of their professional inquiries. But it seems to me that, irrespective of the intellectual credentials of the various schools of thought, the systematic and ultimately science-based production of capital goods of an increasing range and sophistication – which is the core of Landes' study – created problems for the foreign and military policy of states which were either new in themselves or were on such a scale as to invalidate any precedents.

As for 'science' itself, it is ordinarily taken to mean 'natural science', unless otherwise indicated, and is considered as the coherent body of knowledge resulting from the attempt to understand Nature through the method of controlled experiment. 'Technology' is rather more elusive with customary definitions ranging from the ability to use tools to the organisation of social groups for practical ends. It is regarded here as comprising the knowledge and skills, including those derived from habits of work, which are devoted to producing a practical result. Today, the kernel of technology is engineering.

In adopting these usages, I am aware that they beg many questions which agitate historians and philosophers of science, and that there are areas of research in which it is difficult to determine which is science and which technology, but for this study, the difference is assumed to lie mainly in the need to be met: science provides explanations which may be purely theoretical, technology offers its 'explanations' in the form of artefacts, or in relation to their use.

The United States, although now virtually synonymous with science and technology, is not central to the discussion since in comparison with Europe, it was isolated enough during the period of its industrialisation, virtually to be able to dispense with foreign policy. One consequence (still to be detected) was an ingrained tendency to regard the problems of foreign relations as sudden developments – usually unwelcome – which, however, could be 'fixed' by an appropriate and quick reaction. From the presidency of Andrew Jackson until after the Second World War American opinion rejected the traditional European notion that foreign policy was a matter of continuous engagement with other powers in order to defend the international interests of the state and that its essential aim was to reach accommodation through rational argument. The objectives and practices of diplomacy were damned as either Machiavellian or trivial. The crusading element in American policy-making requires that *conflicts* are *won*, not that *differences* are *accommodated*; exercises in game theory replace rational negotiation.

The United States only began to put its foreign service on a professional footing in 1924 and on the requisite scale only in 1947, but even so the 'European' theory which the professionals espoused was (and still is) regularly challenged by individual presidents and by Congress. When President Truman wrote Charles Thayer, one of the most eminent of American professionals, 'Protocol and striped pants give me a pain in the neck' he was expressing a popular, not to say populist, attitude towards diplomacy which is politically effective in the United States. The prevalence of such attitudes, and the duplications built into the American system of government ensure that Foggy Bottom does not have the public esteem and support which, say, the Quai d'Orsay has in France.

Thus, for much of the industrialised era, American developments do not raise the same questions as do those in Europe. After the Manhattan Project and the Korean War, the roles have been reversed: the United States has become the paradigm in terms of which relationships between foreign and military policy and the direction of science-based industry are discussed. The norms and axioms of the discussion are different and have shifted the focus of the debate, which even in Europe tends to use an American vocabulary. But in historical terms, America rounds off the argument outlined here; it is not intrinsic to it. However, the United States and the advanced industrial states of Western Europe do share one particular problem of policy, since they are democracies in which the public adheres to the traditional way of thinking that 'war' is 'war' and 'peace' is 'peace', while the experts responsible for defence policy and military preparedness know that the traditional dichotomy no longer obtains. 'War' and 'peace' are no longer opposites but correlatives. Why this is so, and how the present nexus between the two came to be established, this essay aims to show.

PART I

'Fighting is done with machines
such as were never envisaged by
pagan ferocity or barbarism.'
Erasmus

1. Technique and the redefinition of categories

What moves men to war with one another, and the circumstances under which it is legitimate for them to do so, are questions which have an established place in the European intellectual tradition. Until recently the *techniques* of warfare have been less widely discussed, except when the introduction of a new weapon has temporarily shocked the victims into protest, as happened with the use of massed archers in the fifteenth century and of poison gas in the twentieth. As a form of human behaviour, warfare has relied, traditionally, on the means which were to hand. In consequence, the distinctions between 'war' and 'peace', between the military and civil order of society, which have occupied philosophers, theologians, lawyers, diplomats and statesmen throughout the centuries, have found no parallel in the technology of war. Swords were worn for individual protection as well as for defending the realm; feudal levies mustered with the axes and billhooks they used in their daily pursuits; for centuries, any ship engaged in other than strictly coastwise trade had to be armed; oxen and horses were the common method of traction for the baggage train as well as the plough. Technology, in general, was not specifically related to 'war' or 'peace'. The exceptions, cannon and armour, were clearly implements of war, even in their ceremonial uses; they were, however, extremely costly and small in numbers relative to other weapons or means of defence.

The main materials used were iron, brass, timber and leather, and stone for fortifications. The basic skills required were those of the blacksmith for forging metals, of the locksmith for constructing mechanisms, of the stonemason, and of the joinery trades wherever timber was needed as a raw material. All these were civilian crafts, exercised militarily on demand. Additionally, mechanisms devised for military purposes had to be robust rather than finely tuned, which put them well within the range of existing skills. There was thus no compulsion to develop a specifically military technology, the learning and practice of which could become a full-time job. Designs were traditional, slowly modified by practice and the ingenuity of the craftsman. It followed that equipping an army or navy made virtually no demands which civil employments did not make, and that the time taken to manufacture was not a particular problem. Campaign losses could be made good with relative ease.

The problems of resources required for war were discussed almost exclusively in terms of money. Hence, the need to accumulate 'war chests' or to defray the payments for mercenaries, in which Swiss magistrates for long did such model business. The long wars against Revolutionary and Napoleonic France demonstrated the use of loans to secure alliances. The financing of operations has not become less weighty than it was prior to the Industrial Revolution, but at that time, money seemed the main resource problem. It occupied much more attention than technique.

Industrialisation, in the course of the nineteenth century, changed these priorities. Its immediate impact on the range and quality of weapons was simply to improve the effectiveness of fighting units. The flintlock musket had an effective range of 100 yards and could be fired twice a minute; the field gun fired a twelve-pound round shot to about 1000 yards. These were the basic weapons of Europe until the end of the Napoleonic wars. By the mid-nineteenth century, the musket had been superseded by the rifle which was not a single-shot but a repeating weapon, effective at ten times a musket's range; cannon were now rifled and fired shells; they were, therefore, more accurate and at longer ranges, generally about 2000 yards.

The products of industry not only provided improved tools for killing, but improved means of getting them where they were to be used. The quintessential innovations were the railway and the steamship, followed by the electric telegraph. Steam freed generals from dependence on the traction power of the horse and therefore of the restrictions on manoeuvre which their use imposed. Similarly, in their element, admirals were released for the first time from the vagaries of the wind as a determinant of their strategy and tactics. Industry increased the options of those whose job it was to deploy weapons. It also increased the options of those reponsible for decisions about war and peace and made the judgment of issues much more complex.

Industrialisation took place not in a political vacuum but in a world of states which were already competing with one another. In such a world, then as now, foreign policy is necessarily concerned with maintaining or improving one's place in the competition. Success in this aim is conventionally described as 'security'; the time-honoured methods are negotiation (diplomacy) and the use of force (war). Both are attempts to induce an opponent to comply with one's wishes and in that sense involve leverage, either through persuasion, or a combination of threats and promises, or physical violence. By the time Europe had entered the nineteenth century, both methods had evolved their characteristic techniques, rules and rituals, and the relationships between them had been worked out by precept and practice in the emergence of the European state system.

The first consequence of industrialisation for foreign policy was to increase the number of levers available. It introduced a qualitative difference between states, similar to that between weapons: henceforward, the international order was divided into those states which possessed the materials, skills and facilities to manufacture the improved weapons and techniques and those which did not. Industrialised states had many more options: they could bring their power to bear or influence the policies of other states either more quickly or more intensively or in areas hitherto barred to them. Eighteenth-century captains relied on a dictum that the Mediterranean had only four usable harbours, June, July, August, and Port Mahon! Maritime strategies had to take those conditions into account. Steam power opened the Mediterranean all the year round. There and elsewhere it altered the assumptions and the operational possibilities, and therefore the political leverage which could be employed. Non-industrialised states could either develop their own capacity or become dependent on those who had it. For the manufacturing states, industry thus presented a new means of exercising power and one which was particularly advantageous for as long as there were no technical substitutes or only a finite number of producers. These advantages were transitory, as other states industrialised, but, from that time onwards, the leads and lags in technology gradually entered into judgments about foreign policy. The range and degree of industry entered the debate between 'What do we wish to do' and 'What can we do?'.

These changes were not immediately apparent, nor were the advantages consciously sought and reaped. The main manufacturer, Britain, was moving rapidly towards international free trade and was happily selling to France the designs and models on which an indigeneous French manufacture of engines for the French navy could be based. Nevertheless, politicians on both sides of the Channel noted that the industrial element enforced a revaluation of traditional attitudes and assumptions about what was now militarily possible and consequently what foreign policy should be. The observation was right, even if the deductions drawn for practical policy were frequently wrong. Steam power *did* upset time-honoured assumptions about the degree of security afforded by the Channel and the relationship between the fleets of France and Britain respectively, even if the deduction that 'steam navigation' made it 'nothing more than a river passable by a steam bridge' – as Lord Palmerston put it – overstated the capabilities of the technology and understated the possible counter measures.

Industrialisation might upset basic assumptions, but it did not, by itself, create problems for the conduct of foreign policy which were intrinsically new. Foreign offices, as before, were preoccupied with managing international power relationships, and armed force was conventionally regarded as the main means by which they could be maintained or altered. But to both diplomats and the military industrialisation offered new techniques for achieving their traditional ends. Whether a state aimed to dominate its rivals or to achieve a situation of balance with them, the radius of possible action became longer, and influence, which had hitherto been intermittent, could be exercised more consistently. The products of industry compressed the time between intention and execution, in policy-making as well as during military or naval campaigns. Faster speeds on land and sea allowed better reporting between units and bureaux and consequently closer coordination of the military and diplomatic aspects of foreign policy. The changes, in short, speeded up actions and reactions. Their effects appeared most sharply in the transition from peace to war, that is, at the point at which diplomatic argument gave place to armed conflict.

As inherited from the eighteenth century, the practice of 'going to war' had, broadly, three phases: *mobilisation*,* i.e. assembling the manpower and material necessary for conflict: *concentration*, i.e. bringing these resources into campaign order, and the *march to battle*. These three phases were differently delimited and subdivided by the powers, but were common to all. Each phase had its counterpart in diplomacy. Mobilisation could be total or partial but in either case signified that the state was going onto a war footing: it did not automatically mean that hostilities would follow. It could be undertaken for defensive or bargaining purposes, as by Austria-Hungary during the Crimean War, or simply to observe events. The French Government manned the frontier with Spain with two divisions during the Carlist Wars (1834–1839) and called up forces in the Rhône Valley during the war between Austria and Piedmont in 1848; similarly, units of the Prussian army were deployed in the eastern provinces during the Polish insurrections of 1830 and 1863. During mobilisation, the chancelleries would be busy defining the meaning of the action, testing the sincerity of their opponents for peace and the strength of their own alliances. The next phase, concentration, implied that the mobilised forces had been given their tasks and objectives. It still did not necessarily mean that fighting would begin, although, clearly it was a more ominous portent than mobilisation. Ritual demanded at this stage that war be formally declared before the final phase. Declarations also indicated to civil society that certain aspects of life were no longer operative; for example, the modification or suspension of trial procedures, the introduction of censorship or a moratorium on specific categories of debt. Marching on the enemy indicated that a diplomatic resolution of the conflict was, for the time being, in abeyance, and all the ambassadors of the contending states could do was to ask for their passports.

The time required for the whole process varied with circumstances. Navies could be mobilised more quickly than land forces, since ships in commission needed only to be ordered to war stations, there to be joined by reservists and ancillary vessels. With armies, the time necessary to complete the cycle depended mainly on the resources which had to be combined. At the beginning of the nineteenth century, Prussia ordered mobilisation on 9 August 1806 and its army was routed at Jena on 14 October. By the end of

---

*Reservists and other conscripts were customarily given twenty-four hours to put their affairs in order, so for High Commands, 'the first day of mobilisation' was the day after the orders were posted up in the streets.

the century, the problems were far more complex and involved detailed preliminary planning, of which Count Schlieffen's is the outstanding example.*

Between Jena and the Schlieffen Plan the distinctions between the three phases began to crumble. The costs of mobilisation became so burdensome that governments made special provision for them and considered whether victory would allow them to be written off or recovered from a defeated enemy as part of an indemnity. The Austrian Government nearly bankrupted itself through its prolonged mobilisation during the Crimean War, but its failure to intervene prevented the recovery of any of the 500 million gulden disbursed. So the expense of mobilisation inclined governments to regard it as the first step towards war rather than as a revocable stage in diplomacy.

At much the same time as mobilisation costs eroded customary usages, 'going to war' came to depend on the use of the railway, which enabled the military to compress mobilisation, concentration and the attack on the enemy, or any two of the three phases, as required. Moltke showed in 1866 that rail transport could be used to compress concentration and the attack on the enemy into one; his troops concentrated on the battlefield because, as he subsequently wrote, an army once concentrated is useless for anything except fighting. In 1870, the French command tried to combine mobilisation and concentration by transporting the serving regiments to the frontier areas and having them joined there by the reservists, in order to get ahead of the Germans. This effort failed disastrously, for lack of competent administrative control.

Compressing the phases on the military side also set limits to the accompanying diplomacy since – so the generals argued – the trains could not be halted while the diplomats deliberated, without producing chaos during which opponents would have an opportunity to strike. The deduction was logical; whether it was factually true or not depended on circumstances, since it assumed maximum operational efficiency on both sides. French incompetence in 1870 would have allowed the Prussians greater diplomatic flexibility, had they cared to use it, but it was jettisoned through reliance on the railway timetable. Where the military stipulated their operational necessities, the diplomats could not gainsay them.

By the end of the century, therefore, mobilisation was beginning to make no sense unless hostilities were to follow. For all practical purposes, the eighteenth-century progression 'mobilisation-concentration-war', with pauses between each stage, had become a swift equation, 'mobilisation = war'. The point was made to the Tsar by General Boisdeffre, Deputy Chief of the French General Staff, on a visit to St Petersburg for the manoeuvres in

---

*See below, pages 125ff.

July 1892, in conversations which issued in the Franco-Russian alliance: 'to mobilise is to declare war, to force one's neighbour to follow suit. Mobilisation necessarily entails the strategic movement of troops and their concentration.' (The reference to the 'neighbour' was illuminating!). When they grasped this trend, governments had recourse to a formal pre-mobilisation phase, with the object of leaving the diplomats as uncommitted to hostilities as had 'mobilisation' before, but the diplomats found themselves hauled along in the wake of the military, who devoted a large proportion of their energy and ingenuity to re-arranging railway schedules in order to clip hours and minutes off the time for mobilisation. General staffs developed a care for the niceties of the process to the point of mania. It engaged the professional honour of the military caste and therefore had psychological consequences which reinforced the technical arguments and brushed the diplomats aside.

The Franco-Prussian War was universally taken as the model. After 1870 it was assumed that success in war required complex planning in which the central element was the railway. Hence, in France, Russia, Austria-Hungary and Germany, no lines could be constructed without military permission, and serving officers became ministers of transport. Hence, also, the elaboration of plans which were so detailed and comprehensive that any action falling outside them could not be undertaken, by definition. So, in 1898, a French military machine oriented towards a war with Germany was totally unprepared for action against Britain in the Fashoda crisis, against an opponent and in a quarter for which no plans had been made. Similarly, the Schlieffen Plan became a touchstone of what was politically possible.* For the German General Staff there could only be one war, and that had to be on two fronts, with France as the first opponent and Russia the second, in that order; no other contingency could be entertained. The tragic outcome of this line of reasoning was seen on 1 August 1914, in the exchanges between the Kaiser and the younger Moltke, when the former (on the basis of advice from the Ambassador in London) correctly saw that there was no political need for an immediate attack on France, to be informed by the latter that for technical reasons, the attack via Luxembourg and Belgium had to be launched as scheduled. (Curiously, at the same time, Moltke's vis á vis, General Joffre was laying down the law in the same terms to *his* nominal superior, the Minister of War, Viviani, who, like the Kaiser was being unreasonably hesitant about starting operations.)[1] Moltke's conclusion was false, as was subsequently demonstrated,** but the outcome of this fateful conversation offers the clearest evidence that during the nineteenth century industrial-

*See below, p. 134.

**see below, page 128, Tirpitz's naval programme diverted funds which the German General Staff considered should have gone to strengthening the army, and for what was in fact not a complementary but a rival strategy. The Kaiser thought he could have both.

isation had gone beyond providing better weapons and had thrown up a new range of constituents in decisions about war and peace.

These became the more complex in that they were not confined to the actions of two mutually hostile states, but were an essential element in the strategies of alliances. After 1892 mobilisation plans had to be dovetailed by French and Russian staffs for a campaign on two fronts against Germany. The German High Command, distrustful of the capability of the Austrian Army and the rigour of its security, did not copy such a coordination of effort. Even so, as experience was to show, the fear of putting an ally at risk was a compelling incentive for allowing the mechanisms of mobilisation to go through.

The more rapid process of technical innovation and the need to follow elaborate timetables raised the stakes for preventive war at the same time as its industrial requirements made concealment more difficult. The introduction of a new weapon increased the temptation to open hostilities before the enemy acquired it, or could counter it or learn to use it tactically. The elder Moltke, in 1868, wanted to use the dispute over Luxembourg to launch a preventive attack on France, before Marshal Niel's military reforms could work through the cadres of the army, and before the Chassepôt rifle could be introduced in too great numbers. Bismarck dissuaded him on political grounds (the ostensible issue, Luxembourg, was not one in which the South German states could be expected to involve themselves). On the 6 July, 1870, the French Minister of War used the same arguments as Moltke to urge on *his* Cabinet colleagues an immediate attack on Prussia. France had superior arms: the Army was 'at its peak' ... 'in a state to win': it should be used forthwith. His advice, unlike Moltke's two years before, was followed, with disastrous results. Bismarck never shared these attitudes: his view was that starting a preventive war was like committing suicide because one feared to die. Nevertheless he publicly toyed with the idea of such a war against France, which, imbued with the desire for *revanche* for the defeat of 1870–71, was engaged in reforming its army through compulsory military service and fortifying Toul, Épinal and Verdun. The consequence was the war scare of 1875.

From that period onwards, the merits of preventive war were much more widely canvassed for reasons which were ultimately technological. The military commonly argued from the inevitability of war to the desirability of starting it under favourable technical auspices. If industry produced weapons which held out the prospect of battlefield superiority and enhanced the chances of victory to the point of certainty, then it was prudent to use them before the envisaged enemy could match them. If industry furnished a new means of improving the strategic situation, then the advantage thus conferred should be maximised. From the Russian point of view, such a change was expected from the construction of the Trans-Siberian railway: for the Japanese, it was imperative that any war with Russia should take place before the logistic benefits from the construction could be reaped by the Tsar's forces. Such reasoning dictated the timing of the Russo-Japanese War of 1904–5.

It is the professional duty of high commands to explore such options; whether they got their way or not depended on the role they played in making state policy as a whole. In Britain, the tradition of subordinating military to civil authority ensured that those who wished to forestall what they were convinced was inevitable had no effect on what actually happened. Admiral Fisher and his journalist friends on the *Daily Mail* were isolated – the German Navy was *not* destroyed by surprise attack. General Robertson, who had similar views to Fisher's about armed conflict with Germany, was reminded by his civilian superiors, as late as 1912, that war, though a *conceivable* outcome, was not inevitable. The distinction was not operative in Continental Europe, where the military was a privileged caste within the state, irrespective of whether it was in form a republic like France, or an autocracy such as the German Empire and Austria-Hungary. Preventive war was freely canvassed and controverted, if at all, on grounds of prudence, not because a civilian was able to insist on the distinction between the conceivable and the inevitable. Behind all the advocacy, however, lay the brutal fact that in a world of technological advance, advantages could only be temporary. In this way, industry enhanced the attractiveness of preventive war and helped to make the resolution of conflict through diplomacy more difficult.

2. Values and technological change

During the nineteenth century, industry galvanised war, increasing its demands on society and causing more enduring physical damage, but the full potential was not realised until the twentieth. Commanders did not always grasp the new possibilities which techniques held out to them. In the Crimea, the Anglo-French forces had rifles but the troops used them in the same way as the short-range, less accurate muskets with which the Russians were armed. In Italy, in 1859, the Austrians had the technically superior rifle but failed to modify their tactics on the battlefield accordingly. At Sadowa on 2 July, 1866, the Prussian needle gun was less important to the outcome of the battle than the faulty tactics and organisational defects of the Austrian command. The Prussians were also superior in handling their artillery although it was technically inferior to the Austrian. Seventeen days later the situation was reversed. The Italian fleet was defeated by the Austrian fleet in the Adriatic, off Lissa, though the Austrians used some wooden ships and deployed inferior firepower. Four years later against France, the superiority of German forces lay as much as in the *use* of the new Krupp cannon as in their excellence (it also helped to have overall command exercised by a Moltke rather than, say, a Steinmetz). In 1866 and 1870 alike, the opponents of the Prussian army failed to assert their superiority in weaponry – the Austrian cannon at Sadowa and the Chassepôt rifle and the mitrailleuse[2] during the Franco-Prussian War, with in each case radical consequences for the configurations of European politics. Merely to possess a superior weapon was not enough.

The generals' failure to assimilate the tactical effects of innovations in weaponry was paralleled in the sphere of policy-making by the governments' failure to draw the logical conclusions of technical advance. The right to make judgments about war and peace belonged to the ruler and as many advisers whom he wished or could be induced to consult. These advisers were recruited from the landowning aristocracy. Those who might have made technique an end in itself or given greater weight to it – the manufacturers and engineers – were excluded from determining foreign policy. The right to command in the field followed from the right to declare war: again this largely devolved on members of the aristocracy – in 1870 the battlefield interventions of William I and Napoleon III were, alike, unhelpful. The ethos governing the use of technique remained aristocratic and rural, not bourgeois and industrial. The aristocrats naturally identified both military and diplomatic aspects of foreign policy in terms of their particular values.

First among these was the ruling idea about warfare itself; war was a grandiose duel, and therefore subject to rules. It was the final and awful arbitrament in human affairs, enterprised in a sense of righteousness under God, who ruled the battlefield and imposed limits on the conduct of individuals. By the nineteenth century, the 'Truce of God' no longer halted military operations on the Sabbath, but the basic concept of limitation remained in the rigid distinction between the military and the civilian. Even Clausewitz, who considered moderation in warfare to be an error, limited the objective to *disarming* the enemy *forces*, and did not go on to advocate *exterminating* the enemy *population*.

Such assumptions were not merely theoretical but governed the conduct of operations. In 1832, Marshal Gérard, attacking Antwerp with French troops, and General Chasse, defending the citadel with Dutch forces, agreed on a line of attack and a line of defensive cannon fire, respectively, in order to safeguard the neutrality of the city. When the citadel surrendered on December 23, no non-combatant had suffered in life or property.* During the Crimean War (1855–56) the distinction between military and civil was upheld by the British Government when it permitted the Russian Government to raise a loan on the London money market to meet the interest due on Russian bonds, and by the French, who *during the course of hostilities*, invited the Russians to participate in an international exhibition of industry and the arts. In view of these and other similar gestures, it is not surprising to find that the Russian delegate to the Congress of Paris attended a celebratory march-past of French troops returning from Sebastopol!

War was considered as a duel on behalf of the state or the nation by those who considered themselves governed by its codes. It was the antithesis of peace but, like peace, operated in a framework of moral ideas; it was not outside the moral order or a negation of it. War had moral limits, and although they might be breached in particular campaigns, the ensuing condemnation by the victim and self-exculpation by the transgressor demonstrated that they both agreed that limits existed. Even the two masters of *Realpolitik* in the nineteenth century, Napoleon III and Bismarck, subscribed to this view, as much out of conviction as out of prudence (though in particular acts of policy it is often difficult to distinguish between the two). War might be the *ultima ratio* but it was also a moral activity, the moral

---

*By way of contrast, it is interesting to note that in the same decade, the American General Scott, besieging Vera Cruz in Mexico, refused to allow women, children and neutrals to be evacuated from the city, on the grounds that, as long as they were in the city, they would exert pressure for its surrender. Scott warned that anyone, without exception, who attempted to leave the city would be fired on.

character of which was defined by the ends for which it was undertaken and the means used. In his anonymous, kite-flying pamphlet of 1859, *Est-ce la paix – Est-ce la guerre?*, Napoleon III discussed the rationale of war, dismissing wars for the increase of territory, since experience – above all his uncle's – showed that what a nation gained by war, it lost by the same means. He concluded that the only legitimate reason for war was 'the defence of the weak against the strong, the maintenance of law and justice against wrong-doing and violence.' Napoleon added that it was not sufficient that war was legitimated in this way, it had also to be inevitable. That is, only when all other means of pacification, exhortation and amicable negotiation had been tried, then and only then, could war be honourably enterprised.

Napoleon was not indulging a taste for philosophy; his pamphlet had an immediate political purpose, to put Austria on notice that France might well intervene militarily in the question of the unity of Italy. But he was not merely being disingenuous; he was trying to lay down principles on which a moral right could be morally exercised. His repudiation of Napoleon I implied that national aggrandisement was no longer an adequate moral basis for bloodshed. The conditions which made war morally acceptable had changed; the only valid grounds were protection or retribution. Later generations, especially those who survived Verdun or the Somme, have naturally tended to regard this language as self-delusive or downright hypocritical. But Napoleon's arguments appealed to his contemporaries because they drew on a body of assumptions common to officers and diplomats throughout Europe, who implicitly and explicitly believed in such concepts as 'honour', as applied to themselves and to the state they served.

Honour was a complex notion which functioned as the moral basis for leadership. It was independent of formal religious belief,* though it tended to be coloured by the dominant forms of the Christian faith and practice throughout Europe. It was grounded in tradition, caste and conscience. Its central concept was not love but duty, derelictions of which were brought before 'a court of honour'. Authority deriving from knowledge was by definition inferior, the mark of the bourgeois, fitted only for employment as lawyers in civil life and artillery officers in the military. Such people were useful, no doubt, even necessary, but were incapable of true leadership because they traded in book-learning and were inclined to ask questions.

Honour stipulated that duty was paramount, and once established should be rendered without further question. On this both soldiers and diplomats were agreed, though they otherwise tended to interpret the requirements of the concept differently. For the diplomats honour had to be 'maintained', whereas the officer corps was prone to regard it as something to be

---

*The independence was most strikingly demonstrated in the Indian Army before 1947, in which 'honour' was a substitute for a national bond between officers and men and covered the differing religious beliefs and practices of Sikhs, Muslims and Hindus.[3]

'vindicated'. The distinction made for two entirely different, and sometimes opposed, outcomes in questions of policy.

Nevertheless 'honour', 'duty' and their correlatives provided the only acceptable vocabulary in which international behaviour could be explained and ultimately justified. They impinged on even those ideas with which they could formally conflict, such as 'the national interest'. 'Honour' was translated into rules and rituals, such as formal declarations of war, with ambassadors exchanging ceremonial farewell visits. Most important of all, since it was held in common by all the élites, 'honour' facilitated ultimate reconcilation. Policies could, in consequence, be very flexible, since it was universally assumed that makers of policy would have an interest in maintaining the system based on honour which overrode or at least was as important to them as their more narrowly construed political aims. War itself was limited in time and consequence, not merely by the inadequacies of contemporary technology and logistics but through the basic concept governing its practice. As a corollary, those who remained outside the contest could rely on being undisturbed: 'neutrality' was theoretically acceptable and practically possible, and, like war itself, covered a complex set of rules defining rights and duties.

With the temporary exception of Revolutionary and Napoleonic France, which for twenty years introduced a prototype of 'total' war,* the European polity subscribed to these general principles down until 1914. It was not only the Old Diplomacy which was rational, unhindered by the appeal to mass ideology and highly ritualised, the Old Warfare was too, though after 1870, the increasing scale of war and the emergence of conscript armies threatened to fracture the limitations – as they eventually did – and invalidate the aristocratic values from which they derived. This possibility was consciously feared by some leaders in the years immediately before 1914. In a prolonged and intense conflict both the military and the diplomats would lose their primacy and their activities would be exposed to 'democratisation' from other social classes.

Till then, however, aristocratic values predominated and fostered resistance to the innovations which manufacturing industry increasingly made available for military use. Occasionally, this resistance was on moral grounds. One British general opposed the introduction of the rifle in place of the musket on the grounds that it would turn infantrymen into 'long range assassins'. Proposals to drive the gunners defending Sebastopol from their posts through releasing sulphorous gases or to use armoured traction engines against Russian infantry in the same campaign were alike indignantly dismissed as barbarous. In the main, however, resistance to innovation

---

*The Convention decreed on 23rd August 1793 that every Frenchman was *permanently* required for service in the armies. The italicised adverb was an innovation – and a portent. By the next year 1,169,000 men had been registered as liable for military service.

rested on the corporate inertia of high commands. The first examination of the military possibilities of railways in Germany – a country which was to owe its unity to their use – was by a civilian, the Rhineland industrialist Friedrich Wilhelm Harkort, who in 1836 published in Berlin an essay on the subject : his views were promptly ridiculed by army spokesmen: Alfred Krupp in 1849 was informed by the Prussian War Ministry that his cast-steel three-pounder cannon was unacceptable since the existing methods of manufacture and quality of the results satisfied all reasonable needs and left hardly any room for improvement. The British Admiralty long hesitated over the adoption of steam propulsion in warships (partly on account of the fuelling problems) and then of the screw instead of the paddle-wheel. The readiness of the French officers to accept change remained untested, with the exception of steamships, until the Second Empire, whose ruler was both interested in military technology *and* in a position to enforce his views, but the case of the Chassepôt rifle indicates that corporate unresponsiveness to innovation was not absent from the army which regarded itself as first in Europe. The new weapon was forced on the High Command by Napoleon III.

Even after France from 1859 to 1860 and Prussia between 1866 and 1871 had shown what could be done, resistance to change remained a feature of military life, though it must be recognised that after 1870 most battles were fought in colonies and made no technical demands. To contemporaries, the success of the Prussian system was so overwhelming that high commands 'froze' the process of adaptation. In his plan to destroy the French forces before turning on Russia, Schlieffen relied on the technology available to the elder Moltke (except for machine guns and siege mortars) thirty-five years before: the adoption in France of the famous '75' field gun became a sufficient reason for *not* exploring the problems of the manufacture and use of howitzers. These were professional matters guarded from outside interference, especially from diplomats who, however socially exalted, ranked as mere civilians.

With few exceptions, those concerned with making and carrying out foreign policy at the highest level were not prepared by their social origins or intellectual background to exploit to the full the possibilities which indus-trialisation created. It should not be inferred that these social reasons offer a *complete* explanation for the failure: the innovators generally shared the same background. The answer, also, lies perhaps in the bureaucratisation of decision-making. In peace time the highest virtue is to keep the machine going; innovators rarely get promoted quickly. In the long peace between the powers in Europe, after 1870, incentives to innovate were lacking. Thus, in 1914, lancers on horseback entered a conflict in which machine guns and artillery were already seen by some to be the dominant weapons. Cavalry benefitted from the success of von Bredow's 'Death Ride' at Vionville-Mars la Tour on 15 August 1870 which 'won it a renown during the next forty years at the hands of military historians who were to cite it to prove that cavalry was not an anachronism in battle'[4]. The cost was an average casualty rate of thirty-three per cent, with some of von Bredow's squadrons losing over fifty per cent of their strength. The percentages might well have been higher had not the French infantry already fallen back from the guns, leaving them unprotected, and the French artillery run out of ammunition. Such specific evidence, and the lessons of earlier cavalry disasters on both sides in the same campaign, was freely discarded or discounted by a leadership derived from landowners which tended to consider that a man, a horse and a sabre made up a spiritual unity whose reflexes were superior to shell-fire.* The proprietors and their sons provided the cadres of officers: the tenants or labourers, the rank and file. The common assumption was that warfare was an extension of the hunting field, requiring much the same skills and techniques – an ability to ride hard and a good eye for ground. The Crown Prince of Prussia has been much excoriated in the literature for calling his brother officers, in August 1914 *'Auf, auf, zu einem frisch-fröhlichen Krieg'* but it is possible he was only recalling the words of a familiar hunting song, *'Auf, auf, zum fröhlichen Jagen, frisch auf ins freie Feld'*. War was a chase: the 'kill', the clash of armies. The survivors honoured their dead and shared the glory. The long-term problems of supply and raw materials did not trouble the devotees of the sport. Urged to consider them in August 1914, the younger Moltke revealingly dismissed them with *'Wir haben einen Krieg zu führen.'* Diplomats, being recruited from the same social groups, in large measure accepted this view; war, like peace, had its rituals and its limits.

It was not until military failure had cleared Moltke and those who thought like him in all combatant armies out of the way that leaders who comprehended the technical complexities of war and their interrelations with social policy were able to take over. The process took eighteen months to two years – roughly half the War, and even then was not complete. Moltke himself broke down under the strain in September 1914; his successor, Falkenhayn, lasted till August 1916. His opponent, Sir John French, left the scene at the end of 1915, but *his* successor Haig had no grasp of war as a totality either. Joffre went at the end of 1916, but Nivelle's ideas produced only a mutiny in the appallingly battered French army. The imaginative powers of most of their colleagues went no further than the technical improvements in the means of killing.

The pacemakers in the new conception of war were Ludendorff and Groener, among the military, and individual civilians, such as Rathenau, Albert Thomas, and Lloyd George, formerly a rabid anti-militarist. The

---

*The American General Sheridan who observed the actions on the Meuse at Sedan reported that though the French cavalry behaved most gallantly, they were sheltered from fire till the last moment and had to charge over only four hundred yards of ground, the result was their destruction as a military body by the Prussian gunners who held their fire till the last one hundred and fifty yards.

emergence of new ideas about the meaning of war for society marks the beginning of the end of the link between the officer class and land ownership which had in the main reinforced a restricted approach to war. Those who possessed land or whose army careers were supported by rents were more aware of property rights and the whole nexus of legal and moral considerations they subsumed. The new leaders extended the notion and practice of mobilisation from the military sphere to the society; victory called for a comprehensive effort: nothing should be allowed to stand in the way. Ludendorff is the exemplar of the new approach. He was not of noble origin. He made his career (unlike the elder Moltke and Schlieffen) not through intellect but through energy and willpower. His path through life was impeded by no traditional values: he believed blindly in himself and in 'efficiency' untrammelled by other considerations. Socially considered, Ludendorff was a radical figure and is the ancestor of our contemporary officer cadres who express only contempt for property rights.

By 1916, it became clear that the war differed in kind from previous wars; it was not simply bigger. August 1914 had not been, as expected, August 1870 on a larger scale, with the scene of the action shifted because the French had fortified the earlier route. In contrast to 1870, war had changed from being the concern of the army as an élite to being the business of society as a whole, and from the limited and rational application of force to unrestricted violence.* War had become a mass phenomenon, involving the nation and a national effort. The change widened the gap between military and diplomatic action. The diplomats were left struggling to adjust their concepts and practices to the new realities. In Britain, civilian control of objectives was, not without considerable difficulty, maintained. In France, it was asserted only after 1916: in the first weeks of the War, the Chamber of Deputies abdicated its responsibilities and had to struggle to get them back. In Germany, civilian authority over all objectives of state policy was abandoned altogether.

The course of events in Europe from the end of 1915 onwards, (particularly the failure of the peace proposals in 1917) suggests that the advent of the professionals such as Ludendorff was not an unalloyed blessing, since under the impact of sustained mass violence,* the European political and social order was shattered. It must be stressed, however, that this consequence followed from the strategies chosen, which turned on the scale and range of industrial capacity. There was nothing ineluctable about the change. For the Western Allies, containment on the Western front combined with a major effort elsewhere would have placed less concentrated strain on industry and society. It was never tried and other theatres,

---

*'Violence' because it had broken out of the framework of legitimating rules as they were accepted in 1914.

significantly known as 'sideshows' were treated commensurately with this assessment in men and materials and confided to the more troublesome or less competent generals. The arguments against any alternative strategy were formidable and rooted in the politics of the Anglo-French alliance. The Allies deprived themselves of flexibility and suffered the consequences – unheard-of wastage of manpower and materials for minimal advantage. On the German side, the leadership, divided on so much else, almost unanimously agreed that though 'the knock-out' blow against France had failed, the thinking behind the strategy was basically sound, and accordingly demanded the dominant effort in the West. Only a few professional voices were raised in dissent. Old General Haeseler, protected by age and seniority, argued as soon as the trench systems were completed that victory was unattainable and that a peace should be negotiated as soon as possible. General Hoffmann, in the East, found his command treated as a 'sideshow' though he was fully aware of the devastating political results more rapid victories on fronts other than the Western could achieve. In his view, political and military dividends for Germany and its allies were sacrificed for objectless slaughter in the West and for 'limited fights around Ypres'. Verdun and the whole front should fall as a by-product of total victory in Italy; the destruction of the Allied lodgement in Salonica would secure the Balkans and the Eastern Mediterranean. For Hoffman, most intelligent and articulate of critics, it was 'the war of lost opportunities'[5]. However, Haeseler was ignored and Hoffman rejected as intolerably prejudiced and self-seeking. His superior, Falkenhayn, so far from wanting to defeat Russia, advocated a negotiated peace in the East to free his hand against France in the West.

Generals and politicians on both sides alike mesmerised each other with the idea of a decisive victory achieved on the battlefields of Flanders. The leaders of the advanced industrial states, France, Britain and Germany, were not driven by blind impersonal forces to break up the European order they knew: *that* was the consequence of the strategy they consciously adopted.

For by 1918, the leaderships had absorbed finally the lessons presented by the process of industrialisation in the previous century. What had happened may be variously interpreted: either that the assumptions governing behaviour finally caught up with technological opportunity, or, alternately, that the dominant ethical and cultural values capitulated to efficiency, taken to be the uniquely valid criterion of action. In either case, the moral ethos of war had vanished; God was either indifferent or in the lists of the fallen. Technique was no longer responsive to traditional ethics, and the series of rough compromises between what science and industry made available and the non-industrial values of those who were responsible for determining its use came to an end. That the compromises took so long to be rejected was due to the social composition and educational background of the pre-war leadership, the influence of religion on its thinking and the exclusion from decision-making of those whose approach might have been more purely technical.

It was also relevant to the question that the leading industrial state for most of the previous century, Great Britain, had the least incentive to explore the new possibilities since its policies did not involve land war against other industrial states in Europe. The policies of Prussia and France did, and it was through their respective searches for strategic and tactical superiority that the implications of the new techniques began to be systematically explored. The process was the easier in that both states were militarist, in a way in which Britain was not: military assumptions automatically commanded precedence in the making of policy and generated the axioms against which alternatives were tested.

Industrialisation allowed warfare to increase in range and scale, making the controlled movement of mass forces possible, and to create situations in which the responses sanctioned by tradition no longer applied. However, its effects were not confined to the sphere of technique. Industrialisation demanded more careful and more extensive planning; the need to plan encouraged a state of war-preparedness which in times of specific political crisis could rapidly develop into a war psychosis, under the influence of a press which was either manipulable or popular. These features could be observed before 1914 but till then were held in check by the rigid distinction between 'war' and 'peace', the limited concept of war itself (military planning aimed at short-term decisions, not long-term exhaustion) and the relative openness of nineteenth-century society compared with that of the twentieth. These constraints vanished with the First World War.

3. Industry as a science-based system: questions for government

The effects of industry on traditional diplomacy and military operations were so far-reaching because what was being applied to these activities was not a number of particular inventions but a *system* in which inventions themselves were only one element. They remained useful novelties unless they could be produced at will, in series, that is in reliable copies of the prototype and in numbers related to the demand for them. Translating inventions into a series of products depended on three basic requirements: the ability to bring together certain kinds of knowledge (for example, of the composition and behaviour of materials or of workshop practice); reliable access to raw materials and to sources of power; and possession of the equipment for manufacture. Series production also presupposed the existence of engineering, metallurgical and other similar skills, and a supply of labour. All these had to be combined systematically – a task carried out by enterpreneurs able to meet the capital requirements and supply the market. The functions of entrepreneurs could be carried out by individuals or corporately, privately or by the state; in all cases, however, combining knowledge, materials and skills around sources of steam power rapidly altered time-honoured patterns of occupations and structures of existing societies, encouraging shifts in population and creating factories and large towns. This was an entirely new phenomenon on the scale and at the speed with which it took place, though it made itself felt at different rates in different countries. From the beginnings of the nineteenth century onwards, governments acquired another yardstick – industrial development – by which to measure each other's progress or reckon comparative strength, especially for strategic purposes. Assessment was the easier since all states were more open than they have since become; industrial secrecy was minimal and, compared with our current practice, not very effective. The emerging emphasis on the virtues of private economic activity automatically challenged the principles of secrecy ingrained in the state.

The components of 'strength' were not just physical assets such as factories, or facilities such as improved communications, but also developments in knowledge. Initially, the inventions and innovations which characterised industrialisation derived from practice, not from theoretically-established premises. James Watt, who made the series production of efficient steam engines possible, was by trade an instrument maker, though he acquired considerable theoretical knowledge from his contacts at Glasgow University, whither he was driven by the hammermen of Glasgow who prosecuted him for opening a workshop without having served an apprenticeship.* Henry Maudslay, who perfected the screw-cutting lathe and virtually founded the machine-tool industry, was a blacksmith. John Wilkinson, who first devised an accurate boring mill, for Watt's cylinders, was a practical iron master. He subsequently ordered from Watt and his partner Boulton the first steam engine on the new principles.

The only nucleus of mathematically trained engineers was to be found in France, thanks to the work of the *Ecole des Ponts et Chaussées*, founded in 1747. The graduates of the School, however, employed their talents mainly on military projects or constructions such as canals which were related to them. Their work in this sphere, supported by the *corvée,* ensured the mobility of the armies of France. Outside France, no scientific engineering tradition existed at all and the work of academic mathematicians had no impact on the efforts of iron masters and mechanics, who worked by trial and error. Modern industry was built up neither from investigations of theory nor experimental research. Research-directed experiment only entered the scene in the middle of the nineteenth century, when its value was first realised in dye-stuffs manufacture. Then, significantly for the future of both countries, the results obtained by an English pioneer, Henry Perkin, were rejected in Britain and applied in Germany.

Practice-derived craft knowledge did not disappear. It lingered on most tenaciously in Britain, where the same instinct for the practical which so admirably inhibited the more intense and other-wordly forms of philosophical speculation impeded progress in the more mundane field of engineering. The perceptiveness to invent did not falter: what was lacking was a realisation that the products, manufacturing processes and working methods alike of industry could benefit from speculative inquiry. Nonetheless in the long run, even Britain could not remain unaffected by theory and consciously-controlled experiment.

Throughout Western Europe, the rate of improvement in technology accelerated, as one new process or invention interacted with others. Men began to learn how to translate ideas into products by means of systematic engineering on a large scale. The production of iron and steel was transformed, and – important for the future development of weapons – steel ceased to be virtually a semi-precious metal and became an economic working material.

The inventions and innovations which changed the techniques of war were not confined to one country (though Britain and France predominated) or to

---

*The University was not within their jurisdiction.

heavy engineering and metallurgy. The extraction of anilene and phenol from coal tar, discovered experimentally in 1834, revolutionised the science of explosives, while the invention of nitroglycerine in 1847 added a formidable new power to the repertoire of destruction. Over roughly the same period, the invention of the Morse telegraph and the setting up of the first international telegraph bureau made couriers obsolete and foreshadowed the age of Moltke. Meanwhile, still before 1850, Carl Zeiss had founded at Jena his optical works, the products of which eventually enabled armies round the world to aim straight. All these developments represented the results of scientific experiment, applied on an industrial scale. The old rough and ready reliance on practice was of no use. It was a portent for the future that exploration at the frontiers of technique was connected with war.

In a more general sense, however, any advance in science and technology merely increased 'the means to hand' for the purposes of war. Progress in medicine and hygiene diminished death rates from wounds or from campaign epidemics and enabled the wounded or sick to be returned to duty. More remotely, compulsory elementary education and training in mechanical aptitudes enabled the new systems which technology provided to be used for war. A telegraph could not be operated by illiterates and the use and maintenance of breech-loading guns demanded mechanical skills. Advances in medical science and in education did not derive from their potential military application but they slowly improved the military potential of society.

The net result of the specific and the general advances in science and technique was that 'military' became more clearly differentiated from 'civil' use. The merchant fleet ceased to be so easily transformed into the navy, since the standards of design and performance between mechantmen and naval vessels diverged. The P and O liner which altered the social position of the British in India by cutting the outward voyage to Bombay to six weeks was built with a view to economy of operation and comfort for the passengers, neither of which were thought essential in vessels of war. Similarly, the tools and equipment used to make weapons gradually ceased to be suitable for civil as well as military production. They tended to be installed to meet a military requirement and could only be amortised through producing what they were designed to produce. When military orders slackened, such equipment became a burden on the overall costs of the entrepreneur – which, variously, led manufacturers to bargain for subsidies or induced them to support politically a strong military policy. In either case, the problem of finding a continuous and therefore profitable or at least loss-reducing use for the assets took them into departments of state. Such differentiation took place at the heavy end of the engineering industry: chemicals and light engineering could be more easily adapted to war or peace.

The differentiation of 'military' from 'civil' was gradual but by the last quarter of the nineteenth century, the 'military' market was sufficiently autonomous to make special concentration on it worthwhile for a few entrepreneurs. By that time, too, the more perceptive minds among the military and diplomatic élites had begun to realise that their policy options were related not just to innovations but, more fundamentally, to the rate of technical progress in manufacture. This correlation raised entirely new questions for government. The state as such could, if it wished, ignore the production of goods for strictly civilian consumption, except as a possible source of additional tax revenue. It could not be indifferent to the production of weapons or to the introduction and use of systems (*par excellence*, the railway) which affected its strategic possibilities since both weapons and railways were directly related to the continued existence of the state and the integrity of its territory in a competitive political order. That being so, what should be the relationship of this militarily-oriented capacity to the state: how was the state to get the benefits of entrepreneurship?

The answers to these questions were suggested not so much by theory as by circumstance. The previous history of states' development in Europe afforded many precedents for the state ownership of the manufacture of weapons, partly for reasons of prudence but, more generally, from mercantilist convictions about the relationship of manufacture to power. On these grounds, past experience suggested a bias in favour of continuing state ownership. Industrialisation, however, brought a significant change. Small arms excepted, there was, strictly speaking, no armaments industry as such: the new weapons and techniques applied to war were developed at the heavy end of iron and steel manufacture. The facilities which produced cannon were also used for producing locomotives, rails, girders and bridges, boilers and similar industrial goods. Moreover, the centres of this new industrial production were outside the traditional arsenals and shipyards and the nature of their output demanded that they be kept in being, ready for expansion in wartime. Hulls made of iron, instead of wood, could not be caulked and stored on slipways against the time when they would be needed. Similarly, extensive dock and harbour works had to be undertaken and railway tracks laid well in advance of the hostilities in which they might be used. This fact in itself put a premium on contingency planning by the military. There was no point in ensuring that railway lines were laid in a particular direction unless the decision were at least in some measure related to ideas of probable future use. Russian railways, for example, were planned from the beginning by the state, with military purposes exclusively in mind – which created problems for the private capitalists to whom they were subsequently sold since the lines ran nowhere near the towns from which operating revenue was expected. Additionally, the Russian command, realising that railways were capable of facilitating an invasion of Russia, as well as an offensive by Russian armies, insisted that the lines be built to a different gauge from that ruling in the rest of Europe. In the West, the extension and fortifying of the port of Cherbourg fitted in to a strategic plan about the future deployment of the French navy, and made no sense otherwise. The industrialisation of war demanded longer and more thoroughgoing preparations in peace time.

These preparations could, theoretically, have been undertaken by the state, with state-owned foundries in parallel to privately owned ones, but current politics compelled governments to approach private industry. The new techniques were applied to war not in isolation, or out of disinterested professional curiosity on the part of engineers, but in an atmosphere of urgency inspired by rivalry between the two main industrialising states, Britain and France.* Policy therefore could not wait on leisurely experiment or on building up facilities in the state's domain. This was accepted the more readily since the problem was to *adapt* techniques such as steam traction to military use rather than to devise systems from the beginning.** The emergent theories of Free Trade confirmed the wisdom of the state's choice. Adam Smith himself had reservations about applying his views to national defence but they were largely ignored by those who subsequently systematised his ideas into a gospel. Dominance tends to set fashions and Britain's early industrial success recommended the body of ideas from which it was presumed to derive.

In transport, the role of the state flouted the axioms of *laisser faire* since the construction of a railway interfered with the use and ownership of land and accordingly required legislation from parliaments in which landowners made themselves heard. State authorities had an opportunity to consider what it suited them to allow. Practice varied: Britain from the beginning encouraged private ownership and operation: nationalisation had its advocates, including, curiously, Gladstone, but it was not adopted. In Belgium, private entrepreneurs were bought out by the state, while in Russia – as already noted – state railways were sold to private entrepreneurs: various regimes were tried in France, with an eventual compromise that the state was responsible for the track and private firms for the provision of the equipment and the service.

In all countries, the state took powers to ensure that the railways, irrespective of their formal ownership, would be available for its purposes in wartime. *That*, of course, was merely an exercise of traditional authority during an emergency. What was new for the government was to define a relationship which would ensure in advance, during peacetime, that the

---

*see below, Part II.

**The transfer of technology was not exclusively from civil to military production. The development of machine tools, and the technique of manufacturing products so that parts were interchangeable were both related to fulfilling orders from the military, represented respectively by the British Admiralty and the United States Government.

necessary facilities would be available during wartime, although the state did not own and manage them. Arsenals and government shipyards continued as before but they no longer covered the national requirements and additionally relied on private manufacture for 'bought-in' components.

Industrialisation meant that the traditional framers of policy henceforward had to take account of a group of private entrepreneurs who possessed and operated the manufacturing capacity and other facilities necessary to fulfil the aims and objectives of the state. In principle, the authorities could command: in practice they had to bargain – and they on occasion weakened this bargaining position by refusing to buy abroad. But this relationship concerned not only physical assets, it also encompassed the process of innovation and obsolescence. Adapting innovations to the purposes of war relied on the perspicacity of naval and military staffs, the enthusiasm of inventors and on the successful demonstration of the experiments. Military staffs were usually looking for reasons for saying 'no' and failures during trials or imperfect technology frequently provided such a reason. Before the innovation of the screw, paddle wheels were regarded as making a ship especially vulnerable to fire from the new guns which fired shells instead of shot. So the adaptation of steam power to ships of war was not rapid. Again, the explosion of cannon during trials did not promote the acceptance of new techniques of breech-loading even though it permitted higher rates of fire. The odds were further stacked against the inventors since testing was rudimentary and they could get no systematic and scientific response from the military. To that extent, they were designing in a vacuum. Many delays can be charged to military conservatism but not all.

Whether successful or not, innovation was costly – which prompted the question whether it was better to innovate and establish a lead in a particular technology or wait and adapt improvements already tested, preferably by somebody else. The choice was an entirely new one for the state – as was the related problem of obsolescence. Fortresses and sailing ships of the line grew obsolete very slowly. *HMS Victory* was forty years old at Trafalgar. Iron ships and heavy artillery deteriorated far more rapidly, both in performance and relative to improvements in other arms. Governments, which defrayed the costs had therefore to decide what rate of obsolescence to take into account when funding their military acquisitions. In the industrial age, these questions were debated in parliaments and cabinets: *a fortiori*, they entered into the relationship between the state and the private industry which predominantly met its requirements. Viewed in the context of public policy, military goods posed questions which did not arise for civil goods.

The need to rely on a private sector and to manage innovation also began to involve a special relationship between producer and customer. In the accepted theory of the market, a transaction did not demand any more from the respective parties than a willingness to buy and a willingness to sell, and the ability to agree on prices and conditions, themselves determined by competition. The whole process was neutral. The purchase and sale of weapons was not. From the outset, the military refused to be regarded as just another customer: it embodied the security of the state; it was socially superior to the manufacturing classes; it was above the haggling of the market place. The dominant military virtues were loyalty and order, neither of which induced officers to value competition, as such. On the contrary, they disposed the military to favour a secure and known source of supply. If this preference failed to procure weapons at the cheapest price, then, from the military standpoint, the difference between that price and what had to be paid was simply a premium for loyalty on the part of the manufacturer and a guarantee of the reliability of his product. Competition, in the form of, say, shooting trials, might be an admirable method of establishing the performance of rival weapons but did not have to determine the price at which they were acquired. The overriding criterion for government was not the cheapest tendered price but the ability to produce to a standard. Hence pricing policies in weapons manufacture departed from the norms and axioms of accepted theory and market practice for other goods.

Manufacturers anxious to secure an outlet for their products responded to reasoning of this kind not by supplying a cheaper product but by attempting to become a favoured supplier. The route to favour lay through successful innovation. 'Success' in this sphere had two distinct aspects: the first, that the weapon could be proved to perform reliably within the limits of the design, and the second, that the service authorities could be persuaded to adopt it. This in itself was rather more problematical, might take some considerable time and was fruitless without solid technical performance. The dispositions of the *customer* thus tended to limit price competition.

The technology of weapons production had the same effect. The increase in size and range of weapons depended on improvements in metallurgy and in machine tools. The major suppliers were restricted to those entrepreneurs who could exploit these developments – which in turn implied access to capital and technological skills which were themselves costly in terms of current rates of income. The technological and financial requirements reinforced each other to restrict the number of participants in the 'weapons industry', irrespective of any desire for combination among manufacturers. In fact, during the formative years in mid-century, individual manufacturers did compete. Combination followed only towards the end of the century but then typically over materials such as steels rather than the particular weapons which they made possible (munitions were exceptional in this respect). Nevertheless, combined or not, the firms which tendered for business with the government were able to do so because they were in the forefront of technology. It was their command of technical progress and their ability to convince the military of its value that differentiated the leading firms from the mass of suppliers to the state. This of itself tended to narrow the field.

4. The ambivalences of the enterprises

Even so, the acid test of value was war itself, and it was a series of brief wars between 1855 and 1871 which enabled a handful of firms to draw clear of their rivals and become identified with the national armament: Schneider in France, Krupp in Germany; Armstrong, Whitworth in Britain. Their fortunes are discussed below*: here it is important to note that, irrespective of their motives in entering weapons production, their manufacturing operations were rooted in the demands of railway or steamship transport, which continued to provide the mainstay of the respective firms. Railways and weapons were linked not only through the facilities required for manufacture but also through the cycles of demand. The railway market, though expanding in the long term, was far from stable. The demand for rails, first of iron and then of steel and for other components and ancillaries from bolts to bridges, varied with the success of railway promoters and the increase in the numbers of competitive sources of supply. Railway construction was liable to be interrupted by failures in capitalisation and the political ambitions of governments. Foundries and forges had to be put to use, and managements saw in armaments contracts a means of stabilising the use of facilities and of increasing their profitability. Circumstances of this order brought Schneider, Krupp and Armstrong, in the last quarter of the nineteenth century, a formidable rival. 'A serious falling-off in trade ... and the reduction of prices consequent upon severity of competition'[6] in railway materials turned Tom and Albert Vickers of Sheffield towards the manufacture of armaments and the official market. In 1887, after assiduous campaigning in Whitehall, the firm entered the business of making guns and armour plate for the Admiralty. Vickers thus consciously decided to stake its fortunes on the production of armaments, though it continued to supply the civil engineering market as well.

The dual character and commerical ambivalence of the major firms could only have been avoided if they had been exclusively and permanently occupied on state contracts. Since they could not be, and since governments wanted a private sector to exist, private manufacturers suffered from the

---

*see pages 77ff and 112ff.

vagaries of the trade cycle and from fluctations in credit. Hence, managements tended to solicit additional government business to offset any
slackening in general manufacture: contracts from the state also helped them
to avoid going to the banks for funds or made the raising of credit easier.

There were, at that time and since, other undertakings in the arms
business, which have contributed to the industrialisation of war. Schneider,
Krupp, Armstrong and Vickers, however, were on the largest and most
comprehensive scale, generated most of the advances in technique and
became synonymous with 'armaments', in both the industry and politics.
Identification with the national war capacity had unfortunate repercussions
for Krupps, after two world wars. It is reasonable to suppose that, had
Germany been the victor, similar misfortune would have been visited on the
others in consequence of the same identity.

For this reason, also, the operations of the four companies have often been
discussed as if they were powers in their own right, making the foreign policy
decisions which they foisted on their governments or at least directing
attention to those courses of action which would increase the companies'
profits. The view fails to explain what in fact was a far more complex
relationship.

Since politics provided the *raison d'être* of their products, manufacturers of
weapons were closely interested in national politics and in the network of
advisors and committees through which decisions were reached. As individuals however they were not tied to party organisations and programmes,*
but saw politics in terms of a patriotism which transcended party affiliations.
They therefore busied themselves with interest groups such as Navy leagues
rather than political parties in the formal sense. Parties, also, were by
definition congeries of interests, not all of which were necessarily in accord
with the ideas and objectives of manufacturers.** They all took care to
interest politicians and officials active in the localities in which their factories
were located, in the wellbeing of their enterprises. Such care was natural and
prudent, but, in the last analysis, secondary: the manufacturers' influence
stemmed from their command of the technique and facilities by which
foreign policy objectives could be met. For this reason alone, it was
considerable. If the French Government considered Germany, another
industrialised state, to be its principal opponent and most likely enemy, then
it had to pay attention to what Schneider was capable of devising or

---

*Armstrong was on one occasion a reluctant and unsuccessful candidate in the Liberal interest:
Friedrich Krupp, Alfred's son, was an inconspicuous member of the *Reichstag* from 1893 to
1898, when he lost his seat, which he made no attempt to regain.

**The most notable exception was Luwig Löwe, who introduced American machine tools in
German armaments' production and manufactured gun sights and revolvers in his factory in
Berlin. Löwe was for many years a member of both the *Reichstag* and the Prussian *Landtag*, and
was one of the leaders of the Progressive Party; he abandoned it in 1877 for the National
Liberals over its opposition to Bismarck's military policy.

producing. This knowledge entered into the Government's calculations as to the most suitable political or military strategy. Conversely, the realisation that the French Government had to come to him, since French industry had no other possible source of supply and the Government's own ban on imports debarred it from looking abroad, strengthened the position and arguments of Eugène Schneider. The same was true in general of Krupp and the German Government, and Armstrong and Vickers in Britain.

Such reciprocity, in the given conditions, is the crux of the relationship. Government could, of course, always vary the conditions, but the limits within which it was free to do so depended on the general atmosphere in foreign affairs; what might be contemplated in *détente* could not even be thought about in times of crisis. Moreover, the relationship did not allow manufacturers to determine foreign policy objectives: that function resided clearly with government. Even Eugène Schneider, who in 1870, had the closest relationship with Government since he was related by marriage to General Leboeuf, the French Minister of War, did not have to urge, on those responsible for policy, a war with Prussia. His successor, also Eugène, in 1912, found that his firm's legal adviser had been elected President of France, but no-one had to persuade Raymond Poincaré, from Lorraine, into an anti-German policy. Nor did Krupp set the aims and axioms of foreign policy. He offered credits to the Prussian Army during the crisis over parliamentary control of expenditure in 1862: he took care to wine and dine important officials at the Villa Hügel in Essen to build up a pro-Krupp faction in the military establishment: he was especially fortunate in that the commandant of the military district in which his works were situated became, in due course, King of Prussia and Emperor of Germany. But the foreign policy of Prussia and Germany, during Alfred Krupp's lifetime, was made by the King and Otto von Bismarck.

Krupp, Schneider, Armstrong and Vickers were content to accept, within their differing institutional frameworks, the policies arrived at by others (as distinct from urging the adoption of particular weapons). As manufacturers they exercised influence: they did not exercise final power. Decisions on foreign policy remained with the predominantly aristocratic élites. From *their* point of view, it was advantageous that the capacity to manufacture technically advanced weapons was within their jurisdiction. It offered a particular means of leverage in foreign relations and avoided the dependence which would result from having to buy abroad. Additionally, the state had an interest in ensuring that the techniques which had or were likely to have a military application were retained as part of the nation's general industrial competence. In the 1880s, British Government spokesmen derived their country's maritime supremacy not just from the numbers and classes of vessels in the Royal Navy but from Britain's capacity to outbuild likely opponents in the event of war. This argument was used as a deterrent, to show the pointlessness of competition. The German Government after 1870 was in no doubt that Krupp cannon were evidence not just of German craftsmanship but of German power. Successive French governments of different complexions took the same view – which is why they assiduously promoted Schneider Creusot abroad. Inevitably, such official recognition of the role of their products in foreign policy increased the potential bargaining power of manufacturers *vis à vis* their own governments.

Into their relationships entered the questions of profits and of exports. They were not, in principle, controversial in the nineteenth century. For manufacturers, weapons were made and sold for profit, as part of their ordinary business. Government, in its turn, accepted that the manufacturer merited a return on his investment, which was usually calculated so as to allow him to cover the costs of research or of special equipment. This was the principle adopted in France, Germany and Britain. In practice the scale of profit realised was liable to scrutiny by officials: furthermore, all three states kept in being their own arsenals and producing establishments to give them yardsticks for assessing costs in the private sector of weapons manufacture. How effective these arrangements were depended on the zeal of the officials and the state of international tension but the apparatus of accountability to the public authority existed and operated; profits were accepted, though their scale could be challenged. It was only during the First World War that the expansion of demand, and the principle that no-one in any industry should be able to profit excessively from a situation for which virtually all precedents were invalid, combined to generate the idea that profits on weapons ought to be restricted. It was only after the War that such profits were regarded as intrinsically immoral.

Exports went through a similar revaluation. They have been taken by many critics to indicate a lack of patriotism or as evidence of a manufacturer's skewing the foreign policy of the state for commercial ends. The explanation is rather less sensational or sinister. Exports derived from the conditions under which production was carried out; in face of a domestic demand which could only be intermittent, foreign outlets helped to ensure the more regular employment of men and facilities. Government, no less than the producer, required that facilities for manufacturing weapons be kept in being and profitably employed. Receipts from exports saved the domestic taxpayer from funding subsidies in slack times; the export customer paid the cost of keeping the facilities going. Government thus had a ready motive for allowing, indeed encouraging, exports, apart from any foreign policy influence they conferred.

Exports also shared out the benefits of technological progress, in military as in civil goods. Through their foreign customers, manufacturers developed technical advances which their own authorities hesitated to commission or adopt. The requirements of Russia as a customer and Krupp's close working relationships with Russian officers promoted improvements in gun design which redounded to the benefit of the Prussian War Ministry, notoriously lax about these matters till 1870. Similarly a cruiser built by Armstrong's for Chile, the *Esmeralda,* was an experiment in combining speed and firepower at sea which went to improve the performance of a similar class of vessel in the Royal Navy. From the point of view of government, such transactions made foreigners bear the costs of research and development, with the attendant risks. Governments, in short, encouraged the export trade because they considered they had more to gain than to lose by it.

Foremost among the gains were prestige and bargaining power. The arrival of a Hohenzollern in Romania as Prince in 1866 saw the end of the French military mission and the introduction of the needle gun into the Romanian army – a by-product of its use at Sadowa. The importance of this type of transaction must not be overstated. The new Romania needed Prussian support against Austria and Russia with or without Prussian weapons and military advice, but the weapons and the training which went with them helped to keep the Romanian army looking towards Berlin for inspiration and guidance. The foreign policy orientation of a state could not automatically be deduced from the origin of its weapons – as to an extent it can now; otherwise, South American states buying British warships would have to be considered allies of the United Kingdom, which they were not, and Italy would have to be accounted pro-French, even though, having equipped its troops with French weapons, it then joined an alliance against France.

The example of Prussia shows that fostering exports involved some risks to the state. In July 1870, von Roon, the War Minister, asked Alfred Krupp to divert to Prussian use cannon ready for delivery to Russia. Krupp was a Prussian subject, his plant under Prussian jurisdiction but he replied that he would have to ask his contracted customer first. The Tsar consented and Krupp supplied the Prussian Government. Such courtesy could not be guaranteed. Ordinarily governments sought to safeguard their position either by insisting that their own requirements would always constitute a valid instance of *force majeure* under a contract with a foreign customer, or by merely commandeering weapons in times of crisis. This the British Government did in July 1914, summarily taking over two battleships already completed for Turkey. The Government exercised its accepted contractual rights but its action pushed Turkey out of possible neutrality into an alliance with Germany – hardly an advantageous outcome for Britain at that time.

Exports were also responsible for the appearance of weapons from the same manufacturer on both sides of a particular conflict – a contingency which twentieth-century commentators have found particularly wicked. It was, however, the logical consequence of Free Trade and of the absence of ideological alliance systems. For the same reasons, the trade in weapons raised the possibility that the manufacturer's compatriots could find themselves under fire from his products. This might easily have happened in the Franco-Prussian War, in regard to both weapons which contributed decisively to French defeats. In April 1865, the French High Command had an opportunity to buy the designs of the needle gun and eventually decided not to proceed with it. The year before, they had turned down the Gatling, the first mechanical machine gun, so they were at least consistent. In 1868, Alfred Krupp offered his cannon to the French Army but his specifications and the evaluations by French specialists were simply filed with the comment *'Rien à faire'*[7].

The overall effect of exports on international relationships was to translate the competition between producer states into the wider world, but from the industrial and commerical point of view, the export market promoted economic and technical benefits. It was for that reason that Krupp was seriously asked by the Russian and French governments in succession to transfer his entire plant to their respective countries. The consequences of his declining to do so are an essential ingredient in the development of Europe in our time. The enterprise remained at the disposal of German policy.

This was, perhaps, the last time such an offer could have been considered. After 1870, the European world was polarised and eventually hardened into the two alliance systems which went to war in 1914. Industrial enterprise was nationalised in the primary sense of being required to operate within national boundaries for national ends, which were increasingly defined by the state rather than being left to the patriotism of the manufacturer. From the point of view of government, industry's international ramifications were justified because they strengthened the home industrial base. Market shares assured by cartel and similar arrangements kept capacity in being at a certain desired level; exchanges of patents allowed a state to tap technology developed elsewhere, which, in consequence was not a charge on the national effort. The state ceased to be the passive recipient of the results of enterprise and worked to bring about the configuration with industry which it, the state, required. This took place even in 'Free Trade' Britain. In 1891, the Admiralty informed Whitehead* that further contracts for torpedoes would be dependent on his setting up a plant in Britain. Whitehead complied, founding a works at Weymouth. In 1906, the whole business came up for sale, and the Foreign Office took the initiative in asking Vickers to buy the assets in Britain and Hungary, to prevent their falling into other hands. Vickers thereupon bought a controlling interest. Naval requirements promoted another breach of the liberal order. So as to enlarge the national capacity, the British Government undertook to guarantee a work load for a group of shipbuilders and engineering firms which wanted to compete with Armstrongs and Vickers. Thus the Coventry Ordnance Works came into being, and were eventually managed by a serving naval

---

*John Whitehead, son of the founder of the Whitehead Torpedo Company, was a British national but the enterprise in which he was a major shareholder was a registered company of the Kingdom of Hungary, located in Fiume (now Rijeka).

officer who resigned his commission for that purpose.* The state, in all countries, began to undermine the liberal economy in regard to its military requirements, even before the War broke out.

The War destroyed it. Capital was conscripted as well as manpower; management autonomy yielded to centralised direction of the economy and rationing of commodities: the 'market' ceased to allocate goods and services. Though much of the apparatus of control was abandoned or allowed to decay after 1918, the dislocations induced by the War persisted and the peace did not last long enough for the old order to be reinstated in the industrialised states of Europe. Their response to the Depression and the onset of the Second World War reaffirmed the changes brought about by the First, which in consequence still shape our contemporary world. In this sense the First World War is more significant than the Second, which extended and intensified its lessons, making them normal rather than exceptional but did not create any intrinsically new ones.

The knell for the old values and practices began to toll at Verdun and the Somme. War changed fundamentally in character and concept. What as recently as July 1914 had been unthinkable had been thought and was acted upon in the pursuit of what was traditionally regarded as victory but in a context in which victory could no longer be obtained on the traditional terms. The difference stemmed from the development of industrialised society. War became 'total' to the point at which, as will be seen, it now ramifies into the whole of society and touches on the limits of the economy and the frontiers of knowledge. This is a matter not only of scale but of complexity. The definitions and arrangements necessary to peace have correspondingly changed in content. The meanings we now attach to 'war' and 'peace' began to take shape in 1916. The Great War thus marks a discontinuity in our culture.

---

*see below, pages 150–1.

PART II

1830–1870

'Their Lordships felt it their bounden duty to discourage to the utmost of their ability the use of steam vessels, as they considered that the introduction of steam was calculated to strike a fatal blow at the naval supremacy of the Empire.'

Lord Melville, First Lord of the Admiralty, to the Colonial Secretary, 1828

1. Technical change and war at sea

Navies experienced the impact of industrialisation before armies. Both France and Great Britain had a long seafaring tradition, and at the time that industry was beginning to turn out the innovations which would change the perspectives of warfare and diplomacy, Britain had virtually no home army, while the campaigns in which French troops engaged in Spain (1823) and Algeria (1830) did not impose new technological demands. There were, in consequence, no stresses on the high commands to promote the adaptation of new techniques. With the navies, it was otherwise; in Britain, the fleet enjoyed social and political approval which did not extend to the army* and funds were somewhat more easily voted; in France, efforts were directed from 1820 onwards to restoring the naval forces to the position they had occupied before the Revolution and Nelson had successively removed them as a fighting arm. For French strategists, steam offered the opportunity of overcoming Britain's superiority in the number of vessels and seamanship at a stroke: an early recognition of technology as a leveller of differences in state power through suddenly superseding the factors on which power had hitherto been based.

Steam was applied to ships of war from the 1820s onwards. Its adoption was, at the outset, hindered by the disproportionate demand of engines and fuel on the available space and the vulnerability to shell fire of engines and paddle wheels exposed above the waterline. For these reasons, the steamship was considered to be useful only for coastal defence, within range of refuelling stations. Otherwise it was a useful auxiliary to sail. The replacement of paddlewheels by screw propulsion (1843–1845) rid steamships of this defensive limitation and enabled far-ranging political and naval strategies to be considered. By 1850 steam had replaced sail for ships of the line.

This thirty-year development produced a number of changes in the composition of fleets. Steam vessels were capable of greater variations in speeds; they could thus be designed more closely in relation to their

---

*The proposal to found an officers club (the United Services Club) was denounced in 1815 as 'a national danger likely to foster the military spirit and the professional pride of officers.'

envisaged use. This factor in itself tended to differentiate civil from naval vessels far more than in the days of sail, in addition to changes in armament and the civilian need for more economy in fuel consumption. In effect, the replacement of sail by steam allowed far more effective action within a more limited radius. Having adequate stocks of fuel in hand therefore became imperative; the steam navy needed colliers and supply ships. The type of fuel also became an important consideration; navies needed to burn coal which had a high thermal content in relation to its weight and which was quickly combustible for steam raising. Other types of dependence resulted from changes in armament and of the related defences. The first innovation, in time, was the Paixhans gun, tested in Brest in 1824 and officially adopted by the French navy in 1837. The gun fired a shell, at high velocity on a flat trajectory; it inflicted damage not by impact (as with solid shot) but by exploding after penetration. Similar guns were introduced into the British Navy in 1839. These were sharper constraints on the military and political intentions of states than had been hitherto experienced. The conversion from sail to steam sacrificed range and some kinds of mobility for vastly enhanced effectiveness within the range of fuel supplies.

The changes brought about by the developments in technology also pointed to the likely use of the new vessels. A steam warship might be considered suitable only for coastal defence, but the Channel was narrow enough for it to become an offensive weapon in those waters. Increases in size and operating range merely translated this offensive capacity to the North Sea and then into the Atlantic. In this way progress in technique shifted the practical distinction between defence and offence. It also entailed political action. Building up fuel stocks demanded coaling stations, on routes of strategic importance. This necessity became a component of international policy, either through acquiring sites, or through treaty arrangements ensuring supply. Direct acquisition usually involved other considerations than merely those of supply: navies in peacetime relied very much on the bunker trade for merchant ships. Nonetheless, the techniques which conferred on industrialised states a far wider range of effective action at sea, made them at the same time more dependent on bases (irrespective of whether they were civil or naval) and allies.

These, however, were not invented for navies. Bases and allies were part of the traditional fabric of arrangements whereby states sought to maintain their security. Steam navies extended the demand geographically, and by doing so introduced two complications into the system. Permanent bases, as distinct from simple revictualling arrangements, were themselves often an element in a local political situation into which the naval state was drawn. Also a base itself could translate into a remote area rivalry between the 'naval' governments concerned. The prolonged wrangles between the British and French Governments over Aden and Djibouti, respectively, is a case in point. In both these respects, bases for navies multiplied the points of possible or actual friction in foreign relations.

The experiments with steam and screw propulsion which occupied the 1820s and 1830s made more headway with civil than with naval vessels. The operational hazards referred to made adaptation a slow process but *that* in itself also indicated an absence of political tensions between the two industrialising states, Britain and France. At the end of the thirties, however, constructional rivalry and cooperation – French steamships relied on marine engines made in Britain – gave place to political and diplomatic conflict, as the Anglo-French *entente* broke down over policy towards the Ottoman Empire. The successful rebellion of Mehemet Ali of Egypt against his nominal suzerain in Constantinople, divided the two powers. France supported Mehemet Ali to strengthen the French position in the Near East and North Africa. His army was organised by French officers and armed with weapons paid for out of the receipts of his cotton plantations. Britain opposed Mehemet Ali, on the grounds that any weakening of the authority of the Ottoman Government could only benefit Russia, and that the encouragement which Britain gave to French ambitions in Algeria should not be extended to Egypt, where they would threaten the overland route to India.

These events marked the beginning of a series of crises in Anglo-French relations which endured as long as the July Monarchy. Hostilities between the two countries were only narrowly avoided. The tactical value of the new power was demonstrated off the coast of Lebanon, when steamships were used by the British naval forces to tow sailing ships of the line into commanding battle stations, in spite of light winds. The French could therefore invariably be out-manoeuvred. No actions were fought; the French fleet was recalled to Toulon. The technical inferiority of the French Navy nullified the advantages in design of its vessels and the acknowledged skill of its Admiral, Lalande. Politically, the inferiority meant that France could not aid its protégé. The operations of Egyptian troops in Syria were brought to a halt through bombardments and the landing of forces. Mehemet Ali was forced to evacuate Syria and to return the Turkish fleet, which had fallen into his hands, but was confirmed as hereditary ruler of Egypt – which left the French position intact, if not quite so unassailable as it otherwise would have been.

The resolution of the crisis in July 1841 only sharpened the competition between Britain and France. The French Navy, rebuilt largely during the previous decade, had been demonstrably out-manoeuvred by the latest technology, and French policy had thereby been unable to attain its objectives. The Navy would have to be converted to steam. For this purpose, it was imperative to cease to rely on imports of engines from Britain, and to encourage domestic manufacture. The firm of Schneider already lay to hand. A new model engine was commissioned, but it blew up on test in 1841. Part of the trouble was traced to design faults, but part to the quality of French iron. This remained a source of difficulty for the emerging engineering industry as a whole. Accordingly, the French Government sought to stimulate the ingenuity of French iron-masters by protecting their efforts through tariffs. In consequence, the price of finished metal goods on the domestic market was some thirty-five per cent above the cost of comparable imports. This is one of the earliest examples of a 'tax' on the general consumer to maintain in being and develop an industry considered vital for national security. French coal was, similarly, unsuitable for coking and the needs of furnaces were largely met by wood until 1864. The fuel needs of the navy were covered basically by imports, especially of anthracite from South Wales.

These policies were generally debated in the press and Parliament, in terms which revolved round the opinions of the Prince de Joinville, son of Louis Philippe and Vice Admiral of the French Navy, who published them anonymously in a series of articles in the *Journal des Débats* and the *Revue des deux Mondes*. These articles provided the strategic doctrine for which the steam navy was being created, and, hence, suggested the foreign policy which it was designed to support. His argument was that in the age of steam, vessels intended for war could not by the nature of their construction be switched to other uses. They either were for war or for nothing. They represented a particular kind of investment. A French steam navy would have two theatres of operation, the Channel and the Mediterranean. Taking Britain as a *'hypothèse convenue'*, the Prince suggested that a steam navy would allow the transport of an attacking force by night to any point on the British coast with impunity. It would also provide for the protection of the French coast from Dunkirk to Bayonne, 'for Britain can do against us all that we can do against her'. The argument admitted the traditional activity of French naval forces, commerce raiding, but only as secondary to the main invasion based strategy. It necessitated a minimum of sixteen first-line ships which should take priority over the elaboration of facilities (*'magnifiques ateliers enfermés dans les monuments grandioses'*). The burden of the unprecedented costs could be eased by spreading them over several financial years. In return France would provide herself with a means of keeping Britain in check and would increase her strength in negotiation.

This rationale of a steam navy was debated by Parliamentary Commissions called to examine budgetary appropriations and additionally incurred costs, in 1841, 1845 and 1846. It was echoed by Orleanist, Republican and Bonapartist spokesmen alike. This, taken in conjunction with the clash of British and French interests in the Pacific and Latin America during the same period, failed to reassure France's cross-Channel neighbour that the intentions were strictly hypothetical. The British reacted by setting aside more funds for the building of steamships and experimented widely and to an extent wastefully with new techniques of construction and operation. Their yardstick was what they knew of French policy. The French were aiming at building a fleet capable, not of dominating, but of preventing all domination at sea. The British wished to protect their already extensive imperial territories and felt vulnerable to invasion. The arms race ensued, with each budget or defence debate on either side of the Channel bidding up the stakes.

A key factor in maintaining tension was the renovation of the port of Cherbourg as a naval base which was, unlike Brest and Rochefort, almost impossible to blockade. The idea antedated the Revolution but was resurrected during the crisis of 1840–41 and from then on involved increasing expenditure on facilities and fortifications against attack by land or sea (the extension of the railway to Cherbourg was put through partly to ease the reinforcement of the garrison). British observers were quick to note that Cherbourg alone cost some £7.5 million in a decade, and contrasted the condition of Portsmouth and Sheerness, which had had virtually no money spent on them since the Napoleonic Wars.

Cherbourg marks a new form of international competition – in construction of strategic facilities. Ordinary harbours no longer necessarily sufficed for naval operations, special ones had to be built and maintained. But the construction made no sense unless it was related to an envisaged strategy, and that strategy could be worked out as easily by the state which was its objective as by the government initiating it. The fact of construction therefore became a threat in itself, and since the essence of a threat is that it should be seen as one, the necessary publicity and the time allotted to the various phases of construction themselves kept Britain uncomfortably aware of the threat over a period of time. The climax of this demonstration occurred in 1858 when Napoleon III showed off the harbour and associated workshops to Queen Victoria and Prince Albert. The message was not lost: Britain could no longer rely on the inadequacy of French harbours – as in the days of Napoleon I – to protect herself from invasion: Cherbourg would allow the French battle fleet protecting the transports to assemble in sufficient numbers to force the passage of the Channel. The traditional British strategy of frustrating the assembly at sea of a large French fleet as its component units emerged from the various harbours along the coast would no longer work.

This intensive naval activity in France promoted what appears to be the first systematic examination of the roles and competences respectively of the state and private industry in regard to covering the former's (vastly expanded) requirements. Between 1849 and 1851, a legislative commission thrashed out the issues in the course of an investigation into the navy. Arguing from British practice and the equal, if not superior, capability of the French, the industrialists urged a policy of relying on private industry, rather than naval foundries, which, they alleged, suffered additionally from being technically backward. Since the naval authorities, faced with the extra expense of ironclad ships, wanted a small but powerful fleet kept in being, they accepted the industrialists' basic argument and recommended closure of some of the state foundry capacity and the stimulation of industrial effort through placing of contracts. In the event, however, some state establishments were retained to monitor performance and set standards. It proved a prudent decision.

2. Anglo-French cooperation and rivalry

The strained relationships between the two states were only modified slowly. The *coup d'état* by which Louis Napoleon became President of France, followed by his subsequent election as Emperor, did nothing to abate the fear of invasion, which, Cherbourg excepted, did not in fact square with the state of French forces. Louis Philippe's building programme had been abandoned, and the French army was reduced in numbers – both results of the chaotic state of French finances. Napoleon himself regarded an understanding with Britain – a quarter in which his uncle had conspicuously failed – as essential, and worked to that end. The interests of the two states in the Near East also began to converge. France disputed Russian claims to protect the holy places in Palestine and the Christians who lived under Ottoman rule. Britain likewise took exception to these claims and had the additional and perennial nineteenth-century concern as to the designs Russia was thought to harbour on India. Britain and France, accordingly, drifted towards each other and into war with Russia.

The Crimean War was, perhaps, the last pre-industrial conflict. The armies were exclusively professional; the field of operations limited, the field leadership innocent of any thought about the tactical use of new weapons; the invaders had their retinue of *Schlachtenbummler*. But such bloody inanities as the Charge of the Light Brigade have obscured the evidences of modernity which the war revealed.

It was the first in which the field commander was directed from home by means of the telegraph. A line from Bucharest to Varna and then under the Black Sea to the Crimea made General Pélissier the first, but not the last, general officer to complain of being snared at the end of a wire. It was also the first war in which rifles appeared (although the allied commanders ignored the advantage they had in this respect over the Russians, who were armed with muskets). The Crimea was additionally the first place in which the problems of terrain were overcome by building a railway, without which the siege of Sebastopol would have had to be abandoned.*

---

*The British command decided to use a railway to overcome the mud which made the 16-mile round trip from the base at Balaklava to Sebastopol take eleven hours and restricted supplies to the besieging troops. Civil contractors arrived in the Crimea in January 1855 to [*cont.*]

The most radical departures occurred at sea. The Russians experimented with torpedoes and both contact and electrically discharged mines. These however were portents of technical change for the future. The Allied naval operations yielded some immediate problems which industry was required to solve, which, therefore, brought industrial considerations into decisions of foreign policy. This consequence derived almost entirely from the technical enthusiasms of Napoleon III.

On 17 October 1854, the fleet bombarding Sebastopol suffered severely from the Russian return fire in the form of shells which pierced wooden hulls and exploded between decks. Napoleon promptly decided to suspend the production of wooden ships and protect the existing fleet with armour plating. He sought to interest his British allies in his solution to the problem of withstanding return fire, which went beyond equipping vessels with protective iron to designing a 'floating battery' of shallow draught and heavy firepower which would be employed to pulverise fortifications from inshore. The British Government agreed to build to French designs and sent naval constructors to study French techniques in ship-building. In return, Britain shared designs of its sixty-eight-pounder gun. Ten batteries were launched, of which three duly arrived in the Black Sea where, protected by four-inch iron plating and manoeuvring under power from 225 hp engines, they put the fortress of Kinburn, near Odessa, out of action, for negligible loss on 17 November 1855.

For the French, the ability to put through such a rapid innovation rested ultimately on the Navy's long-standing connection with Schneider. The floating batteries were also powered by Schneider engines. Britain had larger resources to call on but accepted French design leadership.

The episode is instructive in itself, and in its consequences. Industry was involved in designing a solution to a problem which had arisen not in the course of technical enquiry but in the stress of war. Therefore, the immediate purpose determined the characteristics of the weapon. In view of the disparities between industrial resources and the need for speed, the project was shared between allies. This involved an exchange of technologies (French vessels for British gun). The time from laying down to launching was about three months, which demonstrated for all to see that a new-style fleet was no longer a remote possibility but an achievable goal; such a fleet would be able to perform tasks assigned to it with smaller numbers, greater reliability and in areas hitherto inaccessible. The floating batteries experiment thus prompted a revaluation of the role of the navy in national policy.

The revaluation was first acted upon in France. Napoleon III, in 1857,

---

[*contd. from p. 59*]   build and operate a single-track railway but their civilian employees objected to the conditions and went on strike. They were shipped home and replaced by service personnel who after the war were officially organised as the corps of railway engineers.

embarked on the creation of a steam and ironclad navy which would rival the Royal Navy in numbers and technical advance.

Napoleon's decision to renovate the French Navy did not involve equipping existing vessels with steam engines or screw-propulsion but devising new vessels, with larger ordnance and protected by armour plate. There was a qualitative change, compared with the days of Louis Philippe. To translate the new requirements into ships for service, Napoleon appointed the celebrated designer Dupuy de Lôme as Surveyor of the Navy, with full authority. De Lôme suggested that to achieve parity with Britain, it was not necessary to match her ship for ship: French aims would be accomplished by concentrating on a new class of fast, armoured frigates. The first was *La Gloire,* of 1859: she was the first of three ironclads (wooden hulls with iron armour plate) laid down the previous year, which marked the beginning of the de Lôme programme. Two more were laid down in 1859, and the following year the number was increased by ten. By 1862/3, France achieved parity with Britain in the decisive arm of the fleet; each state had four frigates equipped for action, but the French vessels carried more guns.

Britain's response to the French challenge was to embark on a similar ship building programme, but it was impeded by the as yet unresolved controversy as to the operational merits of iron and wooden ships respectively. The proponents of iron saw the race with France as an opportunity not merely to get ahead in numbers but to carry through a change in the quality of the Navy, from ironclad wooden ships to vessels constructed of iron throughout. The arguments in favour of wood rested on its relative non-fouling properties in tropical waters, where British squadrons reckoned to have to spend time on station. The reconditioning costs of wooden vessels and the expansion of facilities around the world for cleaning iron merchantmen removed the traditionalists' objections. It was generally conceded that iron ships made better platforms for guns and could carry weightier armour. So Britain converted to iron – and by so doing rid itself of a century-long preoccupation with the politics of the Baltic, which had been the prime source of timber and cordage. The debate over the change, however, firmly established that, in view of Britain's existing colonial commitments, the Navy had to encompass a wider range of tasks than the French navy, which was being rebuilt to the old formula of the Prince de Joinville, namely concentration on the Channel and the Mediterranean. Thus cruising range was not so important an element in design.

The Anglo-French naval race, therefore, began under Louis Philippe with the adaptation of existing vessels in greater numbers. It finished, under Napoleon III, with a qualitative competition in vessels designed from scratch. The two contestants had rather different aims. Britain wanted a navy capable of dealing with the French threat *and* with policing Britain's interests round the world. France could work to a more limited strategy. By 1864, Britain had expanded the navy to 934 vessels of all classes, with seventy-two line-of-battle ships carrying over seventy-six guns, compared with only twenty-two in that class ten years previously. In that class, France was quite inferior, with only thirty-seven, but it outnumbered Britain in frigates and corvettes. Thirty-seven battle ships were enough to deter, or if need be, beat off an invasion: the frigates and corvettes could, through commerce raiding, strike at Britain's most vulnerable spot.

In France, the decision to embark on a naval race brought about a new kind of relationship between government and industry. The Crimean War proved false the earlier administrative assumption that private industry would be able to make up the numbers required during hostilities. One Schneider did not make a war machine. French industry was not in the front rank of production methods. The political conditions, that is the desire to rival Britain, did not allow the building up of an entirely state-owned series of production establishments, while renovating the existing plant (which was put in hand) did not by itself provide the scale of output required. The naval authorities met this dilemma by deliberately placing contracts to drive out the inefficient producers and encourage those who were efficient, or were within reach of becoming so. Napoleon III provided a negative incentive to improvement through the Anglo-French Commercial Treaty of 1860, which, by lowering tariff levels on metallurgical imports, cut at the industry's price-fixing arrangements which had protected the least efficient producers, and reduced profits per unit of output.

At the same time, the French Government assisted the metallurgical industry to meet the new competitive conditions by providing loans at low rates of interest to encourage firms to modernise or to experiment with new processes. The official commission supervising the distribution and application of these loans deliberately steered them towards firms engaged in the naval programme – and that programme was fixed at a level designed to promote the maximum use of available capacity. For French manufacturing industry, naval contracts averted the worst effects of the first world slump in 1857, of the Commercial Treaty in 1860 and of the recession of 1867. Measures in this last year were especially significant. Production in naval arsenals was reduced in order to maintain the flow of work to private industry, and the budget for naval construction stepped up to inject an additional twelve million francs into the metallurgical industry.

The French Government had initiated a new form of relationship between state and industry, in which the government through its financial and tariff policies determined the range and quality of manufacture it required to have available for the purposes of rearmament and national defence. This, French manufacturers approved. They were not wedded to the idea of competition (except with other states), tended to blame all their misfortunes on the Commercial Treaty (regarded in Britain as a model of enlightenment) and were pleased to have the state bail them out of the worst effects of industrial depression. Thus the fact that the manufacturing facilities were privately owned was irrelevant to the outcome of state policy, though not to the means employed. Napoleon III conclusively demonstrated that governments could get the results they wanted from the private sector with existing techniques.

Through political rivalry between France and Britain from 1840 onwards, the 'arms race' entered international relations in the industrial age. It was not just a problem of matching a rival in numbers: it was a matter of 'out-performing' a political opponent whom one expected to become an actual enemy. 'Performance' in this context meant designing and producing weapons and investing in facilities which offered superior strategic or tactical options, but long before either were likely to be used. The yardstick for the peacetime preparation now necessary was what the opponent was thought or known to intend. The full rigours of this development awaited subsequent decades.

During the mid-nineteenth century, international exchanges of materials and ideas were far more free than they have been since. Facilities were customarily open to inspection. But, by reason of the investment in facilities and in more complex weapons, an arms race modified political relationships permanently, even when the fears which prompted it died down or were proved illusory. After 1865, Britain and France both had fleets whose character was determined exclusively by the political rivalry which had brought them into being. France, perhaps more than Britain, had deliberately chosen one option, and designed a fleet accordingly – which automatically closed down other options for policy, or made them more difficult to realise thereafter. It is also noteworthy that the fleets were never used against one another, and that therefore the political assumptions on which they were built were not put to the test. It was quite impossible to determine whether the absence of warfare indicated that the deterrent had worked: the more so as the fleets cooperated in 1861 in the seizure of Vera Cruz as a demonstration in support of European bondholders' claims on the Mexican Government.

3. Technical change and war on land

The adaptation of steam power to land warfare, in the form of the railway, did not raise the same intrinsic problems of design, metallurgy or fuel supply. Unlike a ship of the line, the train was not a fighting unit in itself* but merely a means of transporting troops and material far better than by horses and oxen.

As regards manufacture, there was, from the military standpoint, no debate about the relative merits of building in state establishments, such as arsenals or in private plants. The costs of manufacturing the equipment and of keeping the facility in being was borne, wholly or partly, by the day-to-day civil use of trains. For the soldiers, the problem was not merely a matter of getting to a specific destination more quickly, of which the first example was the two-day journey in 1846 by Prussian troops, which gave the *coup de grâce* to the independent republic of Cracow. It was a question of siting the facilities where they would serve the considerations of higher strategy. These necessarily took into account the traditional political rivalries and enmities. General staffs and diplomats became very interested in the activities of concessionaires and in the planning of route, especially where these involved the cutting of major tunnels, which dramatised the strategic effect of railways by threatening to remove traditional obstacles. In the same order of thinking, the location of junctions and the transfer facilities they provided were particularly important. Junctions became the land equivalent of coaling stations.

This approach to questions of construction was less marked in Britain than in Continental Europe, since on an island railways, by definition, could only serve ports – which they did automatically in their 'civil' function. Rail transport could, perhaps, reinforce home defence by adding mobility to coastal artillery, but that was all.

There was also another significant difference; in Britain railways were built when industrialisation was already under way throughout the economy: the military then discussed how they could be used for their particular purposes. In Continental Europe, railways were not one aspect of industrialisation;

---

*Armoured trains or railway-mounted artillery for coastal defence are only a minor exception.

they were, to a great extent, its initiator. As such, they loomed large in the writings of theorists of modernisation, such as the Saint-Simonians in France and Friedrich List in Germany. The railways' potential for foreign policy was a factor in their development from the start. In the aftermath of the Napoleonic wars no publicist was able to undervalue the military aspects of policy, but in the view of the early Continental theorists, security and prosperity were served by the same developments.

French publicists eagerly discussed the necessity for France to be able to transport troops from Paris to the Rhine and from Lyons to the Alps – themes which were prudently echoed by entrepreneurs seeking official sanction for construction.* In Germany, arguments for railways began with the additional defence they offered by allowing troops to be moved quickly up and down the Rhineland against French incursions, but as enthusiasm for railways was taken up by a wider public, the contribution of rail to the more efficient concentration of forces in the Rhineland became a dominant theme in debate. In consequence, by the 1840s when the debates became more general, politicians and entrepreneurs in the two countries were using identical arguments – though with opposing ends in mind!

In all this endeavour, the civilians were ahead of the military. Individual high commands took some time to accept the new technique and accustom themselves to its use. The first systematic official analysis of the effect of the railway on strategy appears to have been the 'Survey of Traffic and Equipment by German and Neighbouring Foreign Railways' undertaken by the Prussian General Staff in 1843–50. Meanwhile the major states all had practice in transporting troops, horses and materials – the Prussians in Schleswig-Holstein in 1848–9 and the Austrians by transporting 75,000 men, 8,000 horses and 1,000 vehicles from Vienna to Silesia in 1850. In the following year the Russians moved a division of 14,500 men, with guns, horses and vehicles from Cracow to Hradish in Moravia. Not all these movements were successful; the Austrian, covering 150 miles, took twenty-six days which presented no advantage in time over marching – but from the subsequent inquest into the failures emerged in May 1851 a decision to construct strategic railways throughout the Monarchy. The Prussian movements were too limited to offer anything but practice in getting in and out of trains – itself a modest but necessary exercise – but the Russian forces demonstrated what could be done since they took only two days to cover 187 miles.

---

*The invasion of 1814 had a traumatic effect on military and public opinion in nineteenth-century France: it was the first successful attempt since French ascendancy in Europe began in 1642. Paris had never been occupied. Marlborough's campaigns had laid France open to invasion in 1710 but the plans were abandoned. In 1792, Valmy not only stopped the invaders but allowed French armies to carry the war into their traditional campaigning grounds of Germany and Italy.

One dimension of strategy, time, was changing for the first time for centuries and inevitably altered the other two, force and space. How fundamental this change was, emerged through practice.

The first international conflict in which these changes could be measured was the outcome of Napoleon III's concern for the unity of Italy – part of his political inheritance and an area of consistent French interest from the time of Charles VIII and Francis I. Like theirs, Napoleon's policy disputed Austrian claims, but Napoleon, unlike his predecessors, had to hand an associate in the form of the Kingdom of Sardinia which, under Cavour, was in process of being modernised with the aid of French finance and expertise.

Cavour had grasped the implications of railways for Italian unity and encouraged their construction.[1] In Piedmont, the principal venture was the Victor Emmanuel company, tactfully named after the King, which in May 1853 obtained a charter to build a line westwards from Mont Cénis to the French frontier. The company was funded by British and French capital, and from December 1855, its shares were admitted to the Paris Bourse – hitherto strictly closed to foreign registrations. The following February the Victor Emmanuel bought out the existing Piedmontese state railways from the east side of Mont Cénis to Turin. By the autumn of 1858 all the constructions and amalgamations were completed, except for a tunnel through Mont Cénis (which, however, the Piedmontese Government undertook to construct at its own expense and then sell to the company at half cost).* In all these transactions, economic and financial measures were intended to consolidate political links between Piedmont and France.

These relationships, for present purposes, crystallised in the Pact of Plombières, of 20 July 1858, when, in negotiations with Cavour, Napoleon engaged himself to declare war on Austria the following May – Piedmont having provoked Austria into action in the meantime through what the victims rightly called 'permanent aggression'. Napoleon also promised to use his influence in the financial world to enable Piedmont to obtain loans in Paris for weapons.

The Plombières arrangements tied diplomatic and military moves to a timetable from the outset, but the schedule was not inflexible and depended entirely on political circumstances. The terms were not formally embodied

---

*The construction of the great tunnels through the Alps caused all conventional strategies to be reassessed. The resistance of British Governments to a Channel Tunnel was ultimately on strategic grounds, it being usually argued that the tunnel might be used by France (or some power in control of the area) to launch a surprise attack without a Declaration of War. The supporters of the tunnel schemes employed Cobdenite arguments, maintaining especially that in the enlightened days of the nineteenth century, no European state would begin hostilities without complying with the usages of the Law of Nations. In 1883, the Government settled the argument by publishing an official paper on 'Hostilities without a Declaration of War from 1700 to 1870', which proved that 'every one of the Great Powers of Europe' (including Britain) had in fact gone to war without formal declaration, in the period concerned. Such candour has on the whole disappeared from state papers in this century.

in a treaty till 10 December; thereafter, from New Year's Day, Napoleon deliberately allowed relations with Austria to deteriorate. This first move in the diplomacy of conflict marked also the beginning of covert military preparations, which went on even though by February the expectation of war had receded, and in April the whole undertaking was all but cancelled unilaterally by Napoleon. During the spring, troops were quietly concentrated in the area between Besançon and Grenoble under cover of normal postings. There was as yet no formal mobilisation. The Austrian Government responded to Piedmontese provocation by ordering the mobilisation of its troops in Italy on 28 February. Full mobilisation took place five weeks later – a procedure complicated by the practice in the Imperial and Royal army of posting units as far away from their home areas as possible. French mobilisation orders were issued in response and troop movements to the South and the Piedmontese frontier began on April 19.

Armed conflict was always the most likely outcome, since that had been the object of the discussions at Plombières, but it still did not *automatically* follow from the manoeuvres so far. On 23 April Victor Emmanuel accepted Austrian terms to disarm. At that point through the display of strength by the Austrians and Napoleon's irresolution for war, the conflict might well have been resolved by international conference had not the Austrian Government cut the ground from under its own feet by summarily demanding that Victor Emmanuel demobilise all his troops within three days. The ultimatum was rejected. Cavour formally requested French help in repelling the Austrian attack. Austrian forces under General Gyulai invaded Piedmont on the 29 April and France formally declared war on 3 May. Napoleon himself landed in Genoa on the 12th but most of his troops went by the Victor Emmanuel railway. Even though the Mont Cénis tunnel did not exist (it was not opened until 1871), they still arrived in Turin, on average, ten days after leaving their depots in the Rhône Valley. On foot and horseback, the journey would have taken six times as long.

The Austrians also had to contend with uncompleted stretches of line – in their case, the link over the Brenner from Innsbruck to Bozen. Nevertheless, the journey of the First Corps (comprising approximately 40,000 men and 10,000 horses) from Prague to Verona occupied only fourteen days, instead of sixty-four. The Third Corps also took only two weeks to reach Lombardy from Vienna. In contrast with the French, however, these were the best, not the average times. Laibach was the scene of total chaos: everywhere rolling stock failed to coincide with concentrations of troops or stores. The Austrian Government had the additional problem that, the railway company having been sold to French concessionaires, senior staff manning most of the lines in the Tyrol and Northern Italy were French nationals; they were placed 'in a state of temporary inactivity'.

On the French side, too, the administration of the system as a whole fell far behind the competence shown in transporting troops to the front in the first instance. There was no pursuit after the battle of Solferino because the ammunition, food and fodder which would have made it possible were still tangled up en route.

But such administrative muddles impressed contemporary opinions far less than the demonstration of the effect of the railway strategy. For the first time in the history of warfare, troops could be delivered to the combat area, fresh for action and in the same numbers as they left barracks.* Over 600,000 men and 129,000 horses went from France to Italy. Large armies were now technically possible.

Railways might have become an indispensable adjunct to war, but they were not yet an inflexible element in the diplomacy of its preliminaries. The French forces were transported to Italy in special trains, without disrupting normal services; and Napoleon's last minute changes of mind did not have to take into consideration the possibility of chaos, if the trains were summarily cancelled. The troops would merely have stayed in their barracks. The experience of 1859 also showed conclusively that the formal ownership of the facilities was irrelevant to their use for war purposes. The lines of Piedmont were in French and British hands, the Austrian lines were in French hands. Foreign capital holdings evidently did not interfere with the execution of state policy.

There were, however, special considerations. The war lasted only nine weeks, from the 3 May to 8 July, so that the full consequences of administrative chaos behind the front could not be experienced. There was insufficient time either to overcome the problems or be overwhelmed by them. More importantly, French policies were coordinated by one man who had the power of final decision.

*Some critics suggested that such pampering would leave the soldiers too soft for action.

4. Railways and strategy: 1859–1866–1870

The discrepancy between the diplomatic and military aspects of foreign policy which the application of industry implied, was forced open by Helmuth von Moltke, who became Chief of the General Staff in Prussia in 1857. Moltke, by then fifty-seven, as a professional soldier in a royal army, worked within narrower limits than Napoleon III, but the enthusiasm for railways he developed while still a junior officer reflected his professional awareness of the impact of speed of communication and transport on force and space. His grasp of these relationships, which he eventually communicated to the army through the general staff system, subserved Moltke's victories. He planned his campaigns, in fact, on a large-scale railway map of Europe. How the new techniques of warfare were evolved, or procured for the army, was not Moltke's concern; it was through his use of them that he demonstrated the new strategic possibilities and the new problems for war and diplomacy posed by industrialisation.

Moltke's opportunity occurred in two short wars – successively, against Austria in 1866 (which upset the balance of political forces in Germany) and against France in 1870 (which upset the balance of Europe). The first was in fact decided, the second virtually so, within six weeks.

War between Austria and Prussia was the outcome of disputes over sharing the gains of their joint campaign against Denmark in 1864; the disputes were important, however, not so much in themselves, but as evidence of Prussian claims to supremacy in North Germany, which caused more deep-seated hostility between the two governments. Both regarded war as one possible outcome. The diplomacy of any hostilities revolved round two factors; the need of Prussia to make Austria appear the refractory party before German opinion, and the difference in speeds of mobilisation – six weeks for Prussia, three months for Austria, for armies of 250,000 men. Austria's problem was, accordingly, to mobilise forces, while attempting to convince German opinion that this was precautionary in a time of tension, as during the Crimean War. Birmarck sought to profit from these manoeuvres to convince a reluctant King that Prussian mobilisation ought to go forward.

Austria first mobilised forces, but for action in Italy only. Bismarck pointed out that Prussians found it difficult to distinguish between those troops intended for Italy and those who might be employed elsewhere. On the 27 April, 1866, the entire Austrian army was mobilised and war declared against Prussia. The latter began to mobilise from 4 to 12 May. The processes on both sides allowed attempts at mediation or other resolution of the conflict, including one plan that the two states should run Germany between them and combine against France to recover Alsace and control the Palatinate. The tortuous political manoeuvres between two states which were engaged in mobilising against each other demonstrate that mobilisation did not by itself determine a head-on collision, and did not rule out other solutions to the problem, even though the Prussian army was getting ready to open a campaign along the borders of Saxony and Bohemia and the Austrian, to advance through Moravia on Silesia.

Moltke's professional enthusiasm for railways now returned strategic benefits: he had five lines at his disposal, while his opponents had only one; he used them to bring his forces into battle formation near where he intended them to close with the enemy. The key element in this strategy was the control of the lateral railway from Dresden to Breslau. The Austrian command abandoned any advantage to be gained from a drive into Prussian territory by insisting on the reserves' joining the main forces before the general advance – a decision which compounded the operational difficulties of having to rely on only one railway. The Prussian strategy took the operations into Bohemia; the fighting was over effectively in a week, culminating in the victory of Sadowa on 3 July.

Although the railway had been intrinsic to the style of campaign the victors had carried through (whereas in Austrian planning it had been simply a superior version of horse-traction), Prussia's performance revealed a number of defects, particularly the absence of any body to coordinate the commissions controlling the various lines and ensure that the separate railway companies, whose facilities were being used, did not, through their parochial attitudes and practice, work against the operation as a whole. Army officers, too, in an excess of professional enthusiasm, tended to order train after train to the front, without considering that they might block lines needed for supplies. Moltke set up a special committee of enquiry, composed of military and civilian transport experts under his own chairmanship. In May 1867, it devised a series of complex arrangements to coordinate military and civil working of railways during war.

Implementing the findings of Moltke's committee was a prerequisite of his preparations for possible (in his personal view, hoped for) war with France, plans for which he began to work out in the spring of 1868. These, in contrast to previous contingency planning, involved an attack by German forces across the Rhine, for which Moltke required four additional railway lines and the renovation of the military telegraph. The success of the operation depended on the speed with which it could be carried out, and therefore on the relative mobilisation times of Prussia against France and against Austria, were the latter to join in. (Moltke calculated that Austrian forces would not be brought to bear for at least eight weeks). Railways also suggested the choice of Prussian objectives. Moltke concluded that the existing railway network *must* tie the French forces to Metz and Strasbourg, as bases for an offensive against Germany. The Prussians would, in consequence, aim to strike between the two, defeating the French forces in detail, before they could advance across the Rhine and enter the – politically unreliable – states of South Germany, and before Austria could have lumbered into action, if allied to France. Moltke's plans were settled early in 1859 and thereafter translated into detailed operational orders for the respective army corps.

Contingency planning of this order drew on the collective memory of two centuries of French domination of Germany. For Moltke and many others east of the Rhine, Napoleon III conjured up a myth and implied a programme. He was considered an adventurer who might readily follow his uncle and Louis XIV in using Germany as a campaigning ground to establish French hegemony in Europe. The supposition was well-founded, although Napoleon, more modestly than his forebears, aimed to be the acknowledged leader and arbitrator rather than hegemonic ruler, making and unmaking states and dynasties. He chose to begin his foreign policy in the Near East and Italy, but the Rhine frontier was never far from his political calculations. In January 1852, immediately after the *coup d'état* which foreshadowed the Empire, he began to concern himself about the Rhine fortresses which had fallen to Prussia in 1815. Later, he manoeuvred in the dispute between Austria and Prussia, with the intention of promoting French influence in the Rhineland, as residual beneficiary of the conflict. When war did break out, in 1866, the speed of the Prussian victory and the conclusion of an armistice left Napoleon's diplomacy trailing behind events. It nullified his initial premise that the struggle would be drawn out long enough to induce the combatants to accept France as an arbitrator which would allow him to continue his manoeuvres in another form and help to promote Austrian-Prussian rivalry. Instead Napoleon could only assert claims for compensation comprising the boundary of 1814 and Luxembourg, which Bismarck turned down. The French attempt to acquire Luxembourg in the next year and the role of France in the affair of the Belgian railways throughout 1868–69 were both expressions of the same desire to re-establish a frontier on the Rhine.[2]

The setback to French policy at Bismarck's hands provoked demands among the French military and their publicists for war against Prussia, to gain through victory the 'compensations' which Bismarck had denied. It was axiomatic that France had a right to the frontiers of 1801, of which it had been robbed in 1815 (no-one asked how France came to possess the frontiers of 1801). Equity demanded that these frontiers be restored: if claims to equity were denied, then the frontiers should be rectified by force of arms: – in which case, the sooner, the better. France wanted '*revanche pour Sadowa*'. The French soldier was so superior to his Prussian counterpart that disparities in numbers were of no importance: the Chassepôt rifle and the mitrailleuse would equip him with superior firepower.

Whether the French government used the army as a threat to gain diplomatic ends or whether the threat was to be quickly translated into hostilities, the deployment of troops and material would rely on the railway. For *any* forward policy by France in the Rhineland, the Prussian success of 1866 suggested the first requirement. In March 1869, Marshal Niel appointed a *'Commission Centrale des Chemins de Fer'*, composed of civil and military representatives to coordinate the use of railways for mobilisation and operations. The Commission's investigations were never put into effect. In August Niel died, and with him (hindsight suggests) the initiative capable of bringing the French military effort up to something like the standards which the adventurous foreign policy of the Empire made necessary. Eventually in the mobilisation ordered on 14 July, 1870, it was of considerable advantage that the General Director of the railway company on which the main burden fell (*Chemin de Fer de l'Est*) had been a member of the Commission, but it did not, inevitably, substitute for a thoroughly tested and comprehensive scheme. The regulations in force did not clearly demarcate the respon-sibilities of railway from those of military personnel or set out the appropriate chains of command.

French contingency planning as a whole suffered from basic organisational defects, professional contempt for the Prussians and confusion as to the role of Austria in any likely war. Austria as an 'armed neutral' or an active ally suggested one strategy (because either would tie down Prussian troops); Austria as a genuine neutral, another. French policy never clearly dis-tinguished between the two. French generals planned to attack Prussia in Germany along the river Main, in order to separate north and south, join Austrian troops in the neighbourhood of Nuremberg and crush the Prussians at or near Leipzig. This plan of campaign is in itself a tribute to the hold of Napoleon I on the French military mind. The political conditions under which it was feasible were never clarified. When in July, the crisis over the Hohenzollern candidature for the throne of Spain blew up unexpectedly to provide the specific occasion for war, negotiations with Austria, on which the strategy depended, were still in train. In the event, French military and political leaders thought that France could operate alone – at least for some time. On 9 and 10 July Napoleon as a precaution ordered the despatch of troops stationed in North Africa back to France, and the inspection of fortresses in the North East. Overt mobilisation was ordered on the 14th and the next day France tacitly declared war on Prussia, in the form of a parliamentary vote in favour of war credits. The formal declaration followed on the 19th.

Scrutiny of the day-to-day events in the week immediately before the opening of the war reveals the more determinate role (than in 1859) of the railway timetable in hampering attempts to moderate the crisis or dissipate it by diplomacy. There was, on both sides, a certain will to peace. The King of Prussia was not anxious to have yet another war, and wanted at most a partial and defensive mobilisation in the Rhineland to protect Mainz, but was advised by Roon and Moltke that, so far from being a retractable step on the way to full mobilisation, partial mobilisation would merely disrupt it, since the same facilities were required by both. (At much the same time, Franz Josef was receiving the same opinion from *his* advisers). In France, politicians like Thiers who considered the candidature issue not worth a war were brushed aside by those who thought that Prussia needed reminding of the France of Jena and that any delay to give time for thought 'would only give the Prussian cannon time to be loaded.' The outcome of these French parliamentary debates buried doubts as to mobilisation on both sides.

To the military-minded in France, delay was only useful to the degree that it permitted French preparations to get ahead of the Prussians. An invasion across the Rhine entailed more rapid concentration of forces; they could only be concentrated after being first mobilised. On these grounds, General Leboeuf, the War Minister, explained to the Chamber of Deputies that war was preferable sooner rather than later 'before the Prussians had changed their rifle and acquired good mitrailleuses.' Moltke, asked by Bismarck on the same day (13 July) whether he required any more time, answered in virtually the same terms.* Both sides declared themselves prepared for war, but 'readiness' did not relate to the same type of combat.

The difference was soon apparent. French generals calculated, on the basis of 1866, that the Prussians would require three weeks to mobilise an army corps and a week to transport it to the frontier areas, and that consequently any attack could only be launched some seven weeks after the date of mobilisation, at the beginning of September. When September arrived the war was more than half over. The mobilisation of Prussia and her allies began on 16 July, and on 3 and 4 August the armies were moving into the attack. Since 1866 – the French commanders discovered by bitter experience – Prussian mobilisation had been cut from five weeks to eighteen days.

French mobilisation produced almost total chaos. Eastern France had been much less developed for railway traffic than the other areas – which was wholly at variance with the aims of Napoleon's policies in the Rhineland. A law of 1868 provided for new construction, but little had been done and by 1870 there were available to the French Command only three routes eastwards out of Paris – and of these only one was double-tracked. The vital Metz-Verdun section was incomplete. On sundry occasions in the last hectic days before the war, General Leboeuf maintained that French forces would be ready to strike two weeks from mobilisation, but he related this time span

---

*Moltke was interrupted while reading a novel of Sir Walter Scott. '*Alles ist fertig. Die Klingel braucht nur gezogen zu werden*' (Everything is ready. We need only pull the bell).

to forces varying from 250,000 to 415,000 men. Leboeuf's intention was to improve on the advantage which his estimates of Prussian movements gave to France by mobilising French forces where they needed to be concentrated for action, in and around Metz and Strasbourg, and marching straightway into Luxembourg.

The idea was admirably conceived but its execution demanded precise administrative control of the very limited rail resources, particularly in the highest echelons. This was entirely lacking. The result was a chaos in which troops were separated from equipment, commanders from their troops, units from brigades, brigades from army corps. Troop trains blocked ammunition trains, and vice versa; stations made ready to receive cavalry received infantry, and vice versa; Metz and Strasbourg became completely choked with traffic. The general who commanded in Marseilles dealt with the problem of reservists for whom he had neither instructions nor accommodation by sending them to Algiers! If the campaign had followed previous practice the French forces might have had time to recover from the confusion, but the Prussian armies used the initiative their use of the railway conferred by dispensing with the customary breathing-space after battle and forcing a series of actions, which, by the evening of 1 September destroyed the French field army at Sedan, forced the surrender of Strasbourg on 28 September and the capitulation of Metz a month later.

The railway was not, of course, the whole story in Prussia's success. Moltke's arrangements worked well in the initial movement of troops; they were markedly less successful in transporting supplies on schedule and to destinations with the facilities to unload them. During much of August, when the Prussians and their allies were inflicting a series of defeats on the enemy, trains with supplies and provisions blocked the tracks on the left bank of the Rhine from Cologne almost down to Frankfurt. The German field troops were saved from the worst consequences of this muddle by the provisions they captured from the French, especially in Metz.

But, clearly, after the demonstration in August and September 1870, war was closely related – even, in some quarters thought to be functionally related – to the railway. What was less regarded by observers was the process by which the logic inherent in the use of railways reached into the diplomacy of preparations for war, rendering abortive some of the options which diplomats traditionally exercised. Moltke's own conviction was that in the railway age, mobilisation terminated the functions of diplomats, who should only come into play again to settle peace terms, if not later: 'Politics must not be allowed to interfere with operations.' In 1866, he used the railway to overcome the three-week lag behind Austria's mobilisation. In 1870, he seized the initiative against France, which German forces never relinquished, through more rapid mobilisation. Both events suggested that adverse military situations could only be avoided if the diplomats stood aside when the trains began to move. This was an ominous conclusion for the future, if military predominated over diplomatic assessments in decisions about how the state should act.

The immediate reaction in Germany was that better technique proved moral superiority and conversely, that the destruction of a Bonaparte – *Der Störenfried* – was a benefit to Europe. German opinion had not imagined – any more than French had – that a Bonapartist regime could be so technically inept in the art of war. But the Emperor's uncle had campaigned in a pre-industrial age: had those conditions continued, Napoleon III's strategy might have worked, since French commanders, who in the field were not inferior to their German *confrères*, would have had time to recover from the administrative blunders. Moltke's use of railways eliminated the chance. The Prussians and their allies won, fundamentally, because he, if no-one else, had thought through the problems of industrialised war and had come to at least some of the correct answers. In the war with Austria in 1859, France had the advantage of being the more developed state: in the conflict with Prussia four years later, the two states were more evenly balanced in that respect; nevertheless, in his German policy Napoleon III was thwarted by the use of technology – by Prussian speed in Bohemia in 1866 and by superior concentration and deployment in Alsace and Lorraine in 1870. In both campaigns, the first lasting two weeks and the second, effectively, a month, the use of technology was decisive *in the event*; if Prince Frederick Charles had arrived too late at Sadowa on 3 July 1866 or the French leadership not thrown away their chances in August and September 1870, the battles might not so easily have furthered Prussian strategy, the railway notwithstanding, and the politics of the two wars developed differently. But these considerations were overlooked or played down in the inquests on both sides. The railway emerged as *the* decisive factor in modern war. 'Don't build fortifications, build railways,' was Moltke's advice. Timetables became as familiar a feature of military life as drill manuals. It also helped the national strategy to appoint former non-commissioned officers to jobs in railway management.*

Yet to the extent that the inception of modern war and its relationship with the industrial structure can be credited to any one man, that man was not Moltke but his defeated opponent, Napoleon III. In the fifties and sixties, he applied his personal curiosity about the possibilities offered by technology to military affairs and possessed the political authority to push through the necessary measures. He grasped the need to construct a system, through

---

*A British traveller Henry Vizetelly, 'could not help being struck by the military tone which characterises the Prussian railway service. Almost all the staff have been soldiers and engine-drivers and guards invariably make a point of saluting the station-master whenever the train enters or leaves a station. It is perhaps these marks of respect received from their subordinates which render the higher railway officials so brusque and peremptory towards the travelling public.'[3]

which innovations could be exploited for the security of the state: 'Innovations that are before their time,' he wrote in a treatise on artillery, 'remain useless till the stock of general knowledge comes up to their level.' The means of integrating innovations into state policy was provided by the structure and performance of industry, both of which could be positively influenced by the state, and tied in with the instruments of its foreign policy. The insight into the need systematically to devise and use these relationships was new, but Napoleon III did not have the consistent drive or the collaborators to translate his ideas into permanency. In consequence, the disasters of 1870 have obscured the originality of his contribution.

5. The main enterprises

Building a national strategy round the existence of a specific industrial capacity and its elaborate artefacts, such as railway systems, implied a regular, if not absolutely continuous relationship between the state and the enterprises concerned. The first to establish itself as an habitual supplier to the national forces was the firm of Schneider at Le Creusot, in the department of Saône and Loire, where there were established but primitively worked deposits of coal and iron ore. They supplied a royal foundry, under Louis XIV. A private company to exploit them on an industrial scale was founded in 1782. Before the outbreak of the French Revolution, it had installed four blast furnaces, two forges and other equipment, the motive power for all of which was provided by steam engines specially designed by James Watt. The works were intended to furnish all the cannon and shot required by the Navy. The Revolution stepped up the demand, but the plant was requisitioned by the government. Napoleon restored the plant to the surviving shareholders, but under both regimes the state was the only customer. After the defeat of France in 1815, orders abruptly ceased, and, the company unable to find alternative business, went bankrupt.

Over the next twenty years, various attempts were made to operate the facilities profitably but none succeeded until, in 1836, the facilities were purchased by two Alsatians, Eugène and François-Adolphe Schneider. Eugène, then thirty-one years of age, was manager of a small ironworks at Bazeilles which was in the portfolio of the Seillère bank. François was an employee of the same bank in Paris. The purchase price was 2.6 million francs; immediately after acquisition the capital was raised by Seillère to 4 million francs. The investment was intended to exploit the opportunities created for metallurgical industries by steam engines in both railways and ships, and the process of implementing the investment yielded an interesting example of the transfer of technology. The centrepiece of the refurbished works was a steam hammer originally designed by James Nasmyth (an assistant to Maudslay) to forge a paddle shaft of unprecedented diameter for a British ship which was, in the event, equipped with screw propulsion. Nasmyth showed his unwanted designs to, among others, Eugène Schneider, whose own engineer built the hammer in 1839–40 (a transfer of technology which Nasmyth only discovered some years later). The first French-built locomotives and the first steamships to ply the Rhône and Saône appeared from the works in 1838. A separate works for marine engines was set up at Chalons sur Saône, from which Messrs Schneider rapidly established themselves in the manufacture of river craft, including engines.

It was this aspect of the firm's business which brought Schneider into contact with the French navy, then embarking on a programme of modernisation and construction aimed at setting limits to Britain's naval dominance. The French naval authorities placed an order for a beam engine for a corvette, which was delivered in 1840. The initial experience proved decisive; thereafter Schneider became the preferred source for marine engines for the navy.

Ventures in the railway market were similarly successful. In addition to locomotives, the firm produced track, bridges (from 1853) and iron-framed buildings for railway stations (from 1858). These products were among Schneider's exports, as well as domestic sales. The first locomotive built for foreign service was delivered to Milan in 1840. Schneider steamboats plied the Danube, the Po and the Nile. From 1859 onwards depots and maintenance shops were built in Rome, Civita Vecchia, Alicante and elsewhere in support of French railway concessionaires. Such activity characterised the work of Schneider et Cie for the first thirty-three years of its existence; its contribution to industrialised war was confined to marine engines. Cannon only followed in 1870. Till then the manufacture of armaments as such remained in state-owned establishments, at Bourges, Puteaux and Tarbes for the army, and Reuilles and Nevers for the navy.

In comparison with Schneider's venture at Le Creusot, the origins of Krupp were much less securely founded in technique. Friedrich Krupp was no ironmaster: he sprang from a well-established family of merchants but he had a personal enthusiasm, amounting to an obsession, with cast steel. In 1812, he set up his first foundry, designed to serve a market created by Napoleon's Continental blockade against Britain, the only other source of supply. Friedrich Krupp began to supply dies and rolls of cast steel to various mints throughout Germany. Ultimate commercial success, however, eluded him, since in spite of persistent experiments, he was not able to guarantee a uniform and unvarying product. When he died in 1826, he left his son, Alfred, then aged fourteen, a run-down business and a legacy of tenacity in the face of technical failure.

Alfred concentrated on improving the quality and consistency of the dies and the rolls, and embarked on a series of journeys among the German states, which the Customs Union of 1834 suddenly transformed into a large single market. By the mid-thirties, also, he acquired steam power for the manufacturing plant. The capital was derived from family connections and modest trading profits. In 1838–9, Alfred Krupp made a prolonged visit to France and Britain, staying incognito in Sheffield in order to study the trade practices and manufacturing secrets of the steel masters. His product range diversified slowly, into cast steel axles for locomotives and into military equipment, steel breastplates and rifled musket barrels. The military authorities were unimpressed. Alfred Krupp thought he might win their patronage with a cast steel cannon. It was delivered to the Prussian Ordnance Factory at Spandau for testing, in September 1847 – and there it stayed for two years. The House of Krupp had entered the world of armaments, with which its name was to become synonymous, but its presence was ignored. Alfred Krupp persisted with his experiments in casting large ingots, one of which, a flawless cube weighing 2000 lbs, attracted much attention at the Great Exhibition in Hyde Park in 1851. He also persevered with making shafts of cast steel and, two years after his London triumph, produced the first seamless (ie, non-welded) railway tyres of that material. The firm became important to German railway development.

During these years of intermittent success, Krupp developed a number of practices which became characteristic. He tried to avoid discarding personnel during slumps in activity by manufacturing for stock and by engaging his workmen in preparing sites for new plant, the installation of which he could not yet finance. This had the natural consequence of building up a loyal workforce, as well as hoarding its skills. *Kruppianer* regarded themselves as an industrial élite. He also maintained a pricing policy related to the quality of his product, in the first instance, rather than to the prices of his competitors, arguing that any excess of his rates over theirs represented a premium for security, which was vital whether the product under negotiation was a railway wheel or a cannon. Krupp vehemently maintained that the exercise of authority and the correlative of accepting responsibility were incompatible with impersonal joint stock enterprise. Krupps had to remain a family business.

William Armstrong brought to the manufacture of weapons even less of a background than Friedrich Krupp, since he was by profession a lawyer, but his bent for the mechanical caused him to abandon the law and in 1847, at the age of thirty-seven, to set out to be a manufacturer. With partners, he founded a works at Elswick, Newcastle-on-Tyne, and began producing lathes and hydraulic cranes – the latter being much in demand by railway and harbour companies. He soon diversified into bridges and, unsuccessfully, into locomotives. In 1854, Armstrongs were approached by the War Office to devise a mine to clear Sebastopol harbour of sunken ships; the mines were successful in tests but were not used. What brought Armstrong into the production of weapons as a continuous business of his firm was the result of his own initiative. Reports of the Battle of Inkerman, on 5 November, 1854, showed that the Russian forces were only decisively but bloodily repulsed after a delay of three hours while two eighteen-pounder smoothbore field guns each weighing two tons were being manhandled over a distance of a mile and a half up the Inkerman Heights. Armstrong saw that the result of the battle could have been achieved with far fewer casualties had the cannon been more manoeuverable and the delay eliminated. He wrote to the War Office in these terms, and was asked in December 1854 to design a gun. Armstrong delivered the first gun in July 1855. It was of iron, rather than steel, since he considered that the existing state of steel casting technique permitted too many flaws for standard mass production of the gun. Steel was, however, used to line the barrel, which was rifled for a three-pound shot. The gun weighed a quarter of a ton. It was the prototype of a series of guns firing twelve and eighteen pound shells, and took Armstrong squarely into weapons' manufacture. Although he started later than Krupp, he was the first to gain acceptance by his own military authorities.

The Crimean War spurred general professional interest in rifled field guns, which Armstrong's experiments vindicated. But other manufacturers were pressing their attention on the War Office, to urge the adoption of alternative systems. Prominent among these applicants was Joseph Whitworth, the pioneer of exact measurement in engineering, who was already producing machine tools for the manufacture of rifles in the government establishment at Enfield. The War Office sifted the claims, and held official trials between Armstrong's and Whitworth's systems. Armstrong's was adopted. The problem was to put it into series production in a hurry, since the deteriorating political relationship with France held out the prospect of future use for the weapon. The short answer, for the state, was to corner the existing expertise. This it did by an unprecedented arrangement. Armstrong gave his patents to the nation, received all his research and development costs since 1855 and entered government service as Engineer to the War Department (in which position he revitalised Woolwich Arsenal). The design capacity was secured to the state; it remained, however, to secure the existing source of manufacture, Armstrong's works at Elswick. This end was achieved through a state grant of funds to extend plant and buildings, combined with a guaranteed flow of orders to maintain it at full operation, against a state monopoly of purchase. These terms were related to a new company with which Armstrong himself was to have no financial connection. Three of his partners entered into a contract with the War Office to found the Elswick Ordnance Co for this purpose. An artillery captain who had formerly acted as secretary to the committee of enquiry into ordnance, Captain Noble, resigned his commission to become joint manager of the new enterprise.

These arrangements stemmed from the desire to manufacture on a large scale a new weapon as rapidly as possible. Carried through between 1859 and 1860, they were highly controversial. Armstrong's appointment was resented in influential quarters in the army, particularly those which considered that the smooth bores which had beaten the French in 1815 were still adequate to the task. Armstrong's competitors reacted to their defeat by promoting doubt about the price and reliability of Elswick guns, in the columns of *The Times* and in Parliament. Whitworth was the main figure in this campaign. Armstrong himself gave evidence to seven government committees of inquiry in five years. Apart from all the technical arguments, he could not easily dispel the suspicion that as government adviser, he could get access to competitors' industrial secrets or could not be impartial in his judgements of their products. A Commission of Enquiry demonstrated the procedures which had been instituted against this contingency, and Armstrong was exonerated.

Armstrong's arrangement with government collapsed, however, when the War Office decided that its artillery requirements could be covered by one source only and that that source would have to be Woolwich Arsenal. The government thereupon bought itself out of the agreement with the Elswick Ordnance Works: the Works took the compensation and the government-funded plant at nominal cost. Armstrong resigned, since he had no wish to be merely the overseer of Woolwich. He returned to Newcastle to merge the Ordnance Works with his own factory, and run the combined undertaking. Woolwich remained the sole manufacturer of guns 'to the pre-Armstrong pattern' till the war scare of 1876. Armstrong, meanwhile, had to find orders for the plant he had inherited. He entered the export market, where he found Whitworth already engaged.

The experiment in new relationships between government and industry fell apart under political pressure in an atmosphere of *détente*, which robbed it of its main recommendation. The price of state manufacture was technical regress. But the decisive issue was the state's contraction of demand, which immediately negated all the arguments adduced in support of a novel arrangement on technical grounds. If the Government could only support one source, it would be difficult to get rid of that source over which the state had basic property rights, rather than contractual ones. The alternative of nationalising Elswick, in the prevailing ethos of mid-Victorian Britain, might well have created an even greater furore; it appears not to have been contemplated.

In a more indirect fashion, the Crimean War fostered a development in technique which was ultimately more far-reaching even than the revolution in relationships discussed above. During the course of the war, Henry Bessemer designed a projectile with a bigger explosive charge and grooving to rotate through the air, in order to overcome one notorious weakness of the existing smoothbore guns, namely maintaining the trajectory of the missile. He approached the War Office with his device, but was rejected. Bessemer took his invention to Britain's ally, in the person of Commandant Minié (of rifle fame) who was impressed but pertinently enquired whether it would be feasible to fire a projectile weighing some twenty-four to thirty pounds from a cast iron twelve-pounder gun. Bessemer's problem, therefore, was to improve the malleability of iron. By the time he had arrived at the answer, the war was over, but his answer, known to history as the Bessemer converter, transcended the malleability problem and enabled steel to be made which was for the first time competitive in price with wrought iron.

Steel guns and steel shells at prices nearer the conventional became an immediate practical possibility. The converter had a number of drawbacks, notably its reliance on a particular type of ore, which caused its inventor much trouble and delayed its acceptance into general use. Two Continental firms which had a keen appreciation of the possibilities the process held out were among the first to adopt it, under licence. The firms were Krupps and Schneider.*

Although his country did not take part in the Crimean War, Krupp at this time also began to be recognised to a degree by the Prussian state, as a designer and manufacturer of cannon. The process began with production for the railways and for steamships on the Rhine and Danube. It was assiduously promoted by the appearance of Krupp at international exhibitions from the London exhibition of 1851 onwards. Paris in 1855 produced the invitation to set up in France (which was refused) and orders for two propeller shafts for the French navy and axles for the Paris-Orleans railway (which were accepted). The Exhibition additionally produced an order for cannon – from Mehemet Said, the youngest son of Mehemet Ali and now Khedive of Egypt, who, over the ensuing four years, took thirty-six pieces. Russia, after the Crimean War, turned to Krupp as a source of expertise and supply, but the cannon he supplied for testing, after surviving 4,000 rounds intact, was then consigned to the Artillery Museum!

Krupp, however, failed to rouse the interest of the Prussian War Ministry, which had eventually tested his cannon on the Tegel range in 1849 and forthwith turned it down, on the grounds that steel was too expensive a solution to a problem which could be solved simply by prolonging the life of bronze barrels and improving the stability of iron. The Prussian War Ministry was not ready for a qualitative jump into steel. It remained unconvinced of the need for ten years, but in 1860 its hand was forced by the Prince-Regent of Prussia, the King's brother who became regent in 1858 when the King was declared incurably insane. Prior to this turn of events, the Prince Regent, as Prince William, had immersed himself in a military career and had been Governor of Westphalia. In that capacity, he had been entertained at Essen. His elevation to the regency, in the most literal sense gave Alfred Krupp a friend at court, and one, moreover, who was determined to renovate the army.

The new ruler's key appointments were those of Albrecht von Roon, as Minister of War, and his friend, Helmuth von Moltke, as Chief of the General Staff. At a slightly less exalted level of command, an enthusiast for steel cannon, General von Voigts-Rhetz became Director of the War Office. The wild enthusiasm generated throughout Germany by the successes of the

---

*They were not alone in appreciating Bessemer's talents. Napoleon III invited him to take charge of French metallurgy.

Italians in 1859 and 1860 was offset, for the makers of policy, by the role of Napoleon III in those successes, which were thought to be the prelude to French initiatives in the Rhineland. Reform of the army, and its equipment was not the unhurried carrying out of professional enthusiasms but an urgent requirement of state security. In May 1859, the Prince Regent forced through an order of 300 steel-barreled guns for Krupp. It was timely. The hoped-for Russian orders lagged, sales returns were slow and the death of a partner removed a substantial slice of the share capital, which the heirs wished to use elsewhere. The order promised a flow of cash and stimulated a more helpful attitude on the part of the banks.

It had other benefits. The mechanism which broke the obstinacy of the War Office was also used, at Krupp's personal petition, against the Ministry of Commerce and the State Railways which had been successfully opposing a renewal of Krupp's patents on his weldless railway tyres. The Prince Regent intervened directly on his behalf. Krupp's new relationship with high authority reached its apogee in January 1861, when the Prince Regent became King of Prussia in his own right. In October of that year, he was entertained at Essen. From that juncture, the fortunes of the house of Krupp decisively turned. The firm's difficulties were by no means over, but Krupp could no longer be ignored.

At the end of 1861, during which Krupp had achieved such a satisfactory relationship with his own military hierarchy, the Russians returned to Essen with a trial order for heavy ordnance of cast steel, which was turned into a firm requirement for 120 rifled muzzle-loading cannon, in May 1863. This, the largest single order to date, was worth about 1.5 million thaler. Solvency was confirmed. The order, however, proved vitally important technically, since, while the guns were being built, Krupp induced the Russian technical officers to experiment with his new breech-loading mechanisms. The Russians, in turn, suggested new methods of improving the gun barrels. The experiments were successful, and so the guns which emerged from the production shops during 1864 and 1865 represented a new generation of artillery. It resulted from the interaction between the technical expertise of Russian officers and the inventiveness of Krupp.

Prussian forces had their first opportunity to test the products of their new supplier, in action, in the war against Austria in 1866. Voigts-Rhetz wrote Alfred in complimentary terms from the battle front, but the unpleasant fact was that two Krupp cannon had blown up at Sadowa – as had two others in Berlin at much the same time. Krupp wrote von Roon, offering reparation and explanation (that he had not supplied the parts which gave way under stress) but the incident provided the proponents of bronze with additional arguments and showed unmistakably that the future of all-steel, breech-loading cannon was by no means secure.

The timing was critical for Krupp in that he was planning to get contracts for ordnance from the navy which Prussia's acquisition of Kiel and the organisation of the North German Federation (following Austria's defeat) brought into the ambit of policy. The preferred source of ships and armament alike was Britain, since the first units were purchased from British yards and a proportion of officers trained with the Royal Navy. The Ordnance Committee of the Prussian War Office and the officers of the state gun factory at Spandau campaigned for a German gun. The models produced from the state establishments failed under test. Von Roon intervened, and Krupp was asked to design a gun, based on the 'Russian' guns, for test against a ninety-six-pounder imported from Armstrong's. Trials were held at the proving ground at Tegel between March and August 1868. The initial results went against Krupp but he successfully appealed against them on the grounds that the test conditions had not been strictly comparable and that the evidence from the trials of his guns in Russia, which were going on at the same time, contradicted the Tegel results. Privately, he argued against reliance on foreign sources. The final tests went in Krupp's favour, as regards both penetration and endurance. He gained his contract to supply: the navy grasped the opportunity to escape from the leading-strings of the army. The bargain between Krupp and the navy was struck – and endured. Krupp became a favoured supplier for the navy because he could deliver the 'right' quality weapon, and because he was not a state establishment under army control. The two factors were related, one to the other. Inter-service politics would only work for Krupp as a private manufacturer provided he could sustain the navy's case for independence by the quality of his output. Neither could the King nor Voigts-Rhetz be asked to exercise their influence on behalf of the second-rate. These furnished additional reasons, apart from the compulsive concern which Alfred Krupp inherited from his father, for staying in the forefront of technique.

He was alerted to the possibilities of Bessemer's process through his London agent, whose brother happened to be one of Bessemer's closest friends – one of the simpler forms of 'technology transfer'. Negotiations opened in 1855, but the State of Prussia refused to cover by patent any acquisition by Krupp against other German manufacturers. So he could only protect himself by establishing an unassailable lead. A few initiated staff began building a 'wheel rolling mill' and in May 1862, the first charge in Krupp's Bessemer plant was blown. A second converter was added three years later. It was a sign of the future that the management of this advance in technique was entrusted not to a long-serving member of the works but to a young graduate in chemistry, for whose education Krupp himself had paid. In the meantime, to fashion the steel produced into larger units than his rivals could, Krupp had installed a massive hammer, of 500 tons, which was the technical basis of Krupp's interventions in ordnance and the manufacture of steel shafts for the navy. As with Schneider in 1840, the range of options open to the military, in one essential respect, depended on the locations within the state's boundaries of one specific capability. Krupp was also the first in

Germany to invest in the Siemens-Martin process for producing open-hearth steels of a quality comparable with the crucible steels to which the Bessemer plant related. The first of four Siemens-Martin plants went into operation at the beginning of 1871.

The decisions to install both new processes were reactions to economic depression in 1857–59 and 1868–69 respectively (Krupp in glaring contrast to his competitors held that bad times were times for innovation), and to the intermittent nature of government business. Napoleon III, it will be remembered, reacted to industrial depression by slowing down production in state plants in order to keep private industry going. The Prussian state was not so obliging. Krupp continued to explore the export market, offering products made of improved steels and concentrating, after his success with Russia, on France. His overtures were not so much refused as allowed to peter out. The director of the French Ordnance Board, General Leboeuf, was hostile to foreign products. He was also related to the Schneider family, though Le Creusot was not at the time producing cannon. His influence was decisive. The French army continued to rely on bronze muzzle-loaders. It was less than a year to the Franco-Prussian War in which the disparity in artillery in both quality and handling was fatal for French policy.

By 1870, rough similarities were appearing in the pattern of relationships between the state and the industry which produced military goods or those, like railways, adaptable for military use. The state retained its own manufacturing capacity in arsenals and dockyards to cover its own requirements, or a given proportion of them, to monitor the progress of weapons manufacture throughout industry in general and to have its own independent yardsticks for comparing prices. The political rivalries in which the states engaged (France and Britain in the forties and sixties, Prussia and Austria with France in the sixties) created a demand for rapid expansion, which outran the capacity of state-owned facilities. The state therefore had to turn to private industry, but it quickly came to rely on private firms not simply to make up numbers but to produce improved weapons. The arsenals were not equipped to carry out experiments with new steels, which private industrialists were able to do in connection with their 'civil' business. Moreover, since they produced only for a military market, state establishments could not spread the costs of innovation over the 'civil' as well as the 'military' output. For these reasons, the state relied on private firms for technical advance. The tendency is illustrated negatively in France before 1870 and in Britain between 1863 and 1877 when exclusive reliance on state facilities left each with antiquated artillery.

In this process, the institutional fact that 'the state' broke down in practice into 'the army' and 'the navy' who were often at loggerheads over the proportion of funds allocated for their respective use, gave the private firms more room for manoeuvre. Above all, since their products were related to a compelling but non-measurable goal, namely the security of the realm, and since that in turn was clearly related to improvements in technique, the more successful the firm as an innovator, the less incentive the state had to interfere.

Such an outcome had nothing to do with *laisser faire* strictly construed: the state retained its powers ultimately to intervene but saw no positive advantage in doing so. Industrialists naturally sought to keep officers and bureaucrats in this helpful frame of mind. Equally, the state could not guarantee to take all the output the improved technique generated. It could either subsidise the facilities during slack periods – which orthodox ministries of finance were reluctant to do – or it could allow or encourage manufacturers to go into the export market – in which case the overheads were covered by the foreign customer. The British Government insisted on being the sole buyer of Elswick output so long as Armstrong was in its service, but it forfeited its capacity to insist when it turned to Woolwich for its requirements. Krupp would have been forced out of cannon manufacture but for foreign interest, and by the time the Prussian War Office grasped the possibilities his firm offered, he was heavily dependent on exports.

6. 'War' and 'Peace' redefined: Cobden

In all three industrialising states, changes in the relationships between individual firms and government were worked out pragmatically, but within a framework of values which gave the state priority when it cared to exercise it. There were, however, larger questions of the overall relationship between industrial capacity, military expenditures and state policy for war or peace which the industrial age raised for the first time or in a new guise. They were analysed by Richard Cobden in the course of a political career extending from 1835 to his death in 1865; a period which spanned the first application of industrial techniques to warfare. His ideas were all rooted in his passion for peace among nations, which reflected profound moral conviction. Translated from metaphysical necessity into the world of action, peace could be ensured only by free trade in economics and non-intervention in politics. The two were mutually related. All other means, historically, had led only to wars, confusion and expense, for which responsibility rested with governments. Peace required 'as little intercourse betwixt *Governments*, as much connection as possible between the *nations* of the world.' But connections between nations should be spontaneous, founded on an unambiguous interest (which could only be trade), and unofficial. Any international organisation for securing peace was to be avoided at all costs; it would become yet another vehicle for diplomatic intervention and would be more likely to sow the seeds of war. Governments intervened in each others' affairs because their interests were defined by the military and the diplomats recruited from the aristocracy, which needed to justify its existence and its continuing hold on state power.

The aristocracy had a professional interest in military expenditure, which was inherently unproductive. In certain closely defined and restricted cases, such as keeping harbours in good repair and maintaining a small standing army against invasion, such waste might have to be accepted: otherwise the preparation and upkeep of military forces was a dead weight on the economy. Moreover, it was even counter-productive since states driven by the fear of being left at a disadvantage emulated each other in military outlays. Hence it was erroneous to think that armed forces guaranteed security: through the competition they engendered they might even be said to foster *in*security. So, in practice, military spending was not only wasteful in itself, it did not even conduce to the end for which it was incurred. Mistrust from time to time erupted into panic, propagated through the press and Parliament by military clubs and officers on half-pay. The consequent increases in military budgets provoked reciprocal mistrust in other states and intensified conflict rather than resolving it.

Cobden was not alone in his generation in advocating such ideas. He had an enthusiastic coadjutor in France, where Frédéric Bastiat represented a traditional line of argument deriving a pacific programme from the fact of industrialisation. But, except for the last two years before his death in 1850, Bastiat was an academic economist working from outside both industry and the legislature. Cobden, by contrast, was deeply immersed in both. His Parlimentary career lasted, with one brief interruption, for twenty-four years. During that time he campaigned incessantly for his ideas in a forum peculiarly placed in British life to give them maximum publicity. They grew out of current politics and for that reason are to be sought in the columns of Hansard and in pamphlets, letters to the press and speeches outside the House.

In 1862, however, Cobden published a more systematic critique in the context of a review of Anglo-French frictions entitled *The Three Panics*. His basic contention is that those who thought that steam navigation had opened Britain to sudden and irresistible invasion from France, had paid excessive attention to, when they had not wilfully misinterpreted, French intentions, by relying on arguments the falsity of which could be demonstrated by considering what the French Government had actually done, or was capable of doing. Any realistic policy should start from a detailed examination of the public accounts of both countries reduced to a common basis. This showed that successive French Governments, far from outspending Britain, had in fact provided themselves with a fleet which, though strengthening France at sea, was quite insufficient to endanger Britain's supremacy. Further, the usual arguments about the feasibility of a surprise attack assumed not only that complete tactical surprise was possible – which Cobden denied – but that the French Government was constantly disposed towards war – which he thought false, provocative and insulting. It involved 'an impeachment of the intelligence as well as the honour of France.' For even if the French did contemplate an unprovoked attack, 'in violation of every principle of international law and in contempt of all the obligations of morality and honour,' then Britain's maritime resources were more than adequate to ward off the immediate threat, while her manufacturing capacity would permit her to add rapidly to her naval arm: 'This not so much owing to our superiority in Government arsenals, where notorious mismanagement countervails our advantages, as to the vast and unrivalled resources we possess in private establishments for the construction of ships and steam machinery.' The true relationship was therefore to be measured not in numbers and types of vessels alone, but in the related manufacturing capacity which could be deployed. Including the industrial factor into the equation of seapower showed the panics of 1847–8, 1851–3 and 1859–61 for what they were – excuses contrived by interested parties for 'repeated augmentation of our armaments'. At the same time, Britain's lead in manufacturing gave her the opportunity to initiate negotiations on limiting naval armaments – which her security and the moral need to make atonement to France alike demanded.

Though scathing about military francophobes, Cobden was no pacifist. He was prepared to assume that some wars might be inevitable or necessary – though he thought that, in practice, the instances were demonstrably few. He approved of wars of defence: at the time of the Crimean War he declared in the House of Commons that if the Russians were to besiege Portsmouth he would be active in defending it. In his reckoning, a defensive war defined itself quite simply – as a response to invasion, signified by the crossing of a frontier. All other wars were totally unjustified. So were the time-honoured related expedients of diplomacy such as spheres of influence and balances of power: they had no permanent effects, just as superiority in armaments conferred no lasting advantage. Cobden advocated non-intervention because it offered the only remaining practicable hope of security.

Neither was Cobden among those radical reformers for whom foreign affairs merely get in the way of cherished social priorities. Throughout his public career, he was immersed in international politics: it was his experience in that field which led him to question the accepted axioms sustaining the international order and to advocate new solutions. They were the more plausible since in his day the state and society were distinct entities, to a degree which no longer obtains.

The Three Panics is more than a closely argued polemic on Anglo-French naval policies. It initiated a line of discussion in Britain which was still influential as late as 1937 when F. W. Hirst, then editor of *The Economist* argued in *Armaments, The Race and the Crisis* that naval and military expenditure was intrinsically reprehensible because it was 'neither repro- ductive nor revenue-producing'. He discussed rearmament programmes entirely in terms of their financial consequences and the danger they portended to balanced budgets. 'The construction of a needed railway, or road, or port, will add to the wealth and revenue of a country: and its cost may therefore well be spread over a number of years. But the practice of borrowing for battleships, guns or bombing planes, which will be worn out and scrapped in a few years, is unjustifiable, unless the country is desperately poor and in danger of attack.'

Hirst denied 'the new hypothesis that peace is indivisible'; was opposed to regional security pacts and the idea of war for 'collective security' (what Cobden had called 'the quixotic mission of fighting for the Liberties of Europe'). He adduced evidence to show that British public opinion largely supported this view, and noted the unwillingness of the Dominions to become involved in another Continental war. For Britain, the only correct policy was 'friendship with all, alliance with none'.

Hirst's only hope of a remedy lay through finance: the obvious costs and social strains of rearmament affected dictatorships as well as democracies and on these grounds he discerned 'some hope that common sense or insolvency may very soon bring about disarmament, or at least put an end to rearmament.' If that failed, he concluded, the economic consequences of armaments were inescapable and threatened the whole world order. 'A democracy may be submerged by revolutionary discontent; and where there are no representative institutions there is always the danger that one or other of the dictators may resort to war as a last desperate alternative to bankruptcy and starvation.' This is not the place for a critique of Hirst's views in relation to the constellations of power in Europe in his day, it is only necessary to note their continuity with Cobden's.

The Three Panics is also important in that it exemplified a mode of analysis which still excites debate. Cobden argues that wars follow not from original sin or from the nature of man but from the existence in society of a group which has an interest in the creation and maintenance of tension. He identified this group with the aristocracy. Hirst, in 1937, defined it more widely. He attributed the British rearmament programme to the malign influence of 'a group of Jingo politicians and service men, encouraged by the armament interest and led by Mr Churchill, the most eloquent of panic-mongers' and 'by economic nationalists supported by protected manufacturers and subsidy-hunters.' Other commentators have preferred other culprits, but the notion of war as expressing a group interest (as distinct from the wickedness of the powerful) and substantiating it by social analysis – now both commonplace – was defined for the industrial age by Richard Cobden.

He also introduced another operational distinction – very much used in the discussion of foreign policy – between taking the declared or inferred intentions of other states and taking what their resources allow them to do, as a datum for policy-making. Cobden demonstrated that if British governments based their policy on what the French could do, rather than on what some Frenchmen said they intended doing, then the British could secure the Channel by a policy of friendship with France rather than by competitive armaments. This distinction between intentions and capabilities is now an elementary opening gambit.

Cobden's reputation and the longevity of his approach have led many to assume that his was the last word of nineteenth-century British liberalism on the subject. But even in his time, his views on armaments and military expenditures did not represent the generality of Liberals who otherwise accepted Free Trade. For Cobden, Free Trade was a means – the only means – to peace: for most Liberals, it was an end in itself – one which maximised profitable opportunities. Furthermore, they rejected his notion of non-intervention, if it condemned subject nationalities to live under oppressive foreign rule.

While willing to organise boycotts by the international financial community of states he classes as oppressors, Cobden was wholly against interfering by force against them to free their oppressed subjects. Intervention produced worse evils and was moreover ineffectual – as Britain's record on the Continent showed. Oppression, under the wisdom of Divine Providence, was self-defeating: injustice produced weakness and injured the parties who committed it. The majority of British Liberals did not take such a highminded view: they agitated, collected funds for weapons, and generally demanded that British governments actively pursue the liberation of subject nationalities especially if they were subject to the Russians or 'the unspeakable Turk'. This took the main stream of Liberal opinion much nearer that of the Continent, where, shortly after Cobden's death, liberals had to chose between the national and the international entailments of their doctrine and chose the former. Unity was more compelling than peace – Continental liberals therefore threw their political weight on the side of military expenditures and jettisoned any idea of wresting control of military policy from the traditional aristocracies. Having made that choice, however, liberal opinion tended to align itself more readily with naval than with army programmes. Ships could not easily be used to suppress civil liberties: naval hierarchies were much less exclusive and happily admitted the sons of the bourgeoisie into the ranks of officers. Such social preferences were only strengthened when, with developments in metallurgy, ironclad fleets with weightier armaments and their ancillary facilities came to make heavier demands on manufacturing industry.

PART III

1870–1914

'He who tries to give intelligent advice
to one who thinks he has intelligence
is wasting his time.'
Democritos

1. The requirements of power after 1870

The Franco-Prussian War of 1870–1871 is more than a conventional milestone for historians, since its outcome not only transferred the leadership of Continental Europe from France to Germany, but promoted far-reaching changes in the aims and conduct of policy in all states. A mere seven years before, Prussia had been the fifth military power in Europe and was second to Austria in Germany. Now it was the core of a new empire stretching from Metz to Memel. The metamorphosis, which seems inevitable to hindsight, startled contemporaries by its suddenness.

The war, however, did more than revise frontiers; it introduced a new element into nineteenth century diplomacy in Europe, in that Imperial Germany and the Third Republic of France were irreconcilable and therefore intractable elements in the system of states. Since the Congress of Vienna in 1815, combinations of all major states could be visualised and were, in fact, arrived at without permanent disruption. From 1871 that flexibility was lost:[1] a combination of France and Germany was effectively ruled out. Imperial Germany thought that possession of Alsace and Lorraine guaranteed an end to two hundred years' use by France of Germany as a campaigning ground. The French government and people regarded the loss of the two provinces as more than a cession of territory, as a degradation which cried out for vengeance. It was not the only issue between the victor and the vanquished but it was the one which in France, till the end of the century, made other differences intractable.

European politics were polarised. Among the six major powers whose interactions constituted European politics, there were, in the fifty years before 1871, fourteen main alignments on issues which brought the states to the verge of war or to war itself. From 1871 to 1914, there were two. Newly emerged states, such as Romania and Italy, whose unity derived from the diplomatic configurations of the sixties, faced the problems of consolidation in a new distribution of political power in Europe. Italian unity had been the product, in different ways, of the anti-Austrian policies of both France and Prussia. Now, any move towards France was automatically one against Germany, and vice versa. The foreign policies of other European states, in military and diplomatic aspects, had to take the polarisation of Europe as a datum. For Italy, it encouraged prudent moves towards Austria, in consequence of which Franz Josef suddenly became, in contrast to 1859, '*il nobile e valorese alleate dell' Italia*.' Austria-Hungary, shorn of its role in Germany, turned its attention to the south-east of Europe, where at this time the Ottoman Empire had embarked on one of its intermittent bouts of reform but where its restless Balkan provinces were already proving responsive to Russian-sponsored pan-Slavism. The rivalry of Austria and Russia in this area was eventually to produce European disaster. The Belgian government clung to its internationally guaranteed neutrality[2] but was aware that the polarisation of politics would make maintaining it more difficult in future. Some French leaders, after 1871, were known to be toying with ideas of annexing Belgium in compensation for being shut out of the Rhineland, while the Germans, nervous of French intentions, requested the Belgian Government to fortify Namur and Liège.

The competition among European states took place in a new framework, within which the prime force was Imperial Germany – even though, under Bismarck its policies were conservative. The framework, however, stretched beyond Europe and the Mediterranean. After 1870, 'foreign policy' no longer implied solely the relationships of a handful of European states to one another within Europe: it covered these relationships as extended round the world through the establishment of colonies or protectorates, especially in Africa, the Far East and the Pacific. The process involved the states not only with each other but also with two extra-European powers, the United States and Japan. Tensions between the European states outside Europe reacted on their relationships in Europe. What, until that time, had been true of Britain and Russia, over the genuine or dubious Russian threat to India, came to relate to the whole complex of interactions between the constituent states of Europe, notably France and Britain over the Sudan and Thailand, Britain and Germany over Samoa and to the four major powers embroiled with each other and with the United States and Japan in China. Options in Europe had to be juggled to take in those in Asia.

Within Europe and in certain states elsewhere, political pre-eminence ensured that Germany became the dominant model. What was the essence of the Prussian achievement in Germany? The question was universally answered by reference to the military organisation of the state and the coordination of military and diplomatic policy. The answer grossly over-stated the case. Military organisation was less than perfect and the coordination of foreign and military policy involved a running fight between Bismarck and Moltke. Nevertheless, German thought and German practice were examined and adopted by other states anxious to rival the new imperial power or, like Japan or Chile, to exercise a similar influence in their own political sphere. Scrutiny concentrated on the war itself – nowhere more so than in France where the lessons received as much study as they did in Germany. In this respect, Moltke became a more influential figure in the seventies and eighties when he was not fighting than during his campaigns, since what he had or was supposed to have accomplished in 1870 and 1871 became the paradigm of the military art. In some states, Ottoman Turkey and Romania, for example, the German model was adopted *en bloc* and in the long run brought a political return in the form of adherence to the German structure of alliances. In others, notably France, Germany provided not so much a model as a corpus of experience from which a distinctively national military organisation and doctrine could be fashioned. In either case, contemporary observers agreed that Prussia had won in the summer and early autumn of 1870 by virtue of the superior use of superior technology, which enabled the armies to maintain an offensive in which tactical reverses could be absorbed.

The conclusion was new. Until 1870, it had been possible to maintain that Prussian victories rested on the possession of a particular 'advanced' weapon – the famous needle gun. By implication, a counter-weapon could be devised – the mitrailleuse. So, in principle, a balance could always be readily redressed. Now, victories were seen as the outcome of a system, in which education, training and the deliberate exploitation of technology were the main elements. The capabilities of manufacturing industry were clearly central to military policy and therefore to all the objectives of the state in foreign affairs. This was the first occasion in which outcome of war was analysed in such terms. The *coup d'oeil* of commanders, the dash of officers and the bravery and steadiness of the rank and file were of less importance to victory than the concentration of armies (which railways alone made possible on the scale required and within the time limits necessary) and the metallurgy involved in making steel cannon. The adversaries in warfare were not weapons and the morale of those using them, but the military systems of which they were the expression. Since, in the world of power, the competitors are unequal, redressing a balance was not a problem of finding an answer to a weapon but of creating a matching system. It could seek to be a mirror image, with fort opposing fort, reserves countering reserves and so on; or it could seek to be a rival, pitting professionals against less highly trained but more numerous conscripts, but, in either case, matching a system was a much more complicated business than producing a weapon. Decisions about war or peace began to take on new connotations.

The grounds on which such decisions could be justified also assumed a more sombre character. War, it came to be thought, was not an instrument of policy which could be taken up or discarded at will: it was intrinsic to the development of human society itself. The argument proceeded from Darwin's *The Origin of Species*, published in 1859. In one of the more curious turns in intellectual history, Darwin's theory of development through the mechanism of natural selection, suggested to him originally by a reading of Malthus' *Essay on Population,* returned to social science via biology, as explaining the differences in the development of states and societies. In this vulgarised version, material success is evidence of biological excellence and biological excellence accounts for material success. This pleasing circularity was easily translated to account for the relations of states. The struggle for existence was not between individuals but between collectivities – states, nations and sects. The fitness of the leaders to lead was 'proved' by the fact, attested by history, that they were better organised to pursue their chosen ends. Those who survived had a right to dominate. One recognised method of selection was war. War, in the industrial age, implied certain preparations which themselves implied organisation which in turn tended to confirm the right to lead of those who consciously adopted these policies. War gave decisions which were 'biologically just'.

Darwin himself, in *The Descent of Man* published in February 1871 spotted the flaw in this conclusion by considering that war, in fact, might well have the reverse effect, resulting in the natural selection of the unfit, since the fittest (the first volunteers, the couragous, the most daring) got themselves killed. He admitted the logic of this argument but concluded that it would be untrue of short wars. He failed to define 'short' but the obvious examples in his maturity, from the Crimea onwards, had all been so.* He did not examine the point at all thoroughly, but, as so often, the epigone ignored the reservations of the master. In Germany and France, Darwin's theories were systematised to a degree which he himself abjured and in that form were widely used to counter pacifist ideas, or even advocacy of the *status quo*. War was a natural and not an aberrant phenomenon; the sharpest and most testing form of 'natural selection'.

The Franco-Prussian War was the first to be analysed in neo-Darwinian terms. The Prussians had, obviously, been the 'fitter' in that struggle – a view which was not only taken by Germans but was shared ruefully or vengefully by the defeated French. In Germany, it was self-evident that unity depended on the army: the force which had achieved it would be necessary to maintaining it. To subsequent generations, 1870 marks the beginning of a process; to contemporaries, it was the end of one. Unity gave the Germans at last the same national status as the British and the French and even the Italians, by putting an end to the traditional French policy of using a weak, because fragmented, Germany as a campaigning ground for French political ambitions in Europe. The work of 1813–14 was completed in 1870–71. This attitude ensured the popularity of the army as an institution – though the appeal was noticeably less in those areas of Germany annexed to Prussia or the Reich from 1866 onwards, where the extension of Prussian military

---

*Darwin, in common with virtually everyone else, misread the signs of 1870–1871 as to the duration of war. It took a month – at the most six weeks – to defeat the regime of Napoleon III. Extracting the same result from the successor regime supported by the French people as a whole, took a further six months and then capitulation resulted mainly from the impossibility of organising effective resistance with properly trained troops, while the Germans were still in France. The German margin of superiority thus sufficed, but at the end of the fighting, the French had more troops under arms in France than their opponents.

law speeded up rates of emigration.

The law provided for compulsory military service for males from the age of twenty for twelve years, three in the active army, four in the reserves and five in the *Landwehr*. Exceptions were authorised on professional or social grounds, so that by no means all these covered by the law in fact served, although a proportion was trained in occupation or police duties (*Ersatz-truppen*) or enrolled in the *Landsturm* for service within the Empire, if attacked. The duty to serve was spread throughout society, and was justified not only by patriotism and security but also as providing a school of useful civic habits such as exactness, punctuality, and a proper pride in oneself. The army was also a school in a more literal sense, regular instruction being given in elementary mathematics and natural science, as well as swimming, gymnastics and so on.

There was no one unified army since the structure of the Empire permitted the continued existence of other states than the Kingdom of Prussia but the position and prestige of Prussia and in particular of its General Staff ensured ultimate coordination in the strategy of the Reich. That strategy was defensive, designed to contain a resurgent France which might be tempted by any suspicion of German military weakness to reverse the decision of 1871. So military planning provided for improved conscription and training and an overhaul of the operational details of the rail network to facilitate superior deployment to the west, without the administrative shambles along the Rhine which marked the campaign of 1870. The only new aspect to the problem of security was the possibility that France, seeking a war of *revanche*, would interest another power in the advantages of defeating Germany.

A mere glance at the numbers and deployments of other forces in Europe showed that the ally could only be Russia. Should an alliance be concluded – a contingency which was thought to be very remote – then Germany would be faced by a war on two fronts, but the inherent disadvantages could be offset by the intelligent use of the interior lines conferred by geography and of the benefits of superior technology in transport and communications. Germany, however, could not conduct two full-scale campaigns at once. The planners' problem therefore resolved itself into choosing priorities between the major and minor theatre and assessing the conditions under which they could best be realised in practice.

Moltke initially decided in favour of a major effort in the west, relying on the indifferent administration of the Russian forces and the poor communications in eastern Europe to give him time to defeat the French army before turning to fight in Russian Poland. Any advance into Russia itself was ruled out. Battles in both west and east had to produce annihilation; victory through attrition would not work in the circumstances. But as France recovered, the prospects of rapid decisive action in the west diminished, and Moltke then sought to use the defensive possibilities of the Rhine to hold French forces while eliminating their Russian allies first. But the decision had to be reached in Poland or the Baltic area where Russian dispositions could be usefully hampered by stirring up the subject nationalities. There was to be no invasion of Russia itself. Germany wanted nothing from the Russians; 'they have no gold and we do not need land.' This very limited aim should be used to bring about a negotiated settlement in the east, and then allow the full weight of Germany to be deployed across the Rhine. All these were contingency plans, discussed and arrived at while Bismarck was, in fact, keeping the Tsar among Germany's allies, but they demonstrate that 'security' translated into far more comprehensive planning than hitherto, and that planning had to rely on the mobility created by the use of railways and their associated technology.

For the French, security was a question of discharging their treaty obligations and renovating their entire military establishment. In September 1870, Thiers, on a diplomatic mission, met the historian Ranke in Vienna; they discussed the news from Sedan. Thiers commented 'This is our Jena, but we shall not need seven years to recover from it'. He was right. By the autumn of 1873, the 5 milliard indemnity exacted by the victors had been paid off, and German troops, in consequence, withdrew from French soil, mourned perhaps only by the restaurateurs and the *filles de joie*, both of which remarked that the occupiers paid promptly for their professional services.

The combination of the loss of two provinces and the searing wound to the pride of a nation which was accustomed to consider itself the instructor in the military arts to Europe turned the Third Republic from the beginning towards militarism. The army was accorded an almost mystical authority which was not questioned until the Dreyfus case. Then hostility arose from only *part* of the nation (not the nation as a whole), which questioned the loyalty of the officer corps to the republican form of government, not the national role of the army as such. Dreyfus' accusers and defenders were united in identifying the external enemy. After 1871, the army in France became a cult: anti-militarist pamphlets were publicly burnt: entry to the military academy of St Cyr trebled, fostered by an agricultural depression which stimulated the flow of cadets from the aristocracy. The successive attempts of Boulanger and Paul Déroulède to overthrow the government failed not because they were military but because they implied dictatorship. France was a militarist republic. It was this all-pervading enthusiasm for the military and the priority it enjoyed in politics and society which made the decades after 1870 for a reactionary and royalist critic like Charles Maurras 'a golden age of national feeling'.

The nature of the defeat in the summer of 1870 suggested the measures which had to be adopted to resurrect the prestige of French arms and assure the defence of *La Patrie*. Conscription replaced the *armée de métier*; the new forces were equipped with improved rifles and field artillery, and with a completely new set of doctrines governing their deployment and use. Now that Metz and Strasbourg were in German hands, the way to Paris was blocked by two new fortified defence zones, Belfort-Epinal and Toul-Verdun. They were deliberately constructed with gaps through which any invader would have to pass; battles would be fought by prepared forces on ground of French choosing. The scheme was devised by General Séré de Rivières, who advocated the construction of a complete defensive system from Calais to Nice. Railways were put under a special branch of the General Staff, headed by General du Cissey. During the war, the centralisation of lines on Paris had impeded the flow of troops and material: so lateral lines were built in concentric rings round the capital. The nearest was the *Grande Ceinture*, about ten miles out of the city and seventy-five miles in length. Further afield, Rouen, Troyes and Orleans became nodal points in the new strategic system. (The *élan* with which all these measures were put into effect alarmed Bismarck, who in 1875 provoked an international crisis in an attempt to induce the French to moderate their rearmament programme.)

The successful application of technique in the form of the railway for mobilising and concentrating armies, and the telegraph and telephone for controlling their operations, removed the two greatest restrictions on the effective deployment of manpower in war. Hitherto discrepancies in population between states had not been decisive in the capacity to go to war since the rudimentary methods of controlling armies on the march or in battle imposed limits on numbers. These limits gone, demographic trends suddenly entered into military planning and into diplomacy. The statistical future became important to policy, and introduced into it yet another 'timetable' effect; planning had to take account of the likely availability of manpower resources twenty years ahead, when the male infants of any given year would reach military age.

Overall numerical strength, though important, was not enough. The primary factor in demographic assessments of policy was the number of males between the ages of twenty and forty at any given time; secondarily, the number in the range from fifteen to twenty. These groups were decisive, both absolutely and relative to the numbers over forty. General staffs considered that an excess of 'over forties' or even parity between them and the primary group, put a state at a disadvantage for the conduct of war. They anxiously began to watch these relationships, since age categories can change more rapidly than populations as a whole. Estimates of potential striking force and of the timing of possible initiatives in foreign policy varied accordingly. Compulsory field service for the primary age groups from twenty to forty ensured that casualty rates would be experienced throughout the crucial groups of entire male populations. The likely consequences to the stability of society remained unanalysed till they were experienced after the First World War.

In 1871 Germany, including Alsace and Lorraine, had a population of

41 millions and France 36.1, but as regards effective military forces they were equal at 740,000 men. This remained the case for twenty years, but the respective birthrates showed, over the same period, a divergence of eight per cent in Germany's favour. Thus by the turn of the century, the German army was superior to the French by 87,000 men. French planners could only meet this foreseeable divergence in manpower by reducing exemptions, by calling up a greater proportion of those eligible for training in any one year, by prolonging the period of active service and by expending more money on arms and fortifications. Through these means, France entered the First World War with an army which at peacetime strength was only slightly inferior in numbers to the German, 582,000 men, as against 596,780. Nevertheless the economic strain of keeping men on active service for three years rather than two, and of diverting resources to military works designed to save manpower, imposed a far greater economic strain on France than on Germany.

If the birthrate, in spite of official and religious encouragement, put France at a disadvantage, the obvious move was to find an ally which could offset it. This consideration dictated what many observers at the time thought to be a curious and unnatural alliance between 'progressive' republican France and 'reactionary' Tsarist Russia. In military terms, the alliance dated from 1892, when the population divergencies between France and Germany had already set in. It may ultimately be traced to the royalist ministry of the Duc de Broglie in the seventies. Intervening republican governments had been more concerned not to provoke Bismarck by establishing an alliance which he could only regard as 'encirclement', but *revanche* undoubtedly required an ally, and only one Continental power fulfilled the French requirements. 'Russia appealed to the extreme right because it was reactionary ... (and was) preferred by the extreme left because it was the alternative to England, for England was seen by both as fickle and insincere, ready to do France down at any turn'.[2] The alliance was therefore negotiated piecemeal over the years 1887 to 1894. Throughout, the French Government took the initiative in the face of sustained reluctance on the part of the Tsar and his diplomatic advisers to commit Russia to a French strategy. The Russian War Minister and High Command were convinced advocates of uniting all Slavs under Russian leadership – a policy which first and foremost entailed a clash with the interests of *Austria-Hungary*. This difference of objective was not considered too important by French negotiators, who reasoned – correctly – that once Russia was tied militarily, its freedom of diplomatic action towards Germany would thereby be restricted. The Russian military were the natural entrée for French policy, so the opening gambit was made in 1887 in the form of an undertaking to supply 500,000 of the latest French rifle.* But rifles by

---

*The French Government, mindful of Madagascar (see below p. 148) prudently obtained from its partner a formal guarantee that the weapons 'would never be used' against France.

themselves were not enough: French policy required that Russia be put in a position to act quickly* against a technologically superior enemy. Facilities were accordingly arranged for Russian engineers to study in France the newest techniques in the production of arms and munitions for ultimate use in Russia. For the necessary investment capital, the French market could replace that of Germany. These attractions were only enhanced when, by arresting Russian nihilists at the Tsar's request and by ostentatiously dissociating themselves from international protests about pogroms and the denial of what would now be called human rights, successive French governments demonstrated that even republican regimes could be relied upon. In 1905, they offered the most convincing evidence to the Tsar when official France prudently failed to support Polish nationalism in the revolutionary upheavals of that year (lest loss of Russian control imperil the base for an invasion of Germany from the area of Warsaw).

By confining the talks to the General Staffs, the French Government not only ensured that discussions took place in the most suitable professional forum but that they outflanked the Tsar's diplomatic advisers, principally the ailing Foreign Minister, Giers, who were reluctant to assume anything like an automatic commitment, were not certain that Germany *was* the enemy (Britain was more likely) and argued that the social and industrial state of the realm demanded an *understanding* with Germany. The crucial military negotiations took place in 1892, and eventually drew the Tsar into an alliance with a republic – which he once publicly declared he would never tolerate. Under the terms of the convention, simultaneous mobilisation of French and Russian forces would bring over two million men into action against Germany. Moreover, the Russian net birthrate had increased rapidly during the second half of the century to 50 per 1000 and was the highest in Europe: German fecundity was outweighed, and the dark and unnatural practices of French women so regularly (and unavailingly) denounced from pulpits no longer imperilled the future of the nation. From that time on, France could outnumber Germany. As one contemporary publicist put it 'We hold Central Europe between the jaws of a vice. At the first insult we shall turn the screw.... On the day when the Cossacks gallop through the streets of Old Stamboul, a French batallion will be presenting arms in front of the Kléber statue in Strasbourg.[3]' The rhetoric summed up French expectations, but it was not entirely clear even to the negotiators that Russia *would* fight for Alsace and Lorraine or conversely, what the French would regard as a *casus foederis* in the Balkans.

These reciprocal opacities apart, there remained the indispensable requirement, from the French point of view, that Russian troops should be

---

*Speed was essential, in the French view, not only to bring pressure to bear on Germany to relieve France but also to extract the best out of the alliance before it succumbed to notorious Russian administrative incapacity.

speedily engaged. This circumstance dictated the appeals and inducements to French investors to put their savings into Russian railways and manufacturing which would improve Russia's military potential. The French rentier responded nobly* to an eventual total of 13 milliard gold francs – but he was investing not just in facilities but in a specific strategy. In principle, technology was the backbone of one, unified war plan.**

This solution to the problem of strategic manpower had two distinct advantages for France: balancing off loans against troops and the facilities needed to equip and sustain them allowed the French Government to tighten its strategic demands whenever their allies needed more money, and 'buying' Russians in this way neatly relieved French Governments of one of their more pressing domestic concerns. During the years up to 1905, budgetary constraints made it impossible to call up and train all those Frenchmen who were legally liable to be conscripted. External loans only affected a small number of investors seeking a profitable outlet for their savings, and were politically popular: income taxes to finance the call-up would have touched a far wider electorate and were political suicide. The Russian alliance compensated France for the unwillingness of its citizens to pay for its defence.

Demography was not, by itself, decisive: even with a smaller volunteer army, the French Government might well have welcomed an alliance with Russia as a means of threatening Germany from the east, but conscription turned what might have been desirable into a demographic necessity. In Britain, which only adopted compulsory military service in the middle of the First World War, demographic trends were not fundamental to military planning. The first line of defence, the Navy, of itself made only finite demands on manpower, which could be met easily from the sea-faring community. On the Continent, reliance on conscripts for the bulk of forces meant that the anxieties of general staffs were closely correlated with population trends. Slow growth in the essential groups meant jeopardising future military power, or abandoning policy options.

---

*Negotiations for financial facilities opened in St Petersburg in September 1887 between the Russian Minister of Finance and the Crédit Lyonnais. The first loan was floated in France on 18 November 1888: it was oversubscribed three times.

**French officers in 1901 were not entirely pleased to find that the Russians had earmarked a large proportion of loan funds to building a railway from Orenburg to Tashkent – for use ultimately against British influence in Afghanistan. Ten years later the French were trying to veto the building of Russian railways towards Austria.

2. New rationales for war; the fittest and how they survive: Schmoller

The creation of the German Empire did not in itself immediately alter the industrial and economic situation in Europe, except insofar as the French indemnity financed a short-lived boom in Germany and the unification of the currencies and economic regulations of the Reich extended the advantages of the *Zollverein* to a wider area. The newly-acquired provinces of Alsace and Lorraine were not welcomed into the Reich, except by the military, since they provided competition in textile manufacture and their iron ore contained too much phosphorous for refining by existing techniques. Technological advance, in the form of the Gilchrist-Thomson process for the extraction of phosphorus, turned the deposits into a major national asset only after 1880. Internationally, the founding of the Reich strengthened the movement towards Free Trade: in 1873 iron duties were abolished and levies on semi-manufactured goods and shipbuilding materials reduced, with a view to their lapsing entirely. To contemporaries, therefore, the unification of Germany reinforced the dominant view that nationalism proceeded from or complemented liberal economic principles, and that the more independent sovereign states there were, the stronger the liberal order would be.

In fact, the new Germany proved to be the last, and – as it proved – temporary example of liberal internationalism at work. By the end of the first decade of the Reich, governments in Germany and elsewhere were beginning to question whether the assumptions of economic liberalism necessarily maximised the welfare of the nation. The lead was taken by France. During the reconstruction of the country in the first months of the Third Republic, it was widely argued that the free trade policies of Napoleon III were directly responsible for weakening the country to the point of disaster in 1870. The argument was totally false but politically persuasive: it betrayed the manufacturers' hostility to the competition which Napoleon III had thrust on them. The opposition under the liberal Empire had advocated protection; it was now the government and, in the person of Adolphe Thiers, the President of the Republic. Thiers was a life-long protectionist and he lost no opportunity to reintroduce tariffs. They did not survive his leaving office in May 1873, but he had made tariffs a permanent item on the Republic's agenda. During the seventies, an intense propaganda created an effective political force for protection, partly in response to depression and falling prices and partly to the need to rationalise a customs' structure dating in some instances from 1791. The agitation produced a new general tariff in 1881, together with a new law on shipping, which included tonnage bounties for ship construction.

One timely and important influence on the debate within France was the adoption of certain protective measures by Imperial Germany in 1878, to support an agriculture faced with a devastating influx of wheat from North America – made possible by the completion of the prairie railway system three years earlier. Agriculture was vital not solely as a source of food within the jurisdiction of the Imperial Government; it supported an estate of the realm which furnished and partly financed the officer corps. The price of bread included a premium for security. The Government also provided a general export subsidy through the fixing of freight rates on the *Reichsbahn*.

Governments of emergent states, such as Italy, also jettisoned economic liberalism, but on grounds which have a contemporary ring, namely that economic growth is incompatible with the open international economy. It was axiomatic in new states that the national market must be reserved for national enterprise; foreign assistance was justified only as a means of bringing a national market into existence; otherwise, relying on 'market forces' made state policy dependent on factors which it could not control. Tariff protection and restrictions on foreign enterprise strengthened the national economy and at the same time the power of the state to control its environment.

The tariff levels which resulted from the rejection of the fundamental assumptions of international economics till then were trifling, compared with those adopted with alacrity by the next wholesale creation of new states after 1918, but they do demonstrate that nationalism and liberalism were no longer synonymous and that the state in the industrial age was succesfully staking its claim to be an economic agency in its own right, in particular in defining and enforcing the terms of the national welfare. In Britain the state was reluctant to do this in any positive sense till 1915, with the partial exception of its defence requirements. Elsewhere in Europe, governments of industrialised states had fewer inhibitions.

They were encouraged in this direction by manufacturers seeking security against the consequences of depressions which, since 1857, had been international in their impact. Industrialists looked to the government as a source of contracts which could counter the vagaries of the trade cycle. They combined to promote their common interests in maintaining output or prices or in securing market shares. The *Comité des Forges* organised the first *comptoir* for centrally fixing prices and quotas in French metallurgical production in 1876. The same year saw the first, though short-lived, potash agreement among producers in Germany. Coking coal followed in 1879 and coal tar dyes in 1881. German industry became extensively cartellised – not the least reason being that cartel agreements could be enforced at law. In France such agreements were not necessary since 'tacit limits on competition were about as effective as formal contracts.'[4]

In due course, considerations of security and the logic of technical development induced the larger manufacturers to combine not only within frontiers but across them. 'Security' might be related to the supply of raw materials or to maintaining market outlets by joining a competitor or to presenting a united front when pursuing a contract, but the net effect was that the major firms ceased merely trading in commodities and began to invest abroad in assets which were locally managed. Their activities and profitability were no longer derived from one country but could depend on price-relationships in a number of countries in which the enterprise operated through a subsidiary. Whether the latter traded in raw materials, locally represented the exporter or supervised contractors, it was bound to be involved in the local political and economic life to a degree hitherto unexperienced. Such involvement was actively promoted by local governments which, to further rapid industrial advance insisted that suppliers set up manufacturing capacity within their territorial jurisdiction.

The practice of investing abroad, as distinct from relying on sale-and-purchase contracts, multiplied the points of possible friction between states. Paradoxically, nationalist policies for independence could only be fulfilled by inviting the foreigner to participate, but nationalist governments, while eager for foreign support in their external affairs, wanted to restrict foreign influence inside their country. Suppliers, for their part, had the problem of ensuring that agreements, once made, would be observed by governments which were ready to plead *raison d'état* for breaking them, or which, experience showed, too easily resorted to converting their contracted debts into issues of bonds which carried much lower rates of interest. This practice increased the likelihood of friction between creditor and debtor. Governments might be indifferent to commercial debts outstanding to their nationals: they were quite prepared to intervene to collect on bonds, since, in the contemporary opinion, a commercial debt was a trading risk but a bond represented the assumption of a more fundamental kind of obligation.

This basic condition drove operating firms into greater dependence on their own governments, either to set up situations or to bail them out of trouble. Government, therefore, acquired an additional power over the firm, if it cared to use it. Management's object was to convince government that the interest of nation and the firm were identical. To this end, industrialists had to spend more time in their own ministries of foreign affairs and concern themselves with those sections of public opinion which could be induced to support them.

By the turn of the century, in comparison with, say 1850 when national unification in much of Europe was either a hope or a programme, industry was more extensive and more complex and impinged on foreign policy to the extent that investment replaced or supplemented traditional import and export business. These changes concerned, especially, industries based on iron and steel production – a sector which included the manufacturers of weapons and the providers of military facilities. Arms manufacturers were not exempt from the pressures experienced by suppliers of civil goods and reacted in the same way, seeking to secure their position by combining, by investing abroad and by establishing close working relationships with their own and foreign governments.

All these aspects of producers' operations incurred severe and widespread public condemnation after the First World War, on the assumption, for instance, that for Vickers to enter into licensing and market sharing agreements with Deutsche Waffen- und Munitionsfabriken in 1901 and with Krupp in 1902 was irrefutable evidence of collusion with the enemy, though the firms' motives were, in each case, strictly commercial: had the Anglo–German alliance sought by Joseph Chamberlain in 1900 been concluded, the agreements would have been acclaimed as patriotic. Similarly from 1901, Krupp, Schneider and Dillinger, with Vickers and Armstrongs were represented, among others, in the Steel Manufacturers' Nickel Syndicate, formed to counter a nickel producers' cartel, at a time when the sole use for nickel was in hardening steel for use as armour plate. The syndicate succeeded in negotiating a lowering of price and bringing down the cost of nickel to manufacturers. On the national as distinct from the industrial scale, governments themselves stimulated share participations, working agreements and other forms of combined action by industry, in support of their own alliance policies. The outstanding example is French investments in Russian manufacture of steel and steel products and in the modernisation of Russian railways, all directly related, from the French point of view, to making Russia a more efficient ally against Germany. One of the most sophisticated endeavours in this respect was the founding by Vickers and some Russian banks of a works at Tsaritsin (now Volgograd) for the manufacture of the French Deport field gun, using steel from Franco-Russian owned plants, with technical management from Vickers and Chantillon-Commetry, which had originally patented the system used in the gun.

The overseas investments of the producers in raw materials displayed no motives peculiar to the share of their output represented by weapons. Krupp invested in Spain, to assure itself of supplies of a particular quality of iron ore, as did Skoda in Cumberland in England for the same reason. More generally, the coal and steel producers of the Rhineland, Belgium, Luxembourg and northern France (the area over which the First World War was largely to be fought) were closely combined to rationalise investments and qualities of output, with the blessing of their respective governments.

Rationalisation applied not just to structures of industry but also, to a degree, to the knowledge which was necessary to future development. An increasingly international technical press exposed basic processes and workshop practice, while individual firms bought and sold technological 'short-cuts' in the form of patents and licences. The compound steel plates manufactured at Le Creusot for the French Navy were made under patents from Charles Cammell, of Sheffield. Such developments were thought by authority to be natural, mutually beneficial and evidence of the spread of international industrial partnership.

All the companies looked to their governments for contracts to tide them over depressions in the trade cycle or slackening in activity. Such contracts had the additional advantage that they were an alternative to raising capital in the market to finance innovations or extensions to plant and to maintain employment of personnel. 'Employment' became a new consideration in the relationship between governments and industry, since it was during this epoch that in Germany and the United Kingdom a revaluation of the social responsibilities of government argued that it could no longer be indifferent to unemployment. As recently as 1869, Gladstone's government had summarily closed Woolwich Dockyard under its programme of 'Peace and Retrenchment' but had not considered it had any duty to the thousand employees, who either drifed northwards into other shipbuilding areas or emigrated to Canada. By the 1880s, government was being called upon to use its power to grant contracts to relieve distress. Manufacturers and their operatives were not slow to stress the advantages to society of this more positive approach, but goverment's most persistent contractual relationships were with the producers of weapons and their ancillaries. The 'social' reasons for armaments began to be canvassed in consequence of the state's assumption of responsibility for welfare. They have been strongly voiced ever since.

Although the manufacture of armaments, after the 1880s, provides the clearest evidence that a new industrial order was emerging nationally and internationally, the extent of the development should not be over-emphasised. Europe until 1914 remained an area in which industrialisation was patchy, with large peasant populations which could hardly be said to be part of an industrial economy at all. But in that economy, freedom of movement for capital and goods was taken for granted: there were no exchange restrictions (in many respects, the European Common Market is struggling to get back to a system which was broken up in 1914). The significant difference between the manufacture of weapons and of goods in general lay not in the behaviour of the firms but in one specific characteristic of their markets. Ultimately, the market opportunities and hence the profitability of armament firms were related to the existence of international tension. The production of other goods, including those made by armament firms, was not. Moreover, the state of international tension at any given juncture took into account the findings of research and the time-scales of production – both of which had to find their way into diplomatic as well as military assessments of policy.

Furthermore, one of the dividends falling to Germany after the Franco-Prussian War was that it displaced Britain as the model of an industrialised society. To contemporary observers, the inadequacies of British industrial and commercial philosophy were disclosed by British performance, from about 1880 onwards, when Britain began to lose ground relative to Germany and the United States (historians still dispute the reasons). More positively, Germany was seen to connect industry deliberately with the national effort in scientific research, especially in chemicals and dyestuffs. The organisation of research for practical ends related to changes in the educational system. The *Technische Hochschulen* came into their own – the Kaiser himself championing them against the traditional humanist learning of the universities. Industrialists looked to them as a source of recruits for technical management, in consequence of which industrial practice itself came under continuous scientific scrutiny. Germany established a lead in the systematic translation of advances in knowledge into 'output' construed as either improved techniques or as superior products. These changes were general throughout industry but were particularly in evidence in engineering and chemicals. Research was applied to markets as well as production. German firms set the style of systematic canvassing for orders which was well adapted to the idiosyncrasies of the specific market.

The displacement of Britain as the model of an advanced industrial society had implications for the analysis of war and peace. Free trade had been advocated not just as a device to improve living standards but as the means of ensuring world peace. Orthodox liberalism considered military expenditures as inherently wasteful and that armaments exacerbated rather than reduced tensions. Free Trade made these burdens unnecessary, because it united men through their necessary mutual exchanges. The Anglo-French Treaty of 1860, the work of Cobden and Chevallier, was thought to be the epitome of these ideas – in Britain. By the last quarter of the century, many liberals in politics and the political sciences were prepared to make minor amendments to the doctrine, but in general it was highly influential in Westminster and Whitehall, even when the government was not Liberal and not led by Gladstone. Reformers who wanted to change the system suffered the tactical disadvantage of being heretics.

The emergence of Germany focused attention on a wholly different set of arguments and recommendations as to the relationship of industrialisation and trade to war and peace. The extreme formulation – the antithesis to Cobden – is to be found in the work of Albert Schäffle and Gustav von Schmoller, both university professors in a country in which professors were rated somewhere between God and His angels. The two professors had differences of emphasis, but they agreed in scouting the possibility of peace in the terms conceived by Cobden and the Manchester liberals, who were condemned for having ignored the fact that the world was composed of states, not of transactions. States required security, which in a complex modern society could only be guaranteed collectively. A military establish-ment, far from being wasteful, was the cheapest means of meeting this collective need. Soldiers were no more unproductive than doctors or priests (or, they might have added, professors of economics). The planned production of arms and military facilities could be used to offset cyclical depressions in economic activity, and was therefore of the greatest social utility. Conscription was not a total economic loss but, on the contrary, a means of training and of inculcating disciplines which were of benefit to the individual and to his employer after service had been completed. These internal benefits apart, armaments and their related facilities were required to protect overseas trade, even without colonial possessions. The latter merely underlined the general need and translated it into specific forms – the establishment of coaling stations and the nature of the fleet. The economic system did not supply the needs of war to the detriment of 'progress' but could, if properly organised for that purpose, confer positive social and economic benefits. These conclusions evoked many echoes in the policies of Imperial Germany and among those for whom Germany became the exemplar of development. The theories of German economists dovetailed neatly into neo-Darwinian views of progress.

3. Enterprises in the new setting: exports

If the army is regarded not simply as an instrument of state security but, in addition, as the embodiment of the unity and honour of the nation, then those who provide the means can expect to flourish in fortune and esteem. From 1870 onwards Krupp's policy was naturally to consolidate the position it had achieved, by keeping in the forefront of technique and by building on its connections with the military.

The campaign itself took Krupp into the design and manufacture of siege mortars and of the first high-angled gun, for attacking balloonists escaping from besieged Paris. With the end of the war, Krupp foresaw that the lead in field artillery which had annihilated the French forces would have to be maintained, since France was bound to attempt to remedy the deficiencies of its arms. The Prussian War Office, from which Voigts-Rhetz retired, was more concerned to save money by recasting the bronze cannon captured in large numbers from the French. Krupp made representations to his old mentor, who was now not only King of Prussia but Emperor of Germany. The Emperor decided that he could not overrule the technical objections of the Artillery Test Commission. French rearmament settled the issue and in January 1874 Krupp got his order, for 2,000 8.8cm cannon, for delivery from 1 June 1875.

The ranges of which his guns were now capable pressed on the limits of the state proving grounds at Tegel, where the arrangements were necessarily in the hands of military officials. Krupp invested in his own testing facilities successively at Dülmen, near Munster, and at Meppen which became the scene of international shooting trials, and hence a 'shop-window' for Krupp's products. This was not the only investment. From 1871 onwards, Krupp systematically integrated his concern, with acquisitions of coal and iron mines in Germany and in Spain. The latter venture took him into the business of transport, building his own steamers and laying out harbours and other facilities. All these investments were financed out of earnings and by short-term loans from the banks, – a course adopted by Alfred Krupp to preserve his independence. It made him highly vulnerable to the collapse of the speculative boom financed by the French war indemnity. In 1873, the withdrawal of short-term money endangered the future of the firm. Krupp was the first of the main manufacturers to experience the peculiar risks attached to using high-cost technology to produce a product which had a limited number of customers, or customers who took far longer to articulate their demand than short-term finance allowed. The incremental costs of the more advanced technology could not be recouped out of higher current earnings.

Krupp who disliked bankers and on moral grounds refused to have anything to do with the idea of conversion into a joint-stock enterprise, applied to the Emperor for a state loan – to be told that, under the new constitution, it was a matter for the Reichstag and that the state had no funds anyway. By the end of March 1874, Krupp required no less than 30 million marks to avoid liquidation. A group of Berlin banks, headed by the Prussian State Bank, embarked on a rescue operation, under conditions which gave the group financial control of the enterprise as long as the debt was outstanding. It was paid off in 1887 – the year Alfred Krupp died. The order for 2,000 cannon had not been enough: indebtedness and the 'outside' control it entailed pushed Krupp further into exports.

In France, too, the war brought about a closer relationship between military industry and the policy of the State. The disasters of 1870 revived the manufacture of guns at Le Creusot for the first time since 1815. Sedan, in this sense, proved as decisive for Schneider as for Krupp. The Government of National Defence, created to replace the Empire of Napoleon III, hurriedly placed orders for artillery. Schneider's newly-installed Bessemer converters were put into operation and within five months the works delivered twenty-three batteries of bronze guns, two of steel (thanks to the experiments initiated by Napoleon III) and sixteen mitrailleuses, all complete with limbers, ammunition wagons and other ancillaries. By the time these equipments were delivered Paris had surrendered and the elections for the National Assembly to decide the question of war or peace were about to be held. The decision was for peace. Schneider, however, had fully demonstrated its capacity and in consequence became the main source of heavy equipment in the postwar rearmament programme. The works were reorganised and overhauled. To the Bessemer converters were added Siemens Martin plants in 1873; the Gilchrist process (which improved Bessemer's) was adopted in 1879. Thus Le Creusot entered the epoch of steel, turning out steel rails, plates and bars of soft steel, for ships and forgings, and ingots for making guns.* A separate gun factory was set up in 1875, and from that time onwards guns were manufactured and sold as a regular business.

For Schneider, the most far-reaching single event in this development was the decision of its traditional customer, the navy, to introduce a squadron of armoured cruisers – a move which prompted the firm to invest in a 100-ton

---

*The slag from the Bessemer plant which had a high phosphoric acid content was sold to the local farmers as fertiliser – an early example of 'spin-off'.

steam hammer. Since it was the first in France, and the capital and running costs discouraged competitors, the hammer tied the navy to Schneider as a supplier – a foreign source being out of the question. This is a significant example of the reciprocal relation between demand and technique. The decision to invest in the hammer and its associated facilities depended on a prior policy decision of the navy in favour of a particular weapon (armoured cruisers) which was related to specific strategy. But the navy became technically dependent on the continued operation of the hammer. Increased demand, in its turn, prompted not only improvements in production techniques but also enlargement of the enterprise. A series of mergers, particularly that with the Canet works at Le Havre, gave Schneider a monopoly of gun construction and a formidably strong position in the manufacture of other military equipments.

The fortunes of both Krupp and Schneider began to turn on their export business, the market for which was during this period enlarged by the polarisation of European politics and the emergence of new states under the patronage of, or in consequence of rivalries between, the Great Powers. Governments turned to Krupp and to Schneider for the weapons and the ancillary systems which they could not make themselves. The German and the French governments both fostered this demand, which gave them an opportunity to extend their general political influence. Weapons were as important to prestige as to keeping manufacturing capacity employed. So, although the German and French armed forces remained major customers, Krupp cannon arrived in Romania and Turkey, and Schneider began to sell armoured turrets to Belgium, Holland, Romania and Spain. The competition between the two firms both reflected and sharpened competition between the two states in which they were located and their policies.

This was not a new development, merely the application of the general rules that, firstly, new states mean new markets, and, secondly, that states with lesser technology offer opportunities to states with greater. In consequence, manufacturers ceased to regard their 'own' forces which constituted their domestic market, as the primary source of return on capital employed. From 1875 to 1891, only eighteen per cent of Krupp war materials went to German forces; the rest went abroad, bringing in a return of RM 250 million. A market of this size resulted from Krupp's identification with the success of Prussia until 1870, and after of Germany, and from the desire of lesser states, anxious to improve their standing in the international competition, to emulate that success. In Europe after 1870, Italy, in the eyes of both Italian and foreign governments, was the most obvious candidate for promotion into the ranks of the major European powers.

During the Franco-Prussian War, the Italian Government took the opportunity of the withdrawal of the French garrison from Rome to occupy the city, which became the capital of Italy. There for the time being the process of unification, begun in 1859, ended. But the achievement of political unity required the creation of more effective institutions, including an army and a navy. An Italian navy had existed from 1861, but the policy set out in the seventies by the responsible minister, Saint Bon Simone, provided for a comprehensive reconstruction of the fleet and of its budgetary support. In particular Italy was to strive for technical supremacy in the naval arm. The policy, continued by successive governments, was an outstanding success. By 1885 Italy was the third largest naval power. But technical supremacy implied reconstructing Italian industry and importing the latest technology. The governments of intending suppliers thus were given an opportunity to strengthen Italy as a power and a potential ally.

'Technical supremacy' was exemplified in the first two capital ships, the *Duilio* and the *Dandolo*, which set new standards for vessels in their class. Their armour was put out to international competition. Schneider's armour plate survived the shooting trials at Muggiano near La Spezia in September and October 1876. These tests proved the value of steel over iron as a material for defensive armour and represented Schneider's first important success. That success not only brought immediate, orders, but led also to orders for later buildings, including the *Lepanto* in 1882. Subsequently the Schneider process was adopted under licence by the Terni Company which at that stage was being expanded and transformed, at the behest of the navy, by two major banks, together with the state. The government's contribution took the form of advances on orders at guaranteed high prices.

The Italian Government also developed new relationships with suppliers over the armament. It had relied on Armstrongs – in consequence of which the Italian fleet included from 1876 the *Europa* which mounted a 100-ton gun; ship and armament were both manufactured at Newcastle. As part of the same policy which ensured that Terni would guarantee the navy's future in iron and steel, the Italian Government decided that it should have an armament production located in Italy, and therefore under its control. Armstrongs were approached to set up in Italy but demurred on the ground that the product would be cheaper delivered from Elswick. The Italian Government thereupon made joint investment in local production facilities an absolute condition of Armstrongs' receiving further contracts. This was decisive. Armstrongs capitulated against an undertaking of a flow of orders sufficient to guarantee the future of the investment. The plant was established at Pozzuoli near Naples, against much nationalist and protectionist opposition in Parliament and, apart from ordnance, produced ships, coastal gun mountings, shot and shell for the Italian armed forces.

The arming of united Italy demonstrated two new methods of ensuring that technical progress was located within national boundaries; one, by manufacture under licence, against payment of royalties, the other, inducing the supplier of technique to 'export' it permanently, by setting up facilities, under threat of denying him access to the market otherwise. This development was strengthened by Italian tariff policy after 1888, when the

Government switched from tariffs for revenue purposes to the outright protection of the economy, including especially the manufacture of iron and steel. The initiatives taken with Schneider and Armstrong, therefore, marked the beginnings of what became a decisive shift in relationships between government and industry.

But the Italian Government found out by bitter experience that the business of arms exports could not always be manipulated to its advantage. Its relationship with Schneider began when relations with France were reasonably amicable. The dispute with the French over the dispossession of the Pope had petered out, and France remained the main source of foreign capital and the main trading partner. Even when tariff changes were introduced in the mid-seventies, Italy sought to exempt France from their more rigorous provisions. The proffered advantages were rejected by the French Chamber of Deputies in 1877. Somewhat less favourable but still preferential terms for France were negotiated four years later. From then onwards, however, relationships between the two states deteriorated rapidly, by reason of conflicting interests in the Mediterranean and East Africa, and a damaging tariff war. It is significant that the purchase of the Schneider licence took place after the first outbreaks of francophobia and thus secured the technique for Italy in spite of increasing political hostility. But Italy was unable to prevent France from supplying those who opposed, or could be induced to oppose, Italian expansion in Eritrea and Somalia. In this area, French activity against Italy involved supplying arms – forty thousand rifles and a million rounds of ammunition – to the ruler of Ethiopia and building a railway from Djibouti to Addis Ababa, with the dual purpose of maintaining the ruler's independence of Italy and providing a strategic link for French forces. The forces proved to be unnecessary: French-instructed Ethiopian troops, armed with French firearms, destroyed the Italian force at Adowa on 1 March 1896. The defeat checked Italy in an area which France hoped to make part of an east-west French empire in Africa. It had more lasting effects, however, in that the defeat entered into nationalist mythology and into Italian policy for decades afterwards and was a potent influence in bringing about Mussolini's campaign in 1936.

4. National strategy and the 'timetable' effect: Tirpitz and Schlieffen

The expansion of industry and the use of more complex technologies brought groups wider than the government and the industrialists into decisions about the manufacture of weapons – the public, not as the assumed general beneficiary of foreign policy but as the specific beneficiary of a particular strategy. Identifying the two far more narrowly ensured that the strategy, in the public mind, defined the overall aims of the state, even though it had no immediate application. Friends and rivals alike could take note of the identification and build it into their own assessments of the future. The consequence was to sharpen international competition. The construction of the German navy offers the classic example.

A *German* navy (as distinct from the naval forces of individual states) had long been a nationalist dream but, in contrast to warfare on land, the maritime performance of Prussia in 1864 and of the North German Federation after 1867 had not been impressive. Neither against the Danes nor the French had naval forces been able to assert themselves. This failing by itself, even without the euphoria attending national unity, was enough to promote inquiry into the kind of navy Germany needed. The conclusions reached reflected the individual concerns of Moltke and Bismarck; the sea was not Molke's *métier*, and Bismarck set himself against colonial expansion; the protection of trade routes did not, therefore, come into question. These two attitudes pointed to the same policy outcome. An Imperial Navy needed only to do the traditional job of naval forces in Germany, but more effectively, namely, to defeat any attempt on the part of France to blockade German ports. So, from 1873, the fleet was augmented by eight armoured frigates. It also began to be mooted that even with this limited role the fleet could be more flexibly deployed if a canal were constructed to connect the Baltic with the North Sea. Thus matters remained during the seventies.

In that decade, however, changes began to occur which were later to cause Germany's strategy to be revised and which accordingly created new objectives for the navy. Progress in scientific exploration and concern that Germans who had emigrated should be kept in contact with the new Reich fostered a popular demand for colonial expansion, which issued in the founding of the German Colonial Society in 1882. In its membership the Society combined the interests of science, commerce and sentiment and generated constant pressure on the Government to protect Germany's overseas trading position and improve it by territorial acquisition. Bismarck bowed to the demand. In consequence, over the years 1883–1885 colonial rule was established in South West Africa, the Cameroons, New Guinea and East Africa. In the following decade, Germany acquired various territories and islands in the Pacific.

Bismarck had not suddenly become enamoured of colonies; his change of front stemmed from his European policies, but it provoked some friction with Britain and brought into being a new German interest which it was necessary to protect. This task implied a larger and different navy – a point which was not lost on the Colonial Society. Nevertheless, the expansion of the navy, when it came, rested on a premise of *European* strategy. The problem was no longer to keep French ships out of the Heligoland Bight or to allow German vessels to blockade Dunkirk. The new axiom of strategy indentified Germany's most dangerous enemy as Britain because it had a large navy capable of blocking German expansion. A stronger German fleet would provide a means of combat and a means of leverage in international politics. Forces designed for coastal defence were irrelevant to this purpose; what was needed was a force capable of unfolding its greatest potential in the North Sea, between Heligoland and the Thames. On this reasoning, the defence of colonial territories although much advertised as a reason for a navy, is, at best, a trifling adjunct to the main strategic task. The premise that Britain must be intrinsically hostile to Germany had a commercial as well as a strategic variant. It was confidently assumed that Germany's new-found industrial and commerical pre-eminence must provoke such envy in Britain that the latter would have to attempt to crush Germany by force to put an end to the competition.

In either version, the theory demonstrates that it is not only amateurs of strategy who indulge in self-fulfilling prophecy; German naval expansion as such threatened Britain no more than that of France, the United States or Italy, which was taking place at the same time, and, conversely, Britain could no more prevent Germany's expansion than it could theirs. The supposition that Britain might strike first without a declaration of war to eliminate the German navy – the notorious 'Copenhagen' argument[5] – ignored the historical circumstances of 1807 and was not voiced by any other navy-building power to which it logically applied. The argument was, in fact, a purely German deduction from the initial premise of inevitable conflict, from which it followed that Germany stood at greatest risk while the fleet was being built. That Britain would react by attempting to destroy the ships in a sudden coup was an article of faith of the apostles of *Weltpolitik* from 1896 – long before Admiral Fisher and his associates appeared to confirm it by their ineffective propaganda for a preventive attack.

The premise of necessary conflict involving transitory risk was the basic concept in German policy towards Britain. It ruled out any attempt at seeking an understanding – if conflict is inevitable, it can be resolved only by fighting or capitulation – but what was logically impeccable was, in the world of action, diplomatically maladroit. Britain reacted to the German programme not by seeking an alliance with Germany on unfavourable terms but by settling her differences with France and Russia.* The leverage worked the wrong way.

The *a priori* reasoning behind the commercial theory was equally flawed. Though German publicists and policy makers were quick to notice the indignant resolutions of chambers of commerce and trade associations in Britain about the effects of German competition, they failed to grasp that Government policy remained dedicated to Free Trade, which gave German capitalists and merchants access to Britain and the Empire on equal terms with British.** German colonial expansion involved cooperation with Britain, as well as incidental, but negotiable frictions. For the proposition that Britain was being overhauled in the markets there was plenty of evidence but the deduction that Britain could only recover by forcing war on Germany contradicted the empirical evidence. British Governments had long since abandoned the idea that trade and war were coterminous, or to be explained in the concepts of Gustav von Schmoller and his associates in the 'historical' school of economics. Even if Britain had the intentions attributed to it, a glance at the state of the British army and its record in and since the Crimea would have confirmed that Britain was incapable of carrying them out. Removing German competition implied destroying the political and commercial order which was practising it. A navy, no matter how large could hardly occupy Berlin, and the small British army was totally unsuited to European conditions; since 1856 it had experienced only colonial campaigns in which its technological superiority had proved no guarantee against defeat. Bismarck, when questioned about the possibility of British intervention in Schleswig-Holstein in 1864, had said that if an army landed, he would send the police to arrest it. His successor, also worried about a landing in Schleswig-Holstein, apparently had less confidence in the police.

In Germany, however, the absence of empirical confirmation was no bar to the theories' acceptance, especially as they were expressed vehemently, if somewhat erratically, by the Kaiser himself who was well informed about developments in naval technology and tactics and who made questions of naval policy very much his own. But naval expansion was a policy, which

---

*see pages 122–3.

**German publicists made great play with an article which appeared in the *Saturday Review* of 11 September 1897 advocating preventive action against Germany, without acknowledging that by that time the *Review* had been taken over by a group of Cecil Rhodes' associates who professed to be anxious about German competition in Africa. Even after the First World War, German apologists alleged that the article represented Britain's 'real' foreign policy: they had, apparently, not noticed the fate of the Jameson raid and of Rhodes himself.

unlike, say, the schemes worked out by the Kaiser's grandfather with Bismarck, involved more than the traditional restricted circle of policy-makers. Now the navy was to express Imperial greatness and it commanded the enthusiasm and the interest of groups in society who expected 'greatness' to confer specific benefits. Industrial advance, universal elementary education and cheap newspapers created an articulate public for foreign policy, to a degree which had not existed during the 1850's and 1860's. Moreover the central elective institution of the Empire, the Reichstag, had to agree to the expense involved. Thus, putting through the fleet building programme ceased to be a decision handed down by the Kaiser or his nominee to a royal arsenal or dockyard and became a matter of political negotiation and of mobilising support among the electorate and their representatives. In this way, the navy became a project for furthering the national identity; it was a sign that strategy was a component of *Weltpolitik*.

The handling of the political negotiations was confided to Admiral Tirpitz, as State Secretary of the Imperial Naval Office, who between December 1897 and March 1898 put through the Reichstag a building programme which followed the theories of Anglo-German relationships discussed above. It provided for the construction of nineteen ships of the line, eighteen armoured vessels for coastal defence and a total of forty-two cruisers. But this process involved Tirpitz in creating and sustaining a favourable climate of opinion through the press, the universities and professional associations. These circles were only too receptive; the navy enjoyed the support of the bourgeoisie, especially the professors, who exerted tremendous social authority. Popular support was coordinated through the Navy League, which was founded on 30 April, 1898, a month after the building programme became law. The League was organised under official auspices. The Kaiser's brother, Prince Henry of Prussia became its sponsor, and Victor Schwein-burg, editor of the Nationalist newspaper *Berliner Neuste Nachrichten*, was elected business manager. This was significant in two respects; it gave the League its own public platform, and it involved Krupp, as the owner of the newspaper, in the League's activities. In fact, Krupp and other manu-facturers who expected to participate in the shipbuilding programme largely financed the League, which the minimum subscription of fifty pfennige opened to a wide membership in all classes. These arrangements permitted the League rapidly to outnumber the other nationalist societies; in three years it achieved a membership of 600,000 and eventually reached nearly a million. The academic community, particularly the economists, were well to the fore, in contrast to the military aristocracy and the nobility, who, Tirpitz complained, refused their support. The League's official journal *Die Flotte*, a flood of pamphlets and an intensive campaign of meetings and rallies carried its message far beyond the members themselves. Its aims were, in general, supported by the Colonial Society and by chambers of commerce, and members of the Reichstag and of local councils in the manufacturing areas concerned. In this manner, naval expansion became a mass movement.

The institution of the Navy League cemented a particular strategy in those sections of public opinion which, under the constitution, was operative in the political process and which expected directly to benefit from the armament programme. By the same token, however, the appeal to the public diffused throughout German society the fears and tensions on which the strategy was based and maintained a state of psychological preparedness for war. This gave the programme a degree of inflexibility which Tirpitz rightly regarded as giving it extra security. The Government made no effort to moderate anti-British feeling, considering that a certain tension in relations was useful to sustaining support for the programme and reconciling taxpayers to the burden it imposed. The contrast with Bismarck's practice could not be more striking. In his time, however much the public might be concerned with foreign policy through parliament or manipulated through the press, it had no direct interest in programmes for procuring specific weapons. Under the Kaiser and Admiral Tirpitz, it had. The German Navy Law of 1898 broke new ground in this respect.

Similarly, although Napoleon III had seen the necessary connections between technical progress, the institutions of finance and manufacture on the one hand and the options consequently open to foreign and military policy on the other, he had not found it necessary to secure a permanent body of opinion in favour of one particular policy rather than another. He, as policy maker, thus retained the initiative in his own hands. After the Navy Law, policy makers in Germany, in practice though not in theory, shared their rights of initiative with the manufacturers of the weapons dictated by the strategy, and with political and social groups who considered that their fortunes depended on that particular programme. Thus the Kaiser and Admiral Tirpitz tied their own hands.

The policies of both Napoleon III and Tirpitz related specific developments in foreign policy to a timetable but its role altered significantly between 1859 and 1898. For Napoleon III and Cavour, the Pact of Plombières, agreed privately between them, was a guide to action, which, other things being equal, would be fulfilled. But, as we have seen, what determined its operation in practice was the will of the signatory with the greater resources. The timetable was neither inflexible nor irrevocable. The German Navy Law had wholly contrasting repercussions. The timetable was established by public law, arrived at because a public opinion was created in its favour and was maintained by organised enthusiasm and official pressure. The programme could be varied in tempo, within limits, but could not be called off without political and social damage; too many people had an interest in its continuance. Where Napoleon III could take account of changed circumstances, Tirpitz could only assert in the face of criticism that he was bound by a law, which there was no will to rescind. He devised the timetable as a tactic to put the shipbuilding programme beyond the contingencies of German politics; from the strategic point of view, it meant that flexibility was sacrificed to the advantages anticipated from steadily increasing a threat. Consequently, German strategy prior to the outbreak of the First World War was stuck with a navy of a particular quality for a task which was narrowly defined, while German diplomacy was left to explain away a development which was intractable.

In the nature of the case, the diplomats' arguments could not be convincing, and their attempts in regard to the Navy Law affected the general credibility of German diplomacy at the time. Officially, the anti-British rationale was muted. Tirpitz denied that the fleet was intended offensively: its function was merely to keep the North Sea open in case of war. He did not identify the enemy but the size and quality of the fleet left little room for speculation and continued to undermine the well-meaning explanations of German diplomats. As with the construction of Cherbourg, the building of the High Seas Fleet made no sense unless it was tied in to a specific strategy – which the object of that strategy could deduce for itself. At a less sophisticated level – in the popular German press – the new fleet was widely publicised as an instrument of humiliation for Britain for her policy in the Transvaal. The agitation did not prevent Eberhardt of Düsseldorf from selling to Britain cannon for use against the Boers (the Boers were supplied by Krupp).

At sea, Britain stood at risk in two respects. The Empire, of which approximately one-quarter had been acquired since 1860, needed to be defended. Britain itself, the Empire's centre of manufacture, required protection from invasion and from interruption of imports from the world as a whole. Britain therefore had more widespread interests and responsibilties than other powers and was correspondingly more vulnerable. For this reason, it was argued, Britain had to be supreme at sea – an axiom which, translated into forces, meant a navy of a size and quality to meet national and imperial responsibilities, backed by an industry which could build ships and arm them more rapidly than any other state. Colliers and coaling facilities had to be provided commensurately (though the latter requirement was generally covered by the merchant bunker trade). As long as Britain held a lead in the vital industries, the axiom was realistic. By the turn of the century, it had ceased to be so. Imperial Germany possessed the materials, the production assets and the technology to rival Britain in construction. Britain's capacity to out-build was called in question.

Even so, Britain's response to Tirpitz's challenge was delayed. The German Naval Law did not precipitate an alignment with Germany but neither was it immediately responsible for a deterioration in Anglo-German relations. The basic fact remained clear for all to see, that the tempo of construction envisaged by the law fixed the precise time when the balance of forces in the North Sea would be changed. The British Government had to respond in time, and it did so by coming to terms with France and Russia, and by embarking on a rival programme of naval construction geared to the rate of construction in Germany. This rival programme aimed not at matching ship for ship but at making a fleet qualitatively superior by building the class of 'Dreadnought' capital ships, the first of which was laid down in the autumn of 1905 and commissioned in December 1906. The *Dreadnought* opened a new era in the combination of speed and firepower. It carried five pairs of twelve-inch guns, instead of the standard requirement of two. Increased gun-power in turn demanded a larger platform from which they could be brought into action. The larger platform also had to move faster, which in the technology of the time demanded larger engines and more space for coal. Thus, for these two technical requirements, the hull had to be larger, and a larger hull demanded a greater area of armour plate. Dreadnoughts were very expensive, with each complete gun mounting costing around £100,000 and the protective armour about £600,000. The original *Dreadnought*, which set new standards for other navies – in particular the German – was completed the more quickly in that the main armament was taken over en bloc from a Brazilian order being completed at the time. (Export contracts customarily contained a proviso under which the Royal Navy could, under certain conditions, exercise a prior claim).

The naval arms race was on, and with more complex instruments than in the race between Britain and France under Napoleon III. In further contrast to the 1860s, the new race related to an identical strategy, namely, a decision at sea by a contest between line-of-battle ships, with the ancillary task for the fleet of protecting the merchant marine of the contending states. From 1906 onwards, the most delicate questions of Anglo-German relations turned on the technical problems of ship-construction. The vital consideration for Britain was the time which had to elapse from the award of the contract to the German yard to the initial trials of the completed vessel. Successive naval attachés in Berlin noted that shipyard managements were constantly trying to reduce the period through the reorganisation of work so as to make the most effective use of labour skills. It was also found that the *Reichsmarineamt* was increasing the tempo of construction by awarding contracts before the related funds had been committed. There were, in addition, distinct and worrying possibilities that Count Zeppelin's new lighter-than-air craft might take naval warfare into a new dimension.

The British Government, having accepted the challenge, had two options: to decisively outbuild Germany and thus maintain a margin of superiority in numbers and quality or to try to moderate the arms race by coming to terms with Germany. The difficulty about the first course of action was that Dreadnoughts represented a diversion of funds from social reform and welfare to which the Government was committed: the problem with the second was that, in the light of the risk theory, any conciliatory move appeared to prove that Tirpitz's strategy was correct. When in October 1913, Winston Churchill, First Lord of the Admiralty, publicly stated that the naval weakness of either power worked against good relations, the Kaiser noted 'a fantastic victory for Admiral Tirpitz. Another proof of the theory I have expounded time and time again that the only way to impress the English and compel them at last to come to an understanding with us is by an unreservedly manly stand for our own interests. England approaches us not in spite of but because of the Imperial Navy.'

Negotiation failed, ultimately, because the two sides had diametrically opposed expectations. Britain sought a far-reaching *naval* agreement, with few political 'strings'; Germany wanted to make as few naval concessions as possible as the price of a *political* agreement. From the German point of view, even an offer to slow down the building tempo was a concession which merited political compensation in the form of Britain's neutrality in the event of war on the Continent. The British Government was willing to promise non-aggression but was not prepared to concede neutrality as a *quid pro quo* for the minimal revisions the Germans offered. In the event, Britain continued to out-build Germany and the Imperial Navy never passed through the zone of risk which in Tirpitz's original theory the discrepancy between the two fleets created.

As it happened, Britain and Germany did not go to war in 1914 over the German Navy. By that stage, Britain considered it a challenge which had been staved off. The naval race did not 'cause' the war; it merely ensured that at sea it took place at a somewhat technically higher level than it might have done without the enforced improvements that the Dreadnoughts and their German counterparts embodied. From our present standpoint, the episode demonstrates that the commitment to a timetable rapidly produced political consequences far beyond the expectations of those who devised the original legislation and that Germany failed to solve the diplomatic problems which it generated. The options in which the timetable was a factor were never properly thought out. The responsible officials assumed too readily that Britain could only react in a way favourable to Germany. Additionally, the policy depended within Germany on a specific group which had an interest in seeing that the tempo of construction was kept as high as possible. Manufacturers who had installed special plant and their workers who operated it were alike concerned that maximum output was achieved. They had a specific interest in that particular strategy in preference to any alternative. This preference was expressed through political representatives and above all through the *Flottenverein*, the pressure group in which manufacturers were involved. It is a nice point whether the propaganda of that organisation or of the Pan-Germans evoked the greater distrust of German policy abroad, but at home it kept up political support which to an extent countered public feelings about the tax burdens the policy imposed.

In the same year in which the Imperial Naval Office sketched out the first lineaments of the Navy Law and Tirpitz was given charge of the scheme, the Chief of the General Staff, Count Schlieffen, completed the first draft of his plan to overcome Germany's geographical disadvantage in a simultaneous war against France and Russia. Like Tirpitz, he aimed at a decision through the annihilation of the opponent, but, unlike Tirpitz, Schlieffen had two opponents acting in alliance. The problem – as for Moltke – was to eliminate one before turning against the other. His priorities were governed by the time he reckoned each of the two allies would take to mobilise and concentrate forces – calculations related directly to the extent of railway construction and the efficiency of its operation since Moltke's time. There was the additional consideration that German industry was located inconveniently near the frontiers, respectively in the Rhineland and in Silesia. The strategy chosen would put one or the other at risk. These were the main 'industrial' elements in the Schlieffen Plan. The rest was merely a matter of procuring the right weapons, especially for demolishing French, and if necessary Belgian, fortifications, particularly those at Liège which the Germans themselves had urged the Belgian Government to build. Skoda eventually supplied the means in the form of mortars.

There were of course many other problems: the division of manpower between east and west; the need for space in which to manoeuvre large armies – a factor which by itself suggested moving through Belgium. Above all Schlieffen had to take into account the measures adopted by the French army since 1870. He juggled with his priorities several times between 1897 and 1906, when he retired. They were slightly, but in the event crucially, modified by his successor, the younger Moltke, who took one decision which proved to be of immense industrial importance, namely not to violate the neutrality of the Netherlands in order to preserve it as a loophole in a possible British blockade.

In contrast to the Navy Law, the Schlieffen Plan did not involve any new nexus with industry or public opinion. It reflected the industrialisation of war only in the sense that the railway became central to the entire strategy. For staff officers, it was the timetable exercise *par excellence*. In Moltke's final formulation, Liège was to be taken on the eleventh day of the attack, Brussels on the nineteenth, the French frontier was to be crossed on the twenty-second and Paris to be entered on the thirty-ninth. On the fortieth, detachments were to leave for the East. There the campaign to hold the Russian forces also depended on the railway, both for concentrating troops and, at the tactical level, to allow them to defeat Russian armies in detail.

The Plan itself required extensions to the existing German rail system. Thirteen main lines to the west were doubled and extra tracks were laid in Pomerania to improve the 'shuttle' between the two fronts. These developments could be passed off as purely domestic, but one particular construction could not. After 1908, the tracks around Eupen and Malmédy, on the frontier with Belgium, were doubled and sidings and other ancillary facilities constructed on a scale quite incommensurate with the density of population or the economic importance of the area. These works were later connected with the Belgian railway at Stavelot, on German insistence, to provide for a traffic whose needs, contemporaries noted, had been wholly met by a twice-daily *'diligence'* from Malmédy. The Belgian Government, relying on its internationally agreed neutrality was in no position to object.

The view Schlieffen himself took of how German diplomacy functioned in relation to his plan is still a matter of disagreement among experts. He himself died the year before it went into operation and his epigone merely assumed that the diplomats would adjust to the *fait accompli:* the Franco-Russian alliance could not be neutralised by diplomacy, the political constellation of Europe could and would be changed only by war. Apart from one half-hearted attempt by the Kaiser himself in 1905, German policy displayed a curious fatalism, discarding all but the military options. The Chancellor, Bethmann-Hollweg, was informed of the intention to violate the neutrality of Belgium and Luxembourg, on the technical grounds of the necessity to outflank the French frontier forts, only on 21 December 1912 – an action which offers the clearest evidence that, in contrast to the situation at the time of Bismarck, the army had become a state within the state, the quintessential element in a society in which the military virtues of discipline, loyalty and obedience were widely acknowledged (and nowhere more than in the anti-militarist Socialist Party!). In Imperial Germany, the military were not required to discuss their plans with the civil authority; the Kaiser was supposed to make the final adjustment of the civil and military aspects of policy but the right of access which the military enjoyed gave them a constant opportunity to work on the Kaiser's personal if theatrical militarism. Civil authority was consistently outflanked. Hence the Schlieffen plan did not have to run the gauntlet of destructive criticism from those who, professionally as diplomats, might have other, less mechanistic views of what Germany's interests required. There was thus no chance that the implicit political difficulties could be made explicit. Objections from Foreign Office officials who were aware of what was afoot were brushed aside. In February 1913, von Jagow, the Foreign Secretary, warned Helmuth von Moltke, Schlieffen's successor as Chief of the General Staff, that a move through Belgium would bring Britain into the conflict – to be told that any change in the Plan was impossible, and to be rhetorically dismissed with the question as to whether civilians would take responsibility for abandoning the only plan which in the judgement of the military would guarantee victory. Moltke's riposte embodied two elements which were constantly used to ward off lay interference; no mere civilian could have any legitimate views on the security of the state, for which the military alone were responsible, and only the plan drawn up by the military was relevant to national survival. In this respect, as in others, Germany's military leaders had moved far from Clausewitz, who insisted that the principal war plans required an insight into political relationships. The younger Moltke's generation insisted that politics would have to subserve military priorities. The civil authority accepted the claim, and capitulated.* As late as 29 April 1914, Jagow announced to the Reichstag that Germany was determined to respect the international covenants by which Belgian neutrality was guaranteed.

Schlieffen's plan and how it was carried out, the role of individuals and techniques and the French response are still controversial topics. The Plan was not published in full till 1956 but its existence was known almost from the beginning. The French General Staff had the opportunity of studying it at leisure, thanks to a prudent purchase from a needy German source. They misread the Plan, assuming it to be a scenario for a war game. This assumption rested on the belief that the German forces would have to contain a high proportion of reservists who would be unable to sustain the persistently offensive role assigned to them. No-one tested the stamina of French reservists under simulated conditions to see whether the assumption was valid or not. In the months of August and September 1914, France paid for relying on *a priori* reasoning by coming to within a hair's breadth of total military disaster, at the cost of the highest French casualty rates of the whole war.

From the present point of view, the Plan is important in that it demonstrated that the ability to conceive and carry out a particular political and military strategy depended on the revolution in transport and communications which scientific and industrial advance made possible. The railway and the telegraph had ceased to be an adjunct to strategy; they had become the core of it. 'Railways,' taught Schlieffen, 'have become a means and tool of warfare without which the great armies of our time can neither be raised nor mobilised nor led into attack nor sustained in battle.' In his plan, Liège was considered a vital objective, not only because it was a fortress but because it was the centre of a railway system leading into northern France. The interdependence between strategy and technique dictated the first overt act of hostility in the war, the seizure by a German motorised detachment of the Luxembourg railway station and post office prior to the formal declaration of war on France.

The centrality of the railway in planning** and its role in the final days of crisis in July 1914 have induced many commentators and historians to conclude that Europe went to war *because of* the timetable, that while the

---

*After the War, the Chancellor, Bethmann-Hollweg, accounted himself virtuous that he had never 'tried to interfere' with the General Staff.[6]

**How far the railway had become the touchstone of modernity in war is shown by the analyses of the Russo-Japanese struggle in Manchuria in 1904 and 1905. It had many of the characteristics of the battles in Flanders from 1915 onwards, but the high commands concluded that since there were no railways in Manchuria, the war offered no lessons for Europe. The premise was invalid, and the conclusion false.

politicians were stumbling or fumbling their way into war, the railway propelled them into it: technology was absolute and ineluctable. The most startling evidence for this judgement rests on the fateful interview between the younger Moltke and the Kaiser on 1 August 1914. Moltke, writing in Homburg in November 1914,[7] recalled that immediately after the Kaiser had given the order to mobilise at 5 pm (on receipt of the news that general mobilisation in Russia had begun) he, Moltke, was recalled to the palace in Berlin to discuss an important development: advice from the Ambassador in London suggested that, under conditions guaranteeing the security of France in the North Sea, Britain might restrain France from attacking Germany, if Germany likewise undertook to refrain from attacking France. This appeared to offer an eleventh-hour possibility of resolving the crisis, at least of avoiding a general war. The Kaiser, the Chancellor and other officials present were in favour of accepting the British conditions, which would mean that Germany could turn its forces to the east. Moltke, in a minority of one, rejoined that that was impossible; that the march to the battle of an army numbered in millions could not be improvised but could be undertaken only after prolonged and careful study; an order to turn the whole force round would deliver to the eastern front not an army but a confused mass of armed men, disorganised and without their supplies. The Kaiser commented, 'Your Uncle would have given me a different answer,' Moltke's reasoning was that what applied to the German army also applied to the French which was under orders to mobilise – in which case the premise of Britain's initiative was invalid: how *could* Britain prevent French forces from attacking an eastwards-facing German army in the rear.

The reply to the British offer accepted Moltke's arguments to the extent that it stated that for technical reasons mobilisation could not be halted but ignored them by adding that nevertheless Germany would not open hostilities if France remained under British control. The Kaiser followed this intention by instructing the division stationed in Trier not to occupy Luxembourg. From Moltke's point of view, this last-minute diplomacy was likely to frustrate the entire military operation through failure to seize control of the railway centre on which it depended. Later the same evening, the diplomacy collapsed and the Kaiser gave permission for the troops in Trier to move.

The technical factor was not the only one in Moltke's mind. By inclination and training he was disposed towards war with France: he believed that the Belgians might protest against, but would not resist, the passage of German troops, and that any British intervention would only increase the Allied casualty lists, in a campaign which would be all over in four weeks or so. There were other military reasons – all of which proved false – for going ahead. But he was, as his account of the interview makes clear, very emotionally involved in its outcome; for him the discussion called in question his devotion to his *métier* as well as his identity as the highest ranking soldier, under the Kaiser, and spokesman for the German army. He felt slighted by the Kaiser's reference to his uncle. He was not therefore giving a cold, or even a cool, technocratic judgement. Yet his notions as to what was technically possible or impossible at that critical juncture have been widely accepted, as either explanation or criticism, since the publication of his papers by his widow in 1922.

The issue was put in its proper technical perspective three years later, in a special supplement to *Militärwochenblatt* entitled '*Aufmarsch nach zwei Fronten*'. The author, General von Staabs, addressed himself specifically to the problem of turning round at least most of the army to the eastern front, while leaving an adequate defensive screen in the west. To this enquiry von Staabs brought the experience of planning and operating railways and associated communications as a former specialist on the General Staff. He admitted the difficulties but showed conclusively that they were not insuperable. He pointed out that mobilising and concentrating troops by rail was not an unbroken and unbreakable process: it contains a number of assembly and dispersal points, in the form of barracks and sidings, which in fact compel pauses and allow changes: further, in accordance with usual practice in 1914, troop commanders had been given times but not destinations – so the General Staff would not have been made to look amateurish if the destinations had been in the east rather than the west. These and similar observations he advanced as a preliminary to examining the requirements of transporting the main forces to the east. The analysis is too elaborate to be summarised here, but General von Staabs took the dispositions as they were at the beginning of August 1914 and set out in detail how they would have had to have been varied so that, army group by army group, the bulk of the Imperial German Army could have been concentrated against Russian troops. He calculated that the transfer operations would take about two weeks. (It is pertinent to note that the Russian First Army crossed the border into East Prussia on 15 August, the Second, advancing from the south, fought its first engagements with German troops on the 22nd; at that time the advance guards of the bulk of the Tsarist forces were assembling on the frontier of Galicia). Von Staabs readily conceded that had German forces won the battle of the Marne and taken Paris the question of whether it was or was not possible to transfer the army more or less *en bloc* to the east would not have arisen and that Moltke's answer to the Kaiser would have been fully justified. But he does show that, to the degree that Moltke's objections relied on the railway, they were, in fact, totally unfounded.

On General von Staabs' evidence, Moltke was not capitulating to the demands of technological rationality, he was merely ignorant of their potentialities. When the Kaiser drew the wounding comparison with Moltke's uncle, he was, perhaps, speaking more truly than he knew. The elder Moltke, however, witnessed the growth of the new technique and moulded his professional thinking round it; the younger simply accepted it, as part of his inheritance of professional knowledge: hence, he knew about railways but had not worked out the problems for himself or initiated a strategy which would have forced him to ask the right questions. But at the crucial meeting on 1 August, he was in the estimation of all present the arbiter of what could or could not be done technically. Clearly, in the process of putting into effect actions already planned, there is a point of no return or some stage when the options are, for the time being, closed. Moltke thought that that point was the publication of mobilisation orders; General von Staabs' more specialised contemporary experience infers that, at least as far as the railhead, chaos could be avoided by relying on the flexibility of the technology. Just how flexible it was, was proved by the rail operations of the next four years, but by that time the very brief opportunity – a matter of hours – in which recognition of that flexibility might have decisively affected policy had vanished.

Although the Schlieffen Plan, as executed, failed to annihilate French forces and German armies in the west were bogged down in a war of attrition it was designed to avoid, the advance through Belgium and Luxembourg and the occupation of northern France yielded one of Europe's most highly industrialised areas* to the German war effort and correspondingly deprived France of its output. The loss was considerable, covering sixty-four per cent of French production of cast iron and fifty-eight per cent of steel. The deprivation of these areas concomitantly threw France on the resources of its industrialised ally Britain, influencing the strategies they adopted and the entire politics of their alliance. The capture of such assets was not a factor which Schlieffen or any of his followers took into account in their planning but it was one which, as it happened, enabled Germany to survive the allied blockade and conduct successfully a defensive war in the west for nearly four years. The Plan, as conceived in the mode of warfare its creator took for granted, failed: attrition, thought Schlieffen, would endanger the fabric of the nation through totally disrupting its economic life (1918 proved him right). Nevertheless, through locating operations where he did, he unintentionally provided the means whereby the next style of warfare could be sustained.

Count Schlieffen might have failed to investigate what became his plan's major economic entailment, but it was submitted to some, if ineffective, scrutiny from an economic point of view. In March 1906, the year after the Plan was finally approved, Admiral Tirpitz raised the question of Germany's capacity to withstand both a continental alliance (as Schlieffen postulated) and at the same time a power with overwhelming naval strength capable of blockading not only German ports but also of restraining neutrals who might

---

*It included the Briey basin: see below, page 135.

otherwise wish to trade with Germany. He also asked about priorities on railways if Germany had to rely on Rotterdam and Copenhagen in place of Hamburg. Tirpitz's letter prompted a general inter-departmental enquiry into the country's capacity for economic resistance. It found that Germany could dispense with imports of foodstuffs and forage for nine months; that more than sufficed for the campaign the army was planning.

Tirpitz rejected this conclusion, suggesting that it would be prudent to investigate the possibilities of withstanding a war twice as long as envisaged by the army. It could not be assumed that the prevailing international law on the subject would protect Germany's neutral suppliers. Further, research in the Admiralty had shown that Germany in fact comprised two economic units, from the point of view of imports and distribution. The railways never had carried food surpluses from the east to the Rhineland, which supplied itself via the Netherlands. If the Dutch ports were closed, would the German rail system be able to transport food and raw materials across the Empire, as well as fulfilling the demands of military traffic. Tirpitz's objections remained unexamined and unanswered.

There in practice the matter rested for six years. The General Staff relied on Schlieffen's logic. It admitted the principle that when national existence depended on an unbroken movement of trade and industry, protracted campaigns were impossible. Therefore, Schlieffen's knock-out blow was the only possible strategy. 'The strategy of exhaustion cannot be attempted when milliards must be spent to support millions.' But in 1912, the anxiety of industrialists and chambers of commerce forced the appointment of a standing commission which although primarily concerned with the mobilisation of the economy, nevertheless necessarily impinged on the problems raised earlier by Admiral Tirpitz. The official doctrine, however, till September 1914, was that the conceivable long-term problems were an added reason for perfecting plans for a short-term decision.

5. 'The Plan' and its consequences: the critique of Bloch

By the end of the nineteenth century, then, during which the major states of Europe had successively industrialised, the process of 'going to war', for whatever reason, had wholly different implications from those in, say, mid-century. The differences were not merely of scale but of degree. Peacetime preparations, of either specific strategies or of the facilities necessary to provide certain options in wartime, became essential in a way in which they were not during pre-industrial epochs. Such preparations, confided to general staffs as the planning agency, involved the military more closely in the civil aspects of the nation. Moreover through conscription, war reached into society at large – which it had not done when armies were small and composed of volunteers. A disposition to think in terms of military solutions, which was the proper concern of the military, was thus generalised throughout society.

Through applied science, war was *beginning* to demand one type of education rather than another. Curricula were not tailored to war, but they did have to provide the types and numbers of specialists which industrialised warfare required. In the given state of knowledge, this posed no difficulty: 'Military' demand could be satisfied from 'civil' technical education; but before the industrial age, the content of education had been virtually irrelevant – as had the extent of its diffusion throughout society. Now education was universal and compulsory, and through more extensive suffrage rights and the popular press the literate democracy was beginning to influence decisions involving peace and war and to demand a greater voice in them – the more insistently because it was aware that the manufacture of the industrial components of war was literally in its hands. Democratic solidarity and coordinated mass strikes could paralyse the war machines and make the plans unworkable. On this premise, Socialist parties erected schemes to make international war impossible.

The implications of these developments were not thought out by general staffs; their awareness of the problem tended to stop at the timetables of mobilisation and the mechanics of killing on the battlefield. Foch's Staff College lectures to French army officers from 1894 to 1900 reveal this limitation. He considered that improving the rates of fire must dictate reliance on the offensive and therefore, the larger a force, the stronger it became in attack. Foch spent much time in demonstrating the necessary proof of this proposition, but his concern in industrial terms was limited strictly to how industry can improve rates of fire; that is, with the tactical application of industrial products. Otherwise, for his generation of military leaders, war was a matter of manpower and more manpower, with the initial battles undertaken by the barracks army and victory ensured by the reserves of the nation in arms. The 'war effort' meant first and foremost service with the colours. It would, of course, call on the full capacity of munitions factories and the suppliers of horses, fodder and blankets, but would involve no further draughts on the nation. The armed forces went to war; the nation at large cheered and supplied.

Even with this restricted and – as events were quickly to show – disastrous underestimate of the problems involved, the scale of the operation, of mobilising and concentrating men numbered in millions, and the systematic recruitment of these numbers from the population introduced the practice of planning in greater detail and planning more widely throughout society. In consequence, planning for war, through ramifying into the civil side of society, began to erode the distinctions between 'war' and 'peace' and 'military' and 'civil' which had been assumed to be hard and fast. It also began to call in question the traditional relationship between war and diplomacy. The common view, held generally right up to 1914, was that diplomacy was the normal way of conducting state business, and war followed its breakdown. But the preparation of plans which made more sustained and more comprehensive demands on society tended to set the tasks which diplomats had to execute and the limits within which they could operate in time of peace. Diplomacy no longer fixed the larger objectives of the state: it followed the Plan.

The change to long-term, detailed planning effectively transferred power from its traditional or titular holders to the bureaucrats, military or civil, responsible for drawing up the plans. The more comprehensive they were, the fewer options were open to policy in any given situation, and the greater the psychological pressure to carry them out. Moreover, because of its complexity, the Plan had to be carried out entirely or not at all. Careful gradations of response to threats or challenges, possible during the pre-industrial era, were progressively ruled out.

The lengthening time scales of manufacture and the need to spread budgetary costs contributed their degree of inflexibility to policy, and reinforced the tendency to regard a plan as a blueprint or a formula which would inevitably produce the desired result. The unanalysed assumption was that the enemy's options would be so cut down that he would have to react as predicted. In this sense, planning was at odds with the qualities which traditionally offset the hazards of war – quickness of decision, adaptability, and the power to improvise. They were all jettisoned in response to the timetable.

There was, in fact, nothing automatic or ineluctable about this reaction: the relevant factors were defined by those who made policy. The factors only became 'imperatives' when the policy makers became prisoners of their own concepts and were incapable of constructing alternatives or had no interest in doing so. The tragedy for Europe was that the timetable and the use of the improved weapons made available by industry were considered as *guaranteeing* the decisive outcome the Plan envisaged. The elder Moltke had been contemptuous of such reactions. 'I have always believed that there are always three courses open to the enemy – and that he usually takes the fourth.' 'Only the layman believes that he sees in the course of a war the accomplishment of an original idea conceived beforehand, considered in every detail and adhered to until the end.' His practice followed this dictum; mobilisation and logistic plans were detailed, operational plans were purposefully vague, to take account of the 'fourth course'.

Moltke's successors and imitators were, in his sense, laymen; their operational plans were as detailed as the logistics which brought the troops to the battle area and sustained them in action. Planning became an end in itself; the Plan did not exist for the policy, but the policy for the Plan. This in itself upset formal institutional balances between military and diplomatic responsibilities for policy. The Ministry of Foreign Affairs might continue to enjoy constitutional parity with the General Staff but was no longer its equal in deciding what was to happen. 'The Plan' became the ultimate argument, to which the highest authorities bowed. In Germany, the coordinator of foreign and domestic priorities was the Kaiser himself. As Supreme War Lord, he was required to be a professional strategist, but William II was never more than an amateur. His essential amateurishness was reinforced by his invariably having to be on the winning side in manoeuvres – which no doubt sustained his *amour propre* but never exposed his judgement to the consequences of his mistakes. He was thus thoroughly in the hands of the General Staff, whose entire professional existence took its meaning from the Plan.

In France, the constitutional arrangements worked in similar fashion. Joseph Joffre, appointed Chief of the General Staff in 1911, went his own way without reference to his titular superior, the Minister of War, Constitutionally, Joffre was *solely* responsible for planning operations: the General Staff accepted his plans as the working basis for planning the concentration of French forces. Neither they nor anyone in government had any authority to require that Joffre submit his schemes for discussion or approval.

In France, as in Germany, the timetable was used, not to indicate a chosen but variable sequence of events but as the inflexible determiner of action in a strategy which was designedly offensive. By the winter of 1910, the War Council had decided that any German attack on France through Alsace and Lorraine would be bound to fail, by reason of the fortified zones and the dispositions of French forces; therefore, it was concluded, any German attack would have to take place through Belgium. The resultant question for policy was whether France should take the initiative in violating Belgian neutrality or only respond to a prior German violation. In either event, the French High Command was adamant that the war would have to take place in Belgium: no-one recommended that French forces should await the onslaught on French territory, in deference to the Treaty of 1839!

Such a campaign depended on railways, particularly those from Paris, the centre of government, to the north-east. Joffre was an engineer who had for some time been professionally responsible for railway planning. He set about preparing the forces entailed by the basic strategy, improving the drafts of reserves, the supply of equipment to the army and its tactical training. His initial plan envisaged using Belgium as a corridor of attack, with Liège, a fortress and rail centre, as a primary objective. To that extent his ideas were a mirror image of Schlieffen's. The question of violating neutrality was not. Joffre personally took a strictly 'military' view, but his proposals were quashed by Poincaré, then *President du Conseil,* who had no more intrinsic respect for Belgian neutrality than Joffre but who thought its violation would alienate Europe and, especially, would deprive France of British support. Discreet enquiries in London bore out Poincaré's contention.

Joffre's response was the famous Plan XVII – designating the seventeenth strategic plan adopted by the General Staff since 1870 – intended to break the German drive at what was assumed to be its weakest point, and then allow the invasion of Germany either via Belgium, if the Germans violated its neutrality, or via the Moselle and the Vosges if the Germans respected it. The railway system was essential to moving the reserves where they would be needed, either in the north-east or the east. Plan XVII, like Schlieffen's, depended on the use of a particular technology but did not take into account the industry on which that technology, in turn, depended. Schlieffen at least considered that military operations had to be kept away from Silesia and the Rhineland. Joffre failed to reveal even this degree of comprehension – as the fate of the Briey basin showed.

The Briey mines ran in a strip about four miles from the Franco-German frontier established in 1871 and parallel to it. Exploration of deep strata from 1884 to 1894 proved the existence of vast ore deposits with a higher metal content than those of Nancy and Longwy, but they could not be worked commercially until serious problems of water control had been solved. From 1903 onwards Briey output grew rapidly. At the turn of the century, Briey supplied 431,000 tons of ore towards a total consumption in France of 6,200,000 tons: in 1913, it supplied eight million tons out of a total of 13,260,000. Growth at this rate also turned France from being a net importer into a net exporter of iron ore. By 1913, it supplied twenty-three per cent of the German requirements and had largely taken over the Belgian market from Luxembourg. Briey's success in the competition rested in part on favourable freight rates on French railways and on attracting immigrant workers in large numbers. (French miners preferred to stay in the more attractive parts of the country.) Insignificant Lorraine villages were rapidly transformed into towns.

Neither industrially nor socially was Briey a hole-in-the-corner development. It was publicised, in fact, as one of the success stories of France. Yet, on Joffre's own admission, pre-war military planning took no account of it. It was not the case that Briey was examined and considered indefensible; it was not considered at all. No doubt, the *Annales des Mines* was not among Joffre's normal reading, but he was a railway specialist whose expertise implied that he realised how essential the iron and steel industry was to modern strategy. Joffre and his staff took the view that the war they had in mind could be fought successfully on the basis of existing stocks. In consequence, no plans were made to defend the area, and in the summer of 1914, after the Battle of the Frontiers had been lost and French troops retreated to the Marne, the area passed almost completely intact into German hands for the duration of the war. It only returned to French control after the Armistice, when the circumstances of its loss provoked passionate debate.* By then the French had digested the bitter lessons of industrialised war, at a cost of one and a half million dead.

In both France and Germany, the Plan took on an almost mystical status: it was the final authority: could perhaps cautiously be refined but not gainsaid.** The British got round this difficulty simply by not encouraging the planning body, the General Staff, to plan, (in the same sense as their *confrères* in France and Germany) with the result that on 5 August 1914, *after* war was declared, the War Council was faced with several mutually incompatible schemes, and in the words of one participant – the Director of Military Operations at the War Office, Sir Henry Wilson – 'fell to discussing strategy like idiots.' Moreover the mind of the Secretary of State for War, Lord Kitchener, did not encompass the idea of a General Staff, whose members were promptly despatched to active duty in France. The Staff College, so far from being a source of consistent analysis of the problems revealed by battle, was closed. The closure was generally approved, since in all branches of the army, the regiment was the centre of an officer's career

---

*In the inquiry, the Secretary-General of the *Comité des Forges* pointed out that Briey ores were not suitable for manufacturing guns or shells.

**Planning in Germany was the easier since, during the entire period 1871–1914, the General Staff had only four chiefs – Moltke, Waldersee, Schlieffen, and the younger Moltke. The elder Moltke exercised special authority as the military architect of victory; his successors' job was to deliver the same result. France had the same number of chiefs of staff between 1900 and 1914, none of whom had an aura of victory to commend them. The outcome in 1914 suggests that continuity was not wholly advantageous to Germany, while discontinuity almost condemned France to defeat.

and the focus of his loyalties. A desire to join the Staff was in itself odd, and required serious explanation.

From 1870 onwards, the quintessential planning tool was the timetable – both long-term, as in estimating male birth-rates, and short-term, as in the ability of railways to deliver troops where they were deemed to be needed. The timetable, however, is a means to an end, and the practice of systematic planning for manpower, troops, weapons or facilities automatically posed the question of what was to happen when the plans were complete. The end date of a specific development automatically suggested the time from which hostilities could begin. But preparedness is not a static condition, and the impending or actual fulfilment of plans psychologically predisposed the planners to put them into effect. It must be emphasised that, at the time, no European leader was pacifist and war was generally accepted as an entirely legitimate, and, in some circumstances, honourable option. For some Germans in authority, 1914 was the best time for war with Russia since they calculated it would then take place some two years before the Russian rearmament programme would be complete. Similarly, the widening of the Kiel Canal to allow the passage of German dreadnoughts suggested the time when they could go into action in the North Sea – a factor which was in the minds of German planners when they demanded the completion of the work by the summer of 1914, about a year ahead of schedule.

In the pre-industrial era, preparedness involved fewer strains on the economy or society. It was essentially a matter of keeping the troops up to scratch by suitable drills and maintaining an adequate supply of war stores for the initial hostilities. By the beginning of this century, the character of war and its demands had changed radically. It was still commonly thought of as the province of specialists, supported by the munitions industry, but the interrelated needs to plan for mobilisation and to involve the opinion of the public, generated persistent tensions both within and between states. This process was ultimately related to mathematical calculations of the balance and composition of forces and the time scales of military production.

That the results might be wholly different was foreseen, before 1914, not by the more speculative minds among the generals, but by a Polish Jewish banker, Ivan Bloch, who in 1898 published *The War of the Future in its Technical, Economic and Political Relations*. The work summed up the thinking and research of over a decade, some of which had already appeared as articles in Polish, Russian and German journals. It ran to six volumes, comprising 3,085 pages, without prefaces. The titles indicate the range of the enquiry: (i) 'General Considerations on Firepower' (ii) 'Continental War' (iii) 'Naval War' (iv) 'Economic Difficulties and Material Losses Determining the War of the Future' (v) 'Efforts Tending to Suppress War' (vi) 'General Conclusions'. An abridgement which, among other questions, discussed the general problem as to whether war was possible, and if so, in what sense, appeared in an English translation in London in 1900. The journalist W.T. Stead provided an introduction, summarising conversations with Bloch himself. This version was reprinted in Boston in 1902. In this manner, specialist readerships and the public at large in all the main powers of the time, save Japan, were able to acquaint themselves with Bloch's views. Their essential thesis may be briefly summarised.

Bloch saw that the 'timetable' in which the experts put their trust to bring about a military decision would be negated by the increases in firepower which the military technology of his day had made available. The rates of killing which the magazine rifle, the machine gun and improved artillery permitted would ensure that between combatant forces a zone would exist in which no-one could survive. Armies would, literally, never come to grips and therefore battles would no longer provide a decision. 'The mechanisms of war had made war impracticable:' it could not produce victory, as conventionally understood, but only stalemate or national suicide. 'War has become a tribunal which by the very perfection of its own processes and the costliness of its methods can no longer render a decision of any kind.' If battle could not produce a decision, then the task of doing so was shifted to the economy: that would involve 'a multiplication of expenditure simultaneously accompanied by a diminution of the sources by which that expenditure can be met.' The consequence was 'the bankruptcy of nations and the break-up of the whole social organisation.' War in short had become 'impossible' and that in two senses: no modern state had any prospect of defeating its adversary by force of arms on the battlefield, and no war was possible, even for the victor, without the destruction of its resources and its society.

Bloch established this outcome not merely as regards the policies of states but across the whole range of military activity – tactics as well as strategies: the relative roles of modern weapons and methods of defence; the training and equipment of forces; their disciplined use and the problems of supplying and administering vast numbers of men so as to maintain cohesion. He also investigated the social basis of war in the main European powers, to consider how vulnerable each was to the war of the economic attrition he visualised. The result was a series of comparative studies of manufacturing and agricultural capacity, wage rates, the incidence of alcoholism and crime, (Jews in Poland showed the highest number of convictions per million of population for swindling and Greek Catholics in Austria for highway robbery and robbery with violence), the effect of requisitioning of horses on agriculture and therefore on the supply of food to the towns (Bloch correlates food demand with concentrations of socialist, i.e. anti-war votes). Through analysis in these terms he indicated possible lines of fracture in combatant states during the long period of increased strain on their resources.

Bloch's method was as important as his conclusions. He deduced the whole of his study from the initial premise of increases in firepower, but quantified each stage of his argument from his knowledge of the costs of technology (derived from his experience in financing and directing railways) and of the lessons of wars from 1870 onwards, as recorded in the specialist literature of the day, supplemented by discussions with leading military and naval authorities. His knowledge of technological developments led him to emphasise the importance of rates of innovation; so long as they were slow it was not difficult to rely on past experience – but progress in science and technology and their application to war since 1870 had, he believed, given new dimensions to warfare to the point of invalidating much if not most of the past. The new fundamental *military* problem was that of managing conscripted masses of troops who could at best be semi-trained for combat and whose morale and health would be vulnerable to prolonged marching and fighting. The new fundamental *economic* problems arose from the increasing interdependence of national economics, the impact on national currencies of the vastly increased costs of keeping armies in the field and navies afloat, and the problem of distributing food and raw materials to maintain civilian morale and manufacturing output. All these changes had been brought about by the industrial system: war was as affected by new demands created by scale and complexity as were the processes of manufacture, finance and distribution.

It is difficult to estimate the impact of Bloch's analysis; six closely argued volumes are in themselves a considerable deterrent, even to a more leisured age, but Bloch himself took part in the peace movements of the day, and his general arguments were known to the delegates to the Hague Conference of 1899. He did not live long enough thereafter to establish his projected Institutes for War and Peace, designed to bring home to ordinary men and women the comprehensive character of warfare in the industrial age. He was engaged in founding the first, at Lucerne, in 1902, when he died. (Institutionalised peace research had to wait another sixty years.) The available evidence suggests that favourable reactions among professionals were confined to the technical services: traditional infantry and cavalry officers resisted a statistical analysis of casualties showing that the bayonet, lance and sword were insignificant weapons: the deadly romanticism of 'cold steel' survived the First World War.

Certain of Bloch's political assumptions were falsified by events. He wrote before the Anglo-German naval race and the *Entente Cordiale* altered the options open to France. Likewise he over-estimated the role of socialists in preventing the outbreak of a general war through strikes. Some of his economic predictions also proved wide of the mark. Bloch was an orthodox economist, for whom bankruptcy was a serious outcome. He did not realise that states, even though formally bankrupt, can either unilaterally repudiate obligations or induce their creditors to renegotiate them at a lower figure – the almost universal practice since the First World War. But in the longer perspective his analysis of future war and its consequences for the economy and society were right. Who, from the present perspective can be realistically said to have 'won' that conflict?

6. Balkan nationalism and industrialised war

The relationship between what the state might want to do and the developments in knowledge which, mediated through suitable institutions, would allow the state to realise its aims emerged during the nineteenth century in response to particular situations. No-one – not even in Germany – sat down and deduced the relationships from first principles; they evolved from the attempt to solve practical questions of state. As time went on, adapting knowledge and technique for this purpose became less random and had to be more consciously organised; but, even so, adaptation was irregular, because the practical questions which required it were themselves to do with changes in the distribution of political power in Europe. There was no smooth synchronisation in the timing of political changes and developments in science and technology. The latter in fact *followed* politics. Deficiencies revealed by war in the Crimea, Lombardy, Bohemia and France all prompted technological developments during hostilities and just after; then application slowed and the powers entered the next conflict with the technology adapted for the last. Since these wars were crammed into fifteen years the technological gaps were short and obsolescence not observable. Nor did the military leaderships think they had to intervene in the processes of technological improvement; as far as they were concerned, industrialisation offered options but in relation to ends which they had already chosen.

Industrialisation, with its military concomitants, did not remain confined to Western Europe. In the last quarter of the century, it was transplanted to Eastern Europe, which, with the exception of Silesia and some areas of Austria and Poland, was (and remained till after the Second World War) dominantly given over to raw materials and agriculture. The process of industrialisation was more explicitly political than it had been in the west in that it coincided with the acute problems of nationalist resurgence. The ideal of independent statehood raised the fear or the expectation that the Ottoman Empire, and possibly the Hapsburg Monarchy, would disintegrate, thus promoting a scramble by other powers for any resultant advantages. The fact that Eastern Europe included, in Constantinople, the capital of an empire which was almost entirely in the Near East gradually extended the political and commercial interests of the industrialised states to the Persian Gulf. None of the states which had emerged in the course of the century had done so without war or without independence appearing as the by-product of conflict between the major powers. The Balkan states emerged as the clients of stronger states, whose support was essential to their continued survival. What actually happened throughout the whole area, then, in regard to industrial projects, was far more closely related to foreign policy than had been the case in the industrialisation of Western Europe, forty years previously. This became particularly evident in the construction of railways.

After the demonstration of the Franco-Prussian War, it was assumed to be impossible and undesirable to build a railway without attempting to serve strategic as well as commercial purposes. All governments were concerned to be able to move troops, if necessary, along the lines from which their nationals, as investors or contractors, drew commercial advantage. International disputes in the 1890s over railway concessions in the Balkans involved anxious comparisons of strategic vulnerability, as well as concern for trade between Central Europe and the Levant. German capitalists orginally devised the Anatolian Railway as the means of establishing their commercial predominance over other foreigners in Asia Minor, but, with the intervention of the military and the diplomats, it was transmuted into the Berlin-Baghdad Railway, designed to facilitate a German or Turkish attack on the British position in Egypt or in the Persian Gulf.

East European governments themselves adapted very quickly to the use of the railway in the military solution of their problems. The Russian campaign against Turkey in 1877–1878 depended entirely on the construction of a railway. Russian mobilisation began in November 1876, but the ability to bring troops into action where they were required demanded an agreement with Romania for the use of Romanian lines. Negotiations were concluded only on 16 April 1877 and thereupon permitted the Russians formally to declare war on 24 April. The timing of the actual declaration depended solely on this technical factor. It was soon found that the routes taken by existing tracks and differences in gauges between Russian and Romanian railways impeded the flow of troops and material – inadequacies which were not exposed as vital to the campaign until Russian forces were held up from July to December at Plevna.* The rationalisation of transport was put in hand from the end of July, and three new lines built to shorten the time from the Odessa area to the front for which Turnovo served as a railhead. Locomotives and rolling stock were purchased elsewhere in Europe, and the campaign was successfully concluded by the emergency construction of new tracks.

---

*A decisive factor in the Turkish resistance was that the Turkish troops had been equipped with the latest technology in the form of Winchester repeating rifles, bought from the United States, to which the Russian forces could only reply with the older, single-shot rifles. They did however possess some Gatling machine guns, but they did not use them in attacking the Turkish positions. Instead they were defensively sited for firing on fixed lines at night.

This demonstration of the efficiency of applied industry on their own terrain was not lost on either the national states or their patrons among the established powers. The laying of railway track became the dispute on which the nationalist rivalries and the ambitions of the non-Balkan powers turned. The Austrians aimed at building and controlling a line running from north to south which would separate Serbia and Montenegro, two Slav states hostile to Austrian policies, and would give the Dual Monarchy an outlet at Salonika, useful for commerce if the Ottoman Empire survived and commanding military leverage if it broke up. Russian policy, conversely, was concerned to link east to west to nullify the Austrian endeavours and to give its client state, Serbia, an outlet on the Adriatic. As in Western Europe, the capital costs of construction enforced combination among financiers and banks but the extreme political sensitivity of the Balkans induced such syndicates to turn to their own governments and induced those governments to bargain with one another to further their own political interest, at the same time as serving the economic interests of their nationals. Industrialisation was not an economically autonomous process in Eastern Europe. It was certainly never so regarded by the recipients, whose governments and diplomatic corps involved in deciding about concessions were habitually heavily larded with soldiers who took a strictly professional view of all developments.

The interrelationship between politics, the railway and national independence was forcibly illustrated in 1908 when the Government of Bulgaria, then an autonomous principality under the suzerainty of the Ottoman Empire, seized a Turkish-owned railway on Bulgarian territory on the grounds that its use by Turkish troops infringed Bulgarian autonomy. The seizure provoked an international crisis, since the railway in question had been leased by the Turkish Government to an operating company financed by German and Austrian capital. Hence one of the major powers with a direct stake in the Balkans (Austria) was involved. Its rival (Russia) was the *de facto* protector of Bulgaria.

The Bulgars chose their moment well. Their action followed shortly after the deposition of Abdul Hamid, so the Turkish administration was in disarray, and the bulk of the army was in Asia Minor. Encouraged by Austria, and with the support of Russia, on 5 October the Prince of Bulgaria proclaimed his country's complete independence, and himself Tsar. The next day, the Austrian Government proceeded to annex outright Bosnia and Hercegovina, which had been under its administration, though still forming part of the Ottoman Empire. The annexation brought about an even more acute crisis, which left the Turkish Government only too willing to propose an indemnity in settlement of its Bulgarian problem. An agreement on the sums involved in March 1909, included £1.7 million for the railway.

The episode demonstrates that, in the Balkans, the security of political entities which were fragile, either because they were riven by faction (as

Serbia) or new and of uncertain status, (like Bulgaria) was the dominant consideration. Consequently, every project for modernising the economy which would help to define the state more clearly was looked at in military terms. Capital goods and expertise were welcomed for that reason.

The situation could hardly have been better suited to the main engineering firms. The Balkans offered a large market, in the expansion of which their own governments were interested and to which they could furnish a range of goods, with interrelated benefits to themselves. Krupp as supplier of track and bridges promoted Krupp the supplier of cannon and vice versa. The same held true of Schneider and Vickers. However, in the existing political conditions, their rivalry could not be merely commercial, and their successes and failures were registered by their own governments as evidence of the progress of national policy in the area. The relationship between government and company was reciprocal; the companies were not the pawns of their own diplomats, but neither did they create or drag them into situations which the diplomats in principle abhorred. The situation was 'made' for Basil Zaharoff, whose background and aptitudes were perfectly adapted to the exigencies of Balkan politics – but the agents of Vickers' competitiors were no less assiduous.

In the Balkans, the sale of weapons took on one new feature. Hitherto it had predominantly been carried on with well-established sovereignties, recognised as belonging to the system of European states. Now the trade was being extended to states which aspired to belong to that system and had virtually no resources of their own, except the loans which the older powers, for their own reasons, made available. Otherwise, their credit-worthiness was suspect. The importation of expertise and materials for engineering projects and of naval vessels and their facilities raised rather more fundamental questions about payment than assisting an aspiring national government to raise money to buy rifles and ammunition, as Napoleon III had for Cavour. The Balkan states were not well-established and, being unstable, were a greater risk – the more so since their leaders were not conspicuous for their devotion to the idea of the sanctity of contracts as understood in Manchester and Birmingham. From the supplier's point of view, selling cannon to the Tsar of Russia was reasonably secure business; securing a return on any project in the Balkans which had to be constructed in the state concerned and might take years, was not. Prudence suggested spreading the risk in some way; by sharing it in a consortium, which made the politics of the project more complicated, or by bringing pressure to bear, if necessary, on the Minister of Finance to ensure that contracted debts were honoured. In these respects, the trade in arms and military facilities after 1870 made more complex demands on the system of finance and diplomacy and thus changed its character. The industrialisation of war was transplanted to secure not only political independence but also economic modernisation. The Balkan states demanded the more lethal products of Schneider and

Krupp as well as equipment for complete railway systems. Without Schneider and Krupp, the French and German governments would have had far less leverage than they did.

From this standpoint, the activities of the manufacturers present, perhaps at their sharpest, features which were common to the society in which they lived and operated. In buying newspapers or commissioning articles in the press about defence policy or the success of their products in action, neither Schneider nor Krupp was doing anything unsanctioned by custom in their respective countries, even though the object of interference with the press could only be to improve their profit position. In Britain, Vickers was not in the newspaper business: custom and the generally accepted values kept it out, and the firm had to find other ways of expressing its views on policy. Where industrial interests did own newspapers, it was customary to devise some means of preventing ownership from affecting the editorials. There is no evidence that the interests of Cadbury in the press affected the consumption of cocoa. Some contemporary newspaper owners like Northcliffe did strike bellicose attitudes but did not direct armaments firms.

Similarly, the role of bribery in the export transactions of the arms firms is a special case of a general practice arising from the fact that in very few states before 1914 (or for that matter even in 1980) were (or are) ministers and civil servants expected to live on their salaries. Professional, disinterested bureaucracy was unknown, and monetary gifts or particular favours were sanctified by custom and by expectation. The main engineering firms were all deeply engaged in such societies and behaved according to their rules. Managements did not consider they were called upon to pioneer changes in the mores of the states which were their customers, particularly when any attempt to do so would probably lead to loss of business. Vickers' agent, Zaharoff, became a byword for corruption in the sale of the means of inflicting death, but this judgement itself only indicates that his background in the Tatavla district of Constantinople gave him a sharper insight into the rules, and the possibilities for advantageously varying them, than the agents of Vickers' competitors. The latter, however, showed themselves equally adept at learning them over the years. In the Balkans at least, Schneider's results suggest that its agents and methods were the most effective.

It was their activities in the Balkans, particularly, which were the focus of subsequent hostility to the private arms manufacturers. Their record was taken to prove that they were a primary source of war and a corrupting influence in society. The case is rather more complex than the critics assumed. Political leadership in the Balkans was predominantly in the hands of the military who did not have to be persuaded into using force to solve problems. The Balkan generals devised plans which the western manufacturers certainly helped to realise, though in their role as constructors of railways as much as of cannon. The manufacturers, however, did not create the hostility which provided their commercial opportunities, and which the preparations for and waging of the Balkan wars in 1912 and 1913 did much to augment. The conflict between Greece and Turkey was pre-industrial, and in 1980 is post-capitalist. The Balkan activities of the arms firms have to be fitted into a continuum of conflict from 1821, and to suggest that they were a prime cause of it in the early years of this century overstates their role and their responsibility. The gravamen of any criticism against them is that they gave a particular shape to the strategies and tactical ideas of ministers and officials, who were anyway happily disposed to war as a legitimate means to their political ends.

The precise responsibility of the manufacturers becomes even more difficult to assess when it is remembered that their marketing successes did not necessarily result from their own unaided salesmanship. That Bulgaria was equipped solely by Schneider until the first Balkan War, derived from the policy of the French Government, which tied the purchase of Schneider products to permission to float a Bulgarian loan on the Paris *bourse*. The Russian Government, for reasons to do with its alliance with France and with its own Balkan policies, was anxious that its Balkan protégé should equip itself from a French source. Schneider were willing partners, but their commercial interest in Bulgaria as a market coincided with, and to an extent was defined by, the political interests of the French Government and its alliance partner, Russia. The technique of using the right to raise loans as a means of compelling a suppliant to buy from a national supplier, through explicitly tying the loan to the product, or of inducing him to do so, through preferential interest rates, was general in the bargaining between states.

How free producers were in practice depended upon how sharply the states, whose registered nationals they were, competed in the area concerned. Where the parent states were not in conflict, the activities of firms making armaments could approximate those of firms making and selling unimpeachably 'civil' goods. In Chile, where official missions from Germany and Britain, respectively, reorganised and trained the army and navy, Krupp and Vickers were largely free to do as they liked. Where political conflicts were acute, as in the Balkans and the Middle East, the firms, even though legally and financially separate from the state, became adjuncts to its foreign policy. They offered the state a particular kind of leverage in return for which their managements and agents took on a quasi-official status which enhanced their power in the market. Their relationships with military attachés and ministers of war became especially close. Official military missions to foreign governments strengthened the position of private firms by recommending the weapons and ancillaries required to modernise the armed forces, which were the objects of the missions' care.

The producer's interest was ultimately expressed in the balance sheet. That, as capitalist enterprises, they sought to earn profits is self-evident, but the pursuit of profit was carried on not in the abstract but in a network of accepted values proceeding from the axioms that war was legitimate and that the right to go to war was an attribute of statehood. Advocates of the liberation of subject nationalities, with irreproachable liberal sentiments, necessarily conceded this right and had no logical grounds for complaint when it was exercised. The corollary was that, irrespective of whether the customer was an established state or merely an aspirant to statehood, selling the instruments of war was no more blameworthy than buying them, and might even be considered progressive.

The tremendous expansion of exports before 1914 raised one problem which also entered into the postwar indictment, but which, like the problems discussed above, relates to the intrinsic problems of industrialisation. Improvements in the quality of materials and workmanship gave the advanced weapons exported by Germany, France and Britain a longer operational life. They often proved more durable than the political alignments they were intended to serve. The allied troops who were decimated by shattering fire from British-made weapons at Gallipoli were suffering not so much from the export of weapons as from a political failure to bring the Ottoman Empire into the War on the side of the Allies, or at least to keep it neutral. Two years later, in 1917, when Romania which had been armed by Krupp as an ally of Germany, nevertheless entered the war on the side of the Allies, German troops suffered the same mortification for the same reasons of political failure. Alliances proved to be less durable than artillery. Weapons might be exported to sustain an alliance but could not be withdrawn when it turned sour. Sub-contracting could produce the same result. The Germans sub-contracted the manufacture of Mauser rifles to the *Fabrique Nationale* in Liège, whose employees some thirty years later used their products to great effect against the attacking German troops.

Again, this highlights a problem implicit in the values and procedures of the nineteenth century. If peace is looked upon as being different from war, and if trade is regarded as contributing to the peace as well as the wealth of nations, at what point does the private industrialist or business man decide that his goods promote his private wealth at the expense of the public peace, or that his exports are untimely? The answer commonly given in practice was that the diplomats and the general staff would decide; only they could declare when a competitor became an enemy. The industrialist worked on the assumption that 'the Trojan War will not take place,' and was, indeed, encouraged to do so by the traditional policy makers, who had no intention of sharing their powers of ultimate decision.

Exports might well have contributed to the timing of the outbreak of specific hostilities by enabling political leaders to carry out what they wished to do. But they also ensured that disparities in weaponry did not last very long and therefore restricted the periods of maximum danger, considered solely in terms of weapons. From the 1880s Hiram Maxim hawked his machine gun round the world and assured equal access to its military potential by whoever could pay for it. If however the gun had been developed by one state which acquired the sole rights from him, its government would, for as long as it could maintain a monopoly of that type of weapon, have acquired a new range of policy options simply because it had sole use of a machine for rapidly killing soldiers in large numbers. Under these conditions, France could more easily have embarked on a war of *revanche* for 1870 because it possessed a means of nullifying on the battlefield the German superiority in manpower. The crucial danger of exports arose when a weapon represented crushing superiority for the time being for one side in a situation of political conflict. That Argentina and Chile, arming against each other, should have cruisers under construction in adjacent berths at Elswick made the ships less than wholly useful for the policies they were intended to serve. Their delivery merely improved the quality of weaponry in the southern part of Latin America.

The export successes and production achievements of the private firms have tended to blind subsequent commentators to the fact that they did not have the field to themselves in weapons manufacture, and were not unregulated by government. Governments were alive to the need to limit their dependence on private industry and to have the means to verify its performance and prices. In all the industrialised countries of Europe, therefore, the state continued to own and run its own plants. The production of defence goods derived from a 'mixed economy' long before that term was generally applied to a blend of state and private enterprise.

In Germany, the Empire inherited a number of factories owned by the constituent kingdoms, with a range of production extending from artillery and gun limbers to food canning and uniforms. In official thinking, these establishments alone covered the peacetime requirements of the army: private industry represented a reserve capacity for wartime expansion, facilitated by the peacetime grouping of firms into '*Industrieverbände*' and by the high quality of German technical management. It was also considered advantageous that the state factories were independent of fluctuations in the labour market and of the general state of the economy. The security of the state implied security in production; risk taking was for the private sector. The infantry and artillery branches ran their own technical laboratories, to conduct their own research and monitor the efforts of the private firms seeking the adoption of new processes or of new generations of weapons. The division of labour between state and private sectors could only be maintained if the political strategies of the government involved no disproportionate increase in requirements. In Germany the adoption during the same period of the Schlieffen Plan and the Tirpitz fleet building programme quickly nullified the initial premise of the state sector. By 1913, arsenals and research establishments were receiving only about forty per cent of procurement funds – the rest went to Krupp, Erhardt and the other manufacturers.

In France, the roles of state and private manufacture was an issue of party politics. The state had turned to Schneider in 1870 as an emergency measure, but, after the Commune had been suppressed, decreed that all future manufacture should take place in government arsenals. Politicians of the Left argued that this measure was not just a prudent anti-revolutionary move suggested by the experience of the Commune; it was anti-Republican, since control of the arsenals could be exploited by monarchists for a *coup d'état* and, worse, it was unpatriotic, since by restricting themselves to covering the national requirements, the arsenals deprived France of the profits which flowed from exports. A free regime would allow republicans equal access to arms and benefit the national accounts. These arguments were eventually embodied in the *Loi Farcy* of 14 August 1885, which permitted private manufacture of armaments with minor reservations, subject only to a declaration at the Prefecture and to registration of traffic. Article II reserved to the state a right to intervene in the export trade – which was exercised in 1894 when the French expeditionary force in Madagascar found itself under fire from French-made rifles. In general, however, the *Loi Farcy* made possible a rapid expansion of French armament manufacture and enabled Schneider over the next thirty years to play the same role in French policy as Krupp had come to play in German. But the pressure for private enterprise originated not with the demands of industrialists but in the desire of party politicians to hamstring political opponents. Internal politics had external effects: the Law sharpened international competition in that it galvanised foreign manufacturers into combining or consolidating to defend themselves against a threatened flood of French material in the export markets.

Britain defined the relationship by Parliamentary inquiry. A committee under the Earl of Morley in 1885 reviewed the existing supply arrangements for the army, recalling that the Royal Factory at Enfield had been created in order to check the rifle trade during the Crimean War. Verification by manufacture and testing by experiment were necessary functions of state. Production at Woolwich and in other state establishments needed improvement but a state monopoly was undesirable. Leaving manufacture in private hands would stimulate invention and improve quality through competition: at the same time, it would widen the area of production – which would allow wartime increases in demand to be more easily met.

The Committee's findings applied equally to the navy since at the time the latter's requirements were supplied by the Master General of Ordnance, even though his department, since the Crimean War, had been merged in the War Office. It was another four years before the Admiralty regained independent responsibility for the design and manufacture of its own guns and equipment; and then, for reasons of inter-service politics, it continued to place part of its orders with Woolwich. For either service the Arsenal proved useless as a source of checks on manufacturing costs, since its layout was uneconomical and it contained a large amount of fixed equipment kept in reserve for use in case of war. Under the accounting procedures in vogue, this equipment was charged to current manufacture. These overheads made Woolwich costs higher than those in the private sector.

For vessels, as distinct from armaments, the navy's relationships with manufacture was somewhat closer, since the Admiralty employed its own naval architects who controlled the design and development of ships. Official monitoring of production was therefore the rule, for which Royal Dockyards provided a constant series of yardsticks. They also conducted experiments and made innovations.

In all three countries, the 'mixed' economy provided for a division of labour between the state and private sectors, with reserve powers to the state. International tension in the first decade of the century made governments more careful of their rights and interests but, at the same time, increased the bargaining power of the private firms whenever government projects had to be completed in a hurry. Broadly, the greater the urgency, the less the scope open to the state to haggle. If 'we want eight (dreadnoughts for the Navy) and we won't wait,'* then the government which places the orders has discarded in advance its powers to insist on detailed accountability. Arms races throw the advantage to the manufacturers. Their bargaining strength in the Anglo-German competition was the greater, in that they possessed not only the production facilities but also the knowledge necessary to developing advanced weapons.

These advantages notwithstanding, the position of the private sector was no stronger than the state allowed it to be, and from approximately 1900 onwards, the state was dominant. That this should be so in Germany and France was not surprising: the structure of government and the widespread militarist sentiment throughout society ensured that the writ of the state was accepted in industry almost without demur. But even in Britain the government responded to international tension by creating the relationship with private industry which *it* needed. Since the major challenge was at sea, the government's initiative was directed at firms producing for the navy and, for that reason, covered the major segment of heavy industry. Hence, in all three countries, firms became closely linked with the official makers of policy for reasons which had nothing to do with the actual or alleged venality of officials. In the prevailing circumstances of incipient conflict, government's need for specific weapons and the companies' possession of the technique by which that need could be met, created links on the production side similar to those already established in the field of exports. The companies' freedom of action was accordingly circumscribed. That they were quite happy with this limitation, even actively sought it, only testifies to the predominance of government in the relationship.

---

*A popular political cry at elections and meetings in Britain in 1909.

Governments used their power to promote concentrations among private manufacturers. In Germany production of the heavy units of the Tirpitz navy was predominantly a matter for Krupp, which for that reason diversified into the manufacture of gun mountings and armour plate and took over, at the state's behest, the Germania shipyard at Kiel. Marine engines and the production of faster, lighter craft remained with established firms at Stettin and Danzig. In Britain, the facilities for marine manufacture were principally located on Clydeside, Tyneside, Sheffield and the lower reaches of the Thames. Moreover, the industry comprised many individual firms responsible for specific items despite some joining of forces, notably by Armstrong and Whitworth, in the 1890s.

The prosperity of these firms, and of the areas in which they were located, depended on how the Admiralty defined its requirements. These in turn depended on the currently dominant tactical doctrine. If defensive armour was considered paramount for battleships, then gun makers could expect fewer contracts, at least until they produced a prototype gun or shell with greater penetration: if fast torpedo boats were thought to be the answer to the concentration of firepower represented by a slower-moving battleship, then the smaller shipyards prospered at the expense of the battleship builders. Admiralty policy was translated into rivalry between firms and their scientific staffs and advisers. Firms could secure their future either by producing a superior system, which would negate their rivals', or they could combine to cover the complete spectrum of policy options by building complete ships of war and their associated facilities, rather than individual components such as hulls, armour or guns. Whatever the Admiralty demanded, business would come their way. The first working arrangement of this kind in Britain was concluded between Armstrong-Whitworth, Vickers and Beardmore in 1903 – a combination which comprehensively covered all phases of ship production from design onwards. The desire effectively to dispute the dominance this combination achieved accounted for the founding two years later of the Coventry Ordnance Company by John Brown of Sheffield, Cammell Laird of Birkenhead and Fairfields of Glasgow. Their experience is instructive. The absolutely indispensable condition for the existence of the new concern was a flow of contracts from the Admiralty and the War Office. At that juncture, the two service departments were anxious to have 'their own' manufacturing company, as one which would cover some of their requirements and act as a check on prices charged by other private contractors. They agreed to guarantee Coventry Ordnance, on two conditions; that it kept out of all price rings and that it never entered into any arrangements (other than those of supplier or customer) with Vickers and Armstrongs. Brown, Cammell Laird and Fairfields agreed, and the Coventry Ordnance company began operations. It soon learned the dangers of dependence. The Admiralty decided in favour of 9.2 inch guns in turrets and gave the work to Coventry Ordnance. The company tooled up and had just completed installing and equipping the production lines when the Admiralty changed its mind about the turrets. The management then found that all the orders for the larger turrets had gone to their competitors. It was partly in order to improve relationships between the Admiralty and the company that, in 1909, a Rear Admiral resigned his commission and became its managing director. Even so, the continuing vagaries of Admiralty policy later caused the Directors to confront the Admiralty with the demand that the navy continue to stand by its original pledge to support its company; otherwise Coventry Ordnance would have to close down. Support was renewed, on a scale which proved sufficient to allow the company to begin to show a profit in the first half of 1914.

Concentration among producers at home and cooperation in markets abroad altered the accepted configuration of industry and government. To the extent that private firms could finance their activity and improve and sell their products by returns from the market, they could be independent of government. To the extent that government needed them as repositories of innovation or as reserve capacity, they had leverage against government. But the firms no longer functioned outside national policy, and in some areas, such as the Balkans, were closely tied in with it.

The new configuration prompted a further development in the analysis of war and peace. Cobden had traced the origin of war to the interest of a group, which he defined as the aristocracy; his Liberal and Socialist successors in the first decade of this century redefined the group as industrialists, no longer, as in Cobden's day, at arm's length from government, but working hand in hand with it. It was argued that arms manufacturers and officials colluded for mutual profit, sustained by warfare and the threat of warfare. War, therefore, was a function of the private manufacture and sale of armaments. Peace required breaking the nefarious association between political power and the private trade. Liberals thought this could be done by appropriate laws, Socialists, by abolishing the capitalist system. Both considered that the state had an exclusive right to the skills and the knowledge, as well as the facilities, for manufacturing weapons. It was right that the state should call on private expertise: it was wrong that officers of the civil and military services should enter private business, oriented to profits and of doubtful patriotism. Philip Snowden in the House of Commons and Karl Liebknecht in the Reichstag attacked the relationship between arms companies and the state in these terms. They were correct in noting a coalescence of interests: they were astray in ascribing it exclusively to the drive for dividends. Moreover, as part of their general theory of politics, they assumed that the state was a uniquely benevolent institution, and deduced from that assumption that war would somehow cease to exist when the war-making agency took complete control of the intellectual and physical assets which made war possible.

This line of argument was to be powerfully reinforced after the War, but in

1914 it did not affect public policy. Indeed, the international connections between firms – Krupp's relations with Skoda, and Schneider's investments in Putilov – were the industrial counterparts, respectively, of the alliances of Germany with Austria-Hungary and France with Russia. In the spring and early summer of 1914, whether the alliances would go to war or not was open to question, in spite of the sabre rattling of general staffs and the sensationalist press. The Powers had got through two major crises – over Morocco in 1904 and over Bosnia in 1908 – without armed conflict. The Balkan Wars of 1912 and 1913 had been contained by diplomacy. French opinion had largely written-off the idea of getting back Alsace and Lorraine by military means: *'revanche'* was the sentimentality of a generation which was dying out. French and German banks cooperated equably, and French capital was freely negotiated on the Vienna *Bourse*. Between Britain and Germany the naval race had abated, and final. agreement on the long-disputed question of the Baghdad Railway seemed to show that the most acute differences could be resolved by negotiation. More generally, the view was widespread that advanced industrial states, by their very nature, literally could not afford war as a technique for solving their disputes.

But the alliance systems contained two flaws. Russia was committed to supporting Serbia in the Balkans – which made it captive to whatever the Serbian Government wanted to do. The German General Staff had given *carte blanche* to their Austrian confrères to deal with Serbia, should the occasion arise. On 28 June 1914, a decade of Balkan politics culminated in the assassination of an Austrian Archduke, the heir to the throne, in the Bosnian town of Sarajevo. The assailant was a Bosnian Serb, who was an Austrian subject, and who had been trained in Serbia. He touched off the final clash between Russian and Austrian ambitions and mutual mistrust. Austria, backed by Germany, rejected mediation. Austria was the ally of Germany: France the ally of Russia. The Franco-Russian alliance brought France into the Austro-Russian quarrel over the Balkans. The French move, from the German standpoint, meant invoking 'Schlieffen', in somewhat modified form. The violation of Belgian neutrality brought in a Britain which, notwithstanding the *entente* with France, might conceivably have stayed out otherwise. Europe proved to be more like the Balkans, than the Balkans, Europe.

PART IV

1914–1918

'L'aviation, c'est le sport. Pour
l'armée, c'est zero.'
Foch, 1910

'A pretty mechanical toy.... The war
will never be won by such machines.'
Kitchener, on the tank, *1916*

1. Upheaval in the European industrial system

The war in the west began on 1 August 1914, with the invasion of Luxembourg, and, on 3 August, of Belgium.* Three weeks later the Allied armies were in retreat along the entire front. 'Schlieffen' appeared to be working, fortuitously assisted by a French plan and military doctrine which almost destroyed the French forces themselves, in the manner of 1870, though rather more comprehensively. The course of events along the frontiers of north-eastern France lent credence to the opinion among all combatants that the war would be over by Christmas, but in the week beginning on 5 September, Falkenhayn, who had replaced Moltke, accepted the check administered to the German advanced forces at the Marne and ordered a retreat. His forces went to ground. The war of movement ended.

The static nature the conflict now assumed may be conveniently demonstrated by one small episode. On 12 September, the German forces retreating from the Marne dug themselves in on the slopes to the north of the river Aisne. The commander of the British Expeditionary Force, Sir John French, issued orders that the next day the pursuit was to be continued, with the objective of reaching Laon, fifteen miles to the north, by nightfall. British forces duly carried out their orders and entered Laon – four years later. Till that time, both sides stayed where they were.

This sequence was duplicated along the entire Western Front. In effect the Germans dug themselves a fortress, which the Allies besieged. The systems and defensive works along the entire front were completed on 14 October. The failure to break through the Dardanelles between April and December 1915 ended any attempt at a mobile solution since it was assumed to prove the necessity, if not the wisdom, of concentrating all available forces in one place. Positional warfare took over. Flanks could not be turned, because they

---

*The exchanges of ultimatums and declarations of war did not take place all at once, but were spread over the first two weeks of August – which left Britain, for example, for eight days formally at war with Germany but not with Germany's ally, Austria–Hungary, on whose behalf she had taken up arms. When at midnight on 16 August, the Austro-Hungarian Embassy left London, a representative of King George V saw them off at Paddington, in a special train put at their disposal by the Great Western Railway. At Falmouth, the Admiralty saw them transferred to a neutral passenger ship. The Austrian officials expressed their appreciation of these courtesies in a letter to *The Times*.

rested on the Swiss mountains and the North Sea; therefore, the enemy front had to be pierced. The logic was simple, productive of extravagant losses, and militarily ineffective. During 1915, the limit of Allied advance on the Western Front was three miles. The stalemate only ended in the spring of 1918. Till then, the war was fought out over an area of ground 400 miles long and varying from a few yards to about ten miles deep.

In this area killed and wounded on both sides were numbered in millions. For the answer to entrenchments was artillery. Strategies based on massed infantry had failed to produce the desired results; the guns were now to blast a way through. Sustained artillery barrages would (theoretically) break up entrenchments and make their defenders vulnerable to assault by infantry. 'Artillery conquers: infantry occupies,' as Pétain put it. The new doctrine required a prodigious expenditure of shells. The increase in demand, which was common to all armies, may conveniently be exemplified by reference to British experience. The preliminary bombardment of the battle of Hooge, in May 1915, required 18,000 shells, that for the first battle of the Somme, from 24 June to 1 July 1916, 2,000,000 and for the third battle of Ypres 16 to 31 July 1917, 4,300,000. The expense of this method of warfare was commensurate. The last-named bombardment lasted sixteen days, used 321 trains for transporting the shells to the front and represented the output of 55,000 workers for one year. The total cost of approximately £22 million was only just short of the total costs of the home army in 1914.

Bombardment preceded the attack by infantry. The military gains over five months were forty-five square miles of Ypres mud, with a loss of 370,000 men, equivalent to 8,222 per square mile. That was all. The German defence did not break, and the stalemate went on.

The dominant military philosophy of the time expected heavy casualties. Before 1914 armies were trained on the principle that morale on the battlefield could offset the damage inflicted by bullets, but prewar planning had been related to envelopments or breakthrough assaults designed to destroy the enemy forces and bring hostilities to a swift conclusion. Schlieffen and Moltke on one side, and Maillard and Grandmaison on the other, were devotees of the offensive* and accepted high casualty rates as necessary. In their minds, however, overall losses would be limited by the short duration of the campaign. Had Schlieffen's plan or the French counter, Plan XVII, worked, that might well have been the result. The plans did not work as scheduled, but until the spring of 1918 the leadership on both sides failed to reverse the doctrine to meet the altered circumstances. They

---

*This doctrine translated into differing tactical instructions: both agreed that infantry was the main arm, but the French stipulated that artillery should not prepare the way for attacks, while the German insisted that the two arms fight together, with artillery specifically to be used to clear a path for infantry. The disasters to French troops in the summer of 1914 stem from this difference.

consequently maximised losses of manpower and material for unrealisable and unrealistic objectives.

Static warfare was not confined to the Western Front. Military action following the entry of Italy into the war on the allied side, in May 1915, showed the same characteristics as that in Flanders ten months previously. Italian hopes of a quick dash to Trieste, thirty miles from the frontier, were frustrated by stubborn Austrian defence on the Corso plateau. Operations thereafter reverted to attrition, with the minor difference that trenches and emplacements had to be blasted out of rock rather than dug out of the soil. It took the Italian forces fifteen months to capture Gorizia, less than halfway to Trieste. In such terrain, the counterpart of the Flanders' railways was an intricate system of aerial lifts, drawing their motive power from the same alpine power stations which served industry in the river valleys of Northern Italy. An Austrian breakthrough into Northern Italy could have destroyed the Italian forces and paralysed the Italian war effort at the same time. The Austrian strategy all but succeeded in October 1917 at Caporetto, but Austrian and German forces were held just before they could erupt into the Venetia. On the Eastern Front, though there were some entrenchments, the methods of warfare were not so static, large areas of territory changing hands in the course of operations. It is however significant that these took place between the least industrialised forces in the conflict, Russia and Austria-Hungary, and in a non-industrialised area, East Prussia, Poland and Galicia.

The completion of entrenchments from the North Sea to the Swiss frontier and in the Alps between Italy and Austria yielded a new order of priorities for the embattled powers. Their foreign policies remained, as at the outset, peace after victory, but the related military policy was changed. Victory was to be achieved through attrition and on the Western Front, the theatre chosen by commanders on both sides for the maximum and decisive effort. The choice of place and means automatically concentrated all their options into one, namely reorganising their forces and equipping them to fight the kind of war required. It also exposed the inadequacies of their preparations. Using artillery to blast gaps in prepared positions through which infantry could advance (a total reversal of prewar tactics) demanded shells on a scale which industry was not equipped to supply. The shortages were shown to be not only in numbers but in quality. Miscalculations were compounded by ignorance. In Britain, confident assertions that native production of iron ore (over sixteen million tons in 1913) would easily allow deficiencies to be made good, soon withered when it was discovered that the figure was irrelevant. Prospects of expanding the output of steel for high explosive shells depended on *hematite* iron ore, of which the 1913 output was only one and a quarter million tons. The procurement authorities also found that they did not even know how many firms were capable of manufacturing to the required specifications. It had been assumed that industry would deliver the goods, when called on; existing evidence to the contrary was among the unadopted lessons of the Boer War.

In Germany, France and Britain the acute shortages of munitions prompted a rapid revaluation of the industrial necessities of war, in relation not only to materials but to plant, skills, and standards. In each country, the law governing the manufacture of munitions served ultimately as a vehicle for extending state control over the economy as a whole. Victory through attrition by mass armies disputing a front 400 miles long generated the need to sustain the armies and conscript materials and skills, and for that reason, fostered what amounted to a reordering of industrial society. The immediate problem was to assess the availability of materials and establish and enforce priorities in their use. Matching supply to demand was a function of the bureaucracy. Skills were suddenly seen to be as important to 'winning the war' as service with the colours, but it was difficult to convince army commands, who still thought in terms of infantry offensives, that industrially-skilled manpower should be released. The extreme case is Tsarist Russia, where the call-up of some thirty-seven per cent of the male working population stripped industry of manpower and ensured that soldiers serving at the front lacked either rifles or boots. The military and political results of this disproportion were, in 1917, catastrophic for the regime.

France was not far behind its Russian ally. The call up of 2.9 million reservists in the first two weeks of August 1914 seriously dislocated the economy, causing shut-downs of plant and unemployment. The vital iron works lost sixty-seven per cent of their personnel. The practice whereby graduates of the *Ecole Polytechnique* or the *Ecole des Mines* held reserve commissions in the artillery or the engineers denuded the metallurgical industries of management and research specialists. The wholesale requisitioning of mules abruptly cut agricultural production in the Landes, where no other animals were suitable for draught purposes. But France, in common with the other participants, gradually learned how better to assess priorities. The states with a stronger 'civilian' tradition proved in practice more capable of digesting the lessons. In Germany, carefully arranged schedules were frequently upset by arbitary military intervention, particularly in transport. The 'crash programme' associated with the name of Hindenburg, which mobilised virtually the whole man and woman power of Germany and all its material resources, only exacerbated the confusion. On the allied side, the institutions of control proliferated and produced a similar chaos. The vital difference was that, by 1918, the Allies got rid of much overlapping while in Germany cohesion vanished. On both sides, however, control was exercised by boards and committees of which civilians from industry were members, since they commanded the expertise on which decisions had to be based. They thus became an integral element in the day-to-day formulation of policy.

The need simultaneously to expand and convert the economy marked the end of prudence in public finance. All the combatants had assumed before the war that its costs could be met by raising funds in the market. The only problem specific to war was how to wage it without endangering internal costs and prices and without undermining the confidence of investors, domestic and foreign. Even Germany, which had gone further into these matters than its allies and opponents, banked on the supposition that a Schlieffen-style victory in northern France would preserve monetary stability by causing the international money market to rally to the mark.

In these reorganisations, the relationship of the state to private industry underwent a crucial change. The received idea of 'the market' as a process by which consumers articulated their demands for the satisfaction of their material wants (even if these demands had to be presented within limits defined by combinations of enterprises) went into abeyance. 'Market' was defined ultimately by government. It rationed commodities, granted or withheld licences to produce or import or to acquire materials, intervened in credit policies to finance investments, and demanded to be supplied at fixed prices or within a pre-determined scale. Essential inputs, such as materials and labour, were no longer purchased by the choice of the manufacturer; they were allocated to him, by some central board. The prices in these transactions did not reflect market values but were simply indicators for accounting purposes. The notion of 'profit' changed accordingly. It was defined not as the return the manufacturer could get from the market, variously by meeting a need, by guile, or by the exertion of market strength, but as the margin allowable by government for services rendered. 'Labour' did not change its connotation so drastically, though it was graded and mobilised and its bargaining rights were curtailed, in favour of the compulsory arbitration of disputes. It was also admitted into the management of industrial manpower. The erosion of the yardsticks and practices associated with liberal capitalism worked to the benefit of organised labour, which, on balance, was the stronger for the re-ordering of priorities.

These developments were not all introduced at the same time or in the same degree in each country. Nor did they always work out as intended. The system of allocations in Germany, for example, was designed to give priority in coal deliveries to industries directly concerned with supplying the armed forces, or with munitions. In practice, deliveries were often scheduled to obviate discontent among workers in industrial districts, regardless of the product they made. The changes were not unopposed. As late as 1916, Knut Wicksell, the celebrated economist, was arguing in the *Archiv für Sozialwissenschaft und Sozialpolitik*[1] that the demands of the state and the army could be met by raising the rate of interest. The ease with which prescriptions such as this were ignored demonstrates how far, in only two years since 1914, the operative concepts of production and distribution had departed from the dichotomy between 'military' and 'civil' which had ruled till then. '*Kriegswirtschaft*' became a science. The Germans, characteristically, formulated it as a concept: their opponents practised it all the same, since it was a consequence of the adoption of a strategy of attrition in one dominant theatre of war.

War had become a contest involving not armies only but whole nations. The epoch in which it was regarded as limited in scope and governed by aristocratic values was at an end. War became democratic and comprehensive – a matter of the mass. It also became a matter of industry and organisation. Victory now hung not so much on bravery or training as on solving problems of the balance and range of industry, securing supplies of raw materials and correctly evaluating the use of industrial manpower. Industrial considerations of this order became central to military and diplomatic policy, particularly towards neutrals, and drew the industrial managements into the processes of decision-making. By 1916, the 'war economy' had taken shape in each of the participant nations. Europe was converted to *dirigisme* and protection on a vast scale. A negotiated peace might have frustrated this development, but, as all the combatants chose war to the bitter end, it was, in the context of history, irreversible.

The core of the transformation of the economies from liberal capitalism into 'war socialism' was the attempt to make good the lack of preparation for prolonged conflict. It is often forgotten that the economy before 1914 was more genuinely international than it has been since. Policy makers were soon aware of the limits on their actions placed by the financial and industrial interdependence of prewar Europe. This posed severely practical problems. Most of the aluminium used in Germany was imported from Switzerland, where it was produced from bauxite imported from France. French officials made the inconvenient discovery that the manufacture of explosives in the state-owned plants depended on imports of phenol from Germany. Britain, especially, had relied on imports to cover requirements, so that in 1914, it possessed only one factory for making magnetos and only one for ball bearings. Even such elementary pieces of equipment as pressure gauges came from abroad. For years the magnesite bricks used for lining basic steel furnaces had been imported from Austria.

Such maladjustments speeded up indigenous manufacture and correspondingly focused attention on the supplies and skills available in neutral states. In this respect, Sweden and Switzerland attained a particular importance, inasmuch as they were the major countries whose industrial materials and skills remained available to Germany within the allied blockade. By the same token, they became the peculiar object of allied economic warfare. Equally, both Sweden and Switzerland had to adjust their economic activities to a situation for which there were virtually no precedents. The last wars in which they had participated were pre-industrial. They were faced with the disruption of their existing markets and sources of supply. Swiss watchmakers found profitable alternative employment for their skills in making fuses, gunsights and similar mechanisms. Sweden became a major source of iron ore, the export of which helped sustain the Swedish economy, as well as the German war effort.

The policies of the other Scandinavian states, Norway and Denmark, as well as of the Netherlands, were determined more by their dependence on sea traffic, which made them the more vulnerable to belligerent pressure, especially as they contained the ports through which American trade with Germany was carried on. Until the US entered the war in 1917, it was often more expedient for Britain to attempt to strangle this trade at the ports of transit rather than at the ports of origin, to minimise disputes with the American Government.

The European neutrals, then and later, discussed their position in terms of a series of high-handed violations of their rights by brutal belligerents. In fact, their neutrality was an active not a passive policy. The neutrals remained sovereign states and as such exercised a considerable degree of leverage over the belligerents. Sweden was vital to Britain because until 1917 it provided the main transit route between the western allies and Russia, and was necessary to Russia itself as a source of specialised engineering products and of munitions. If Britain, using leverage offered by its coal supply, pushed Sweden too far, Sweden could easily retaliate against Britain's ally Russia. Similarly, Swiss industry depended on imports which had to be carried over French and Italian railways, but openings for allied leverage were limited by the fact that Switzerland controlled the interchange of products which France and Germany in their respective interests had to allow. In consequence, all the belligerents were forced to make drastic compromise which could only benefit their enemies, and neutrals shared with belligerents the necessity to strike bargains, in which they had to accept the least disadvantageous option. Absolute satisfaction was ruled out. Belligerents were driven to this course because the alternative would have been to take over the neutral state; neutrals, because they wanted to maximise the advantages which the situation offered, in which their disparities in power could be offset against the belligerents' need and the fact that they were committing their main power elsewhere.

The neutrals were thus much stronger than their relative military strength indicated. Their advantages were substantial. The belligerents, with their peacetime traffic in imports and exports distorted by blockade and countermeasures, were the more dependent on the raw materials in neutral hands: nitrates and copper in Norway, iron ore and timber in Sweden, oleaginous products (yielding glycerine for explosives) in Denmark. Supplies of essential materials such as these could, in an unexpectedly protracted war, spell the difference between victory and defeat. For the neutrals, trade in goods for which the demand had become more pressing provided receipts which helped to sustain the balance of payments in times of great trading difficulties. Moreover, they found that their respective countries were already so much part of the industrial system that they had to participate in the exchange of goods and services to the greatest possible extent, in order to keep plant and skills in use and avoid large-scale unemployment.

Active participation also conferred political benefits. The Scandinavian states and the Netherlands were all democracies, whose governments were directly responsive to public opinion. That was divided. Fear of Russia – then an immediate neighbour – induced the Swedish upper classes and the bureaucracy to favour a German victory, (though only a small group argued in favour of entering on the German side). Liberals and Socialists inclined towards the western allies. To avoid splitting the country completely and possibly endangering the monarchy, it was necessary for the Swedish Government to propitiate first one group then the other.

Switzerland was similarly divided. The General Staff favoured Germany, partly for the practical reason that Swiss and German industries were complementary, and the generals had no wish to compromise the industrial base of the Swiss army. Cultural rather than professional affinity made the German-speaking Swiss pro-German. The feeling waned by the end of 1915 in view of the fate of Belgium – whose neutrality had also been internationally guaranteed – but this section of the population never became pro-Ally. Their French-speaking compatriots were not pro-Ally either: they tended to support France – so much so that German-speaking regiments of the Swiss army mobilised in support of neutrality, could only be quartered in French-speaking cantons at the risk of civil disorders. Mutual hostility only faded at the end of 1917, when the collapse of Russia and Romania and the defeat of the Italians at Caporetto engendered the fear that the vast numbers of German and Austrian troops released for service in the west might find their way there via Switzerland. Belgium, it was widely noted, had been used to outflank the French fortifications in 1914: Swiss territory might well be used for a similar strategy against the Western Front, in 1918. Till then, however, the Swiss Government, like the Swedish, managed neutrality in such a way as to maintain domestic political stability. This involved discriminating cooperation with belligerent governments.

There were, of course, differences of emphasis in the respective policies: Sweden, on the whole, made life far more difficult for the British than for the Germans: in Norway (partly through fear of Sweden), the contrary balance was struck. Danish opinion favoured the Allies but in practice Danish policy was dominated by fear of a German invasion – a repetition of 1864. The Scandinavian neutrals ensured that the belligerents could not easily find out what was happening, by collectively ceasing to publish trade statistics from December 1914. Neutral governments used their authority to promote their own interests as they saw them and contested the belligerents step by step, either by refusing to alter the peacetime requirements for the documentation of goods to show ultimate destinations, or by actively encouraging trading practices whereby, for example, goods shipped by British vessels to Copenhagen were simply transferred across the berth to boats bound for German Baltic ports. The Swedish Government went further: it supported a transit system in which goods consigned from Britain to Russia were smuggled back from Finland and reshipped at Lulea for German destinations. The Swedish officials blandly explained that the original conditions of shipment had been met, and that if the goods went astray in Russian territory, that was not their affair.

By such means, and for reasons discussed above, the neutral governments were able to force drastic compromises on the belligerents. Britain had to accept that a proportion of goods supplied to Sweden would find its way to Germany, and that the continued supply of Danish bacon and dairy products for British breakfasts was conditional on uninterrupted Danish exports to its southern neighbour. France, similarly, had to supply Switzerland with bauxite in the knowledge that doing so helped to sustain German Zeppelin manufacture, in order to receive the magnetos which the Swiss ordered from Germany in excess of their own requirements, for reasons of which the German authorities were well aware. For their part, the Germans found that Swedish pit-props and other dressed lumber had to go to Britain as a counterpart of the export of Swedish horses to Germany and the removal of government restrictions on the export of meat and dairy products. The German Government had to see the Norwegian holders of the rights to a nickel refining process, developed in a plant in Norway controlled by German capitalists, go into partnership with the British Government in opening a nickel producing and refining enterprise in Canada. The French Government, in its turn, had to acquiesce in arrangements which made the aniline manufacturers of Basel part of a German cartel. Through the main neutral markets, the German chemical industry supplied a high proportion of the drugs used to treat allied casualties. The war showed plainly that industrial and commercial frontiers by no means coincided with political, and that the cosmopolitan character of prewar Europe had encouraged the creation of a network of ownership rights and interests which hindered clear-cut policies.

In the experience of belligerents and neutrals alike, the demands of industrialised war on a continental scale were inconsistent with the legal standards and axioms of international behaviour worked out during the previous century. Neutrals were no longer outside the combat, insulated from its effects by their political neutrality and military non-interventions, neither were they just dragged into it by being components in the industrial system: they had a positive interest in keeping intact the circuit of requirements between the contending states. Whatever their formal status in international law, they were, industrially considered, co-belligerents. Government policies had to bend to this reality. As the distinction between 'civil' and 'military' was being eroded within states, so economic warfare blurred the traditional distinction between 'neutral' and 'belligerent'. In war economies, all goods were in principle 'war goods' whether for domestic use or export. Industrialised warfare took governments into the politics and finance of export markets, as well as into regulating their own producers. The Swedish Government had its counterpart of the belligerents 'trading with the enemy' legislation in the Law on Wartime Commerce by which contracts between Swedish nationals and aliens, whether governmental, corporate or individual, were illegal, unless agreed in advance by the State Commerce Commission created *ad hoc* as an instrument of state policy. In Norway, the government assumed the sole right to import cereals and flour products, and monopolised the whaling business, as fats became scarcer. In Switzerland, control of imports and exports was vested in the *Société de Surveillance Suisse*, though in law it was a private association not a department of state. The liberal order was abrogated, even in countries which were not themselves fighting.

Problems of raw material supply disclosed by the hostilities determined many of the ideas about the shape of any peace treaty, either in the form of compensation or of reinsurance. The course of the war allowed Germany two opportunities to put such schemes into effect, both under the stress of attrition on the Western Front. The collapse of Tsarist Russia in 1917-18 and the defeat of Romania, which had entered the war on the side of the Allies in August 1917, were both used by German negotiators to exact economic concessions to meet the immediate needs of industrialised war under conditions of blockade, although longer-term considerations were not absent. Neither campaign originated in economic reasoning. That Germany was at war with Russia stemmed from the structure of alliances before the war and in particular from the military undertakings which the General Staff gave to their Austrian counterparts in regard to the Balkans. Germany had managed to get out of Romania all that it wanted while that country was neutral, and would have been spared a campaign had the Romanian Government elected to stay out of hostilities, but it did not. The Romanians declared war on Germany and Austria-Hungary at a juncture when it seemed they had fewer political benefits to offer than the *Entente*.

Yet, by the end of 1917, the strain of the war within Germany and Austria-Hungary was such that victory had to be construed in terms of immediate economic benefits, especially those of supply. Overcoming the shortages and improving the structure of industry also entered into long-term calculations, embodied in the concept of *Mitteleuropa* and annexationist plans in the West.* Both, by reason of the defeat of Germany, remained unrealised.

---

*The representations by German industrialists that the iron ore deposits of Lorraine should be annexed together with the fortresses of Verdun and Longwy to protect them, derived from prewar estimates by both French and German government engineers that the ore fields on the German side of the frontier were being the more rapidly depleted, with exhaustion in sight by 1943–53.

2. The application of new technologies: war as a 'total' activity

The aims of policy, on both sides, required that the enemy forces be defeated. This meant breaking the deadlock on the Western Front – which in military terms could be achieved either by using some new device to overcome the defences or, in the longer term, by destroying the industrial and, possibly, social support of the military effort. Both were tried.

The stalemate on the battlefield enhanced the blockade of Germany instituted by the Royal Navy in August 1914. What had been almost a traditional reflex of British policy became a much more vital element in strategy – and one which, for some time, appeared to many contemporaries to be the only one which held out any hope of a decisive outcome. German hopes of breaking the blockade at sea, and attacking Britain at its most vulnerable point, rested on the use of the submarine – a weapon which had been considered of only marginal importance in Tirpitz's naval programme. Submarines had been slow to develop throughout the previous century in spite of the interest in their use of one professional group, the *Jeune Ecole* in France. What turned the submarine from a rather hazardous technological novelty lacking any consistent doctrine as to its use into a threat which was all but to defeat Britain in war, was the invention of the diesel engine. Rudolf Diesel's experiments were supported by M.A.N. and Krupp, and the first model suitable for series production was made in the M.A.N. plant in Augsburg in 1897. By 1908, an automotive version had been developed in Switzerland by Adolph Saurer AG of Arben. The *Reichsmarineamt* took an interest in the possibilities for naval purposes, and by 1913 the first serviceable submarine version went into a U-boat constructed at Krupp's Germania yard. Proving trials, which were protracted by the need to eliminate technical difficulties, showed by the outbreak of war that the performance and fuel consumption of the diesel engine had turned the submarine from a coastal defence vessel into an ocean-going one, capable of attacking the enemy far from its base. The most spectacular single demonstration of the diesel submarine's capabilities in range and endurance occurred, not in striking against enemy shipping, but in penetrating the British blockade in June–July 1916 on a trading mission to the United States, at that juncture still neutral. The trading submarine, the *Deutschland*, arrived in Baltimore with a cargo of dyes. American customs officials after meticulous inspection declared that the *Deutschland* was indubitably a merchant vessel – and British diplomatic protests were nullified. It returned to Germany with several hundred tons of nickel and rubber. Another voyage followed, in which similar cargoes of high value in relation to volume were exchanged; six more trading submarines were put under construction but the entry of America into the war altered the priorities; they were fitted with torpedo tubes for naval operations, designed to prevent American forces from being effectively deployed in Europe.

This case points to the main problems to which the use of submarines gave rise, namely, the political context of their operations. The successful elimination early in 1915 of the last of the problems which trials disclosed in the submarine diesel engine enabled German policy to embark on a systematic war on commerce, designed to break the blockade, but since no power had seriously considered submarines as an offensive arm, before the war, their role had to be worked out through practice. As commerce raiders, they were unrivalled, but this role had traditionally been ascribed to cruisers – surface vessels which could carry skeleton crews to take command of prizes and which could, in the event of sinking, escort their passengers and crew 'to a place of reasonable safety'. Hence the rules of international maritime law governing attacks on commerce were built round the capabilities of the existing commerce raider and were known, consequently, as 'the cruiser rules'. The submarine, however, in contrast to the cruiser, could neither man prizes nor escort personnel to safety, and was itself vulnerable to armed merchantmen. Was it to be employed like a cruiser or not? Its use as a commerce raider created political uncertainties which German diplomacy never satisfactorily resolved. It was one thing to force Italian factories to close through submarine attacks on vessels transporting their raw materials: it was another to convince neutral opinion, America in particular, that the rules elaborated for surface raiders had not in essence been broken, or that modified rules for submarines were reasonable.

The German leadership was united as to the legitimacy of submarine warfare in defending Germany's vital interest: it was divided over the precise use of the weapon. Broadly, the diplomats took the view that the reactions of neutrals should determine the scope and limits of use, and that the cruiser rules should apply. The admirals, Tirpitz and Pohl, argued that the characteristics of the submarine alone should determine its use, which, if unrestricted, would bring about a quick decision in Germany's favour. Hindenburg and Ludendorff ultimately supported them, on the grounds that attrition on land ruled out a rapid solution in that quarter, and that Germany's ability to succeed in its aims was directly related to the pressure of the British blockade.

Between the spring of 1915 and January 1917, the debate oscillated between these two points of view, principally in response to estimates of the importance of America to German policy. Could unrestricted submarine warfare be undertaken without bringing the United States into the war on the allied side? When the US had to be encouraged or propitiated, the cruiser rules had the better of the argument; when the predominant opinion was that America could be shrugged off they were ignored. The other variable in the debate was Britain: was the object of submarine warfare to force her to lift the blockade – which was consistent with limitations on the use of the weapon – or to drive her out of the war by the total disruption of her seaborne carrying trade – for which limitations were unnecessary? The offensive submarine was a weapon without a settled doctrine and no clear role in foreign policy.

Experience showed the consequence of this confusion. The first unrestricted campaign, begun in February 1915, had to be abandoned the following September for lack of overwhelming, and therefore decisive, numbers, and in face of neutral protests which were important to German policy as long as Germany was not self-sufficient in the materials needed to sustain the war and as long as the land fronts showed no signs of a decision. Faulty assessments of American reactions and the emergence of Hindenburg and Ludendorff as dictators of German policy brought about a final determination in favour of a submarine policy based on technical considerations alone – viz, the availability of allied and neutral tonnage, the rates of sinkings against those of new construction and the time it would take for American capacity to be deployed for war. The diplomats abandoned the argument – as so often in Wilhelmine Germany. At the Crown Council at Pless on 9 January 1917, civilian objections capitulated to the military view that submarine warfare, provided it were unrestricted, would drive Britain out of the war 'in six months at the most,' before the Americans could arrive. The submarines opened their campaign on 1 February; the diplomats were charged merely with explaining the reasons for it.

The second unrestricted campaign was theoretically mounted against armed merchantmen but soon transcended this limitation; any merchant vessel in designated waters was likely to be sunk on sight. The political consequence of the German action was that the United States promptly broke off relations (on 3 February) and formally entered the ranks of Germany's enemies two months later. The near-exhausted *Entente* states knew that, in a war of material, the advantage was overwhelmingly theirs. Even though bringing American power to bear took a long time – the forces which arrived in France were largely kitted out with French equipment – unwearied American troops participated in the decisive fighting in the summer of 1918.

For Germany, using submarines against strictly military targets, and otherwise for trading, both to exchange vital commodities and to reap the considerable propaganda benefits in keeping the US officially neutral, would appear to have been the better option. That it was not pursued evidences a failure in political perceptiveness. From a purely technical point of view, the submarine was highly effective, whether its use was restricted or not; a fleet of 150 vessels, of which about half were at sea at any one time, inflicted tremendous damage – sinking an average of 369,000 tons of shipping a month from February 1917 to October 1918[2] – and tied up some 4,000 Allied ships in countermeasures, apart from aircraft and dirigibles. Its failure in the overall strategic pattern decided on at Pless has led subsequent commentators to overlook its short-term successes in crippling the allied effort by cutting the supplies of raw materials to Britain's war industries and, on a smaller scale, to Italian factories, and inhibiting the cross-Channel transport of coal, which, from 1915, was the mainstay of French industry.

For the Allies in their turn, the internal combustion engine as the motive power in the tank and the aircraft held out a prospect of gaining the decisive initiative on the battlefield and therefore breaking the deadlock. The idea of arming automotive vehicles for combat seems to have occurred almost as soon as the vehicles themselves had appeared on the roads. The Kaiser, for example, promoted experiments with a steam-driven land fortress. But the introduction of oil-powered engines in the eighteen eighties and nineties solved the problems of weight and fuel supply which inhibited steam cars, and manufacturers were quick to demonstrate the new possibilities. In 1899 de Dion Bouton produced a four-wheeled motorcycle with a Maxim gun and six years later his compatriot firm Charron Girardot et Voigt demonstrated a chassis with a revolving turret – which was sold to Russia. In the same year, Daimler and Erhardt both made their first armoured cars. The first combat use of the new vehicle took place in 1912, when Italian forces were in action in Tripoli. These efforts were all with conventional road wheels. Tracked vehicles also appeared in the decade before the First World War, stimulated in Britain by a War Office competition for vehicles capable of hauling heavy loads across the country. By 1914 and 1915, Daimler and Lancia respectively were at work on armoured vehicles.

The conditions created by artillery barrages and defensively sited machine guns prompted experiments into the use of armoured vehicles – armoured to withstand machine gun fire, and tracked to enable them to progress over the churned-up terrain on the battlefield. The tactical motive, to cut down the losses in manpower which the attacker suffered in the adopted form of combat, accounted for the use of the 'tank' prematurely and in too small numbers. This offers the most positive example of the difficulty the leadership had, among all the combatants, of translating the characteristics of a weapon into a doctrine for its use. (After the war, the tank became a touchstone of those who understood the lessons of 1914–1918 and those who did not.) Nevertheless, its introduction shifted the possibilities of decisive combat one stage further away from sheer manpower – the concept with which the war began – and towards the machine. Land strategies, and therefore certain aspects of policy, were linked with the possession of a new branch of manufacturing. The motor car industry, that is light engineering, became important to war, and the size and range of the firms in the industry became a concern of national policy.

The manufacture of tanks and armoured fighting vehicles did not involve the industry in any new nexus with the state. In contrast, the construction and use of aircraft did. The internal combustion engine took warfare into a new dimension, the air. The use of heavier-than-air craft was discounted by military commands before the war. Foch flatly stated in 1910, after witnessing some trials, that he thought flying was a good exercise but void of military value. Even the more forseeing considered it of possible use only in reconnaisance. That remained a major feature, but before the war was over, the role of aircraft diversified into strategic bombing, tactical support of the army, and the interception of enemy aircraft. As the purposes varied, so did the machines; they were built to suit each of these tasks. Concomitantly a new industry was brought into being at the behest of the state. The United Kingdom, which at the end of the war had the world's largest airforce operating as a separate command and with doctrines independently elaborated for its use, offers an instructive example of this transition.

In Britain, as elsewhere, flying was widely regarded by established military opinion as, at best, a mildly eccentric hobby. It was thought to offer some help in spotting artillery fire, but military pilots had to learn to fly at their own expense and obtain the certificate of the Royal Aero Club at a fee of £75 – a device not only to relieve the Treasury of the cost but to ensure that the private flying clubs did not fail for lack of support. In similar fashion, the Admiralty relented about aviation, but only in 1911 and then to the extent of allowing *four* officers to learn to fly, provided the navy did not have to bear the cost. Machines and tuition were provided free by private enthusiasts who were members of the Royal Aero Club.

The government was more directly concerned with the manufacture of the aircraft. In 1912* it sponsored a competition for the design of airframes; a series of monoplane accidents procured a ban on monoplanes for military purposes and the setting up of an Aeronautical Inspection Department to supervise both manufacture and maintenance. The next year, the airframe competition was followed by one for engines. It was won by a design which, though reliable on the ground, never in fact flew because its weight and fuel consumption adversely affected its performance. The engines adjudged second and third were, significantly, both adaptions of foreign makes, French and Austrian. It was equally noteworthy for the future that the testing and

---

*Government had already sponsored an institution to conduct research into the problems of aeronautics by setting up a special aerodynamics department at the National Physical Laboratory, which from 1909 analysed problems of air resistance, stresses on materials in the new environment, wing shape, etc. Much effort went into problems of engine failure. Academic science made its contribution in the guise of Professor G. H. Bryan's pioneering enquiry into *Stability in Aviation* – which furnished a mathematical basis for the theory of flight.

adjudication of the entries were carried out by the Royal Aircraft Factory, Farnborough. This was a government establishment, staffed by civilians. Through its experiments, it set standards of design, materials and performance for the nascent aircraft industry. On the demand of the military, the Factory developed and constructed models from which to derive the specifications for the private builders, to whom it also gave technical assistance on their private ventures.

These developments occurred largely in the three years prior to the war, not without resentment from the private firms who considered that they could put to better use the large proportion of total funds which was made available to the Factory and who preferred to produce their own types and ideas rather than compete for government contracts on which they all too frequently made losses. Government-designed aircraft were no more immune to mishaps than those made by private firms, and during 1913 a number of accidents provoked a controversy in Parliament and the press over the merits of the emerging system. It survived the agitation, in which the arguments of private manufacturers were buttressed by those of their friends among the aviation staffs of both army and navy, and retained its authority intact. The outbreak of war showed that in spite of progress made, the system was inadequate to the new challenges. About eight firms were working for the War Office, but none had received orders for more than six aircraft. In August 1914 there was neither an up-to-date model capable of being put into series production, nor any experience in industry of manufacturing on such a scale. There was no indigenous engine manufacture at all, engines for operational use being imported from France. At the end of July, when opinion in Whitehall began to think that the crisis set in train by the Sarajevo assassination might well result in European war, British officials went to France to buy every available Farman aircraft and Renault and Gnome engine, to make good the deficiencies. Purchasing was interrupted by the French Government, until it was assured that the United Kingdom would, in fact, enter the war. The unforseen consequence was that, in this respect if in no other, Britain standardised on her ally's design and manufacture from the outset. But the air force which crossed to France in August 1914 was got together by mobilising private enthusiasts *with their machines*, which brought the total strength up to four squadrons. Its transport reflected the same situation; vehicles were not standardised and most still bore the markings of their peacetime trades. The armament available for combat was the regulation service rifle.*

---

*Its inadequacies were more quickly revealed by combat on the Western Front than at home. Ben Travers recalls in his memoirs *A-Sitting on a Gate* (London 1978) that at the end of 1915, as an officer in the Royal Naval Air Service, he met Winston Churchill, First Lord of the Admiralty: 'Information had reached him that the Germans were about to launch the first Zeppelin airship raid on London. He had come to inspect the one Hendon aircraft   [*cont.*]

The war integrated the aircraft, its armaments and ground support into a fighting system, the effectiveness of which was directly related to its technical performance. Inferiority in this respect meant surrendering the initiative and consequently those wider policy options which the initiative confers. So, perhaps more closely than with other arms, policy was tied to the rate of innovation.* This was rapid; in 1917 none of the aircraft which took the field in 1914 was flying. New types and marks succeeded each other in response to demands for improved manoeuvrability and rates of climb, better integration of weapons with the machine and more reliable operational conditions for the crew. The air war resolved itself into competitive escalation between types and into diversification in the roles undertaken by aircraft.

The initiatives conferred by technique were not always realised; they were sometimes surrendered for other reasons. On 1 May 1916, the British fleet at Jutland had only one torpedo-carrying aeroplane, having left behind the *Campania*, a liner converted into an aircraft carrier, in Scapa Flow. In April of the next year, on the Western Front, the Royal Flying Corps was badly beaten over Arras, when its technically superior machines were flown into battle by insufficiently trained pilots – the official view of the RFC commander, General Trenchard, being that they would learn to fight by fighting. The Royal Naval Air Service first began to consider the possibilities of strategic bombing as early as 1915 but had to yield its first bombing force to the demands of the Western Front, where current tactical doctrines of the continuous offensive caused high losses in men and machines. The strategic option was put in abeyance until the Independent Air Force was established in June 1918. Until that time German manufacturing and chemical plants in the Rhineland, which were within range of aircraft based in Northern France, were able to sustain the German effort in the Western Front virtually unscathed.[3]

Britain, in fact, derived nothing like the full benefit which its manufacturing superiority justified. The nascent industry of 1914 employed some 350,000 men and women by the end of the War. The Royal Aircraft Factory began itself to produce aircraft, as well as guide other manufacturers. Total output of the industry was 30,782 aircraft in the first ten months of 1918 – by which time expansion of the air force had already been curtailed by lack of pilots. Excessive losses in France and a high rate of training accidents

---

which had been finally detailed and equipped to engage the enemy, and to admonish its pilot and crew. I was the crew ... He questioned me about my armament, and I exhibited the rifle with which I had been served out for the purpose of shooting down the Zeppelin. I didn't tell him that I had never handled a rifle in my life, and hadn't the slightest idea how to reload it'.

*The problem of firing forward was solved early in 1915 by Roland Garros, who worked out mathematically that only seven per cent of bullets fired from a fixed machine gun would strike the airscrew and could be deflected by protector blades. Garros' aircraft, thus modified, was captured by the Germans after a forced landing – and another transfer of technology took place.

inhibited the flow of volunteers. Building aircraft drew new technologies into the service of war – notably the knowledge of lightweight materials (aluminium and therefore bauxite entered the category of 'essential raw materials'), investigation into alloys for use in engines under combat conditions, and optics (for bomb sights). It also demanded continuous, systematic research. This was the province of the Royal Aircraft Factory and to a lesser extent the Aerodynamics Department of the National Physical Laboratory. Additionally, an official advisory committee on aeronautics suggested promising fields of enquiry. In 1917, the state gave up designing aircraft and engines, on the grounds that relying on private industry would tap a wider pool of inventiveness, but retained and extended its lien on the industry through research and inspection. It controlled its current existence, in that the government, in the form of the War Office (for the Royal Flying Corps) and the Admiralty (for the Royal Naval Air Service) was the only customer, and, after early competitive chaos, allocated materials for production for each service. No civil aircraft were produced; there were no civil airlines. The returns to private manufacturers could not be based on market value for the simple reason that no market existed. Production costs were taken as a basis instead, and with that concept necessarily went the right to inspect manufacturers' accounts. The demands of state policy now stretched into the manufacturer's use of his factors of production. His accountability was no longer restricted to providing a workable system which met the defined requirements, and to that extent his autonomy was abridged. After 1917, the authority of the state, as sole purchaser, was exercised to concentrate manufacture, to produce fewer types of engines and airframes from fewer but larger plants. For this purpose, the state built and equipped 'national factories' on its own account, in which private firms were installed as professional managers.

With the production of aircraft, the overall integration of policy entered a new phase. For the first time in the industrial age, the state related the traditional function of choosing the ends of policy to the means whereby those ends were to be fulfilled, consciously and in advance, and itself controlled each stage in the process, if necessary from research onwards. Should the state decide that its political ends could be met by strategic bombing, then the state's requirements governed the design of the bomber. The state might own the facilities on which the aircraft was built; met the costs even if it did not own them, and provided the only customer, the air force. This happened in a country synonymous with private enterprise and *laisser faire*. After the war, the pattern remained in essentials, though scaled down and with slack relationships between its component parts. The aircraft industry never sloughed off its wartime origin.

Prolonged industrialised war promoted mass organisation and centralised government. The state took charge of the economy, ridding itself of all particularisms, as far as it could, and converting to its own use what had hitherto been accepted as the guaranteed rights of private individuals. By the end of hostilities, all the major combatants were operating regimes of industrial conscription, justified by the need to sustain the war effort for so long at such intensity. In the long term, the beneficiaries of this wartime change were the military and industrial managers and organised labour. The mobilisation of rights and the priority given to collective values did not allow any more than the partial restoration of the liberal individualism which had flourished till 1914, and ten years after the peace treaties, the Depression gave *that* the *coup de grâce*.

The re-ordering of social groups and classes is a familiar consequence of upheaval, but the war, specifically, demonstrated that the traditional theories about the relationship of civil to military authority were no longer tenable. Between 1914 and 1918, in the accepted vocabulary of all the European combatants, 'military' and 'civil' came to stand for the 'battle front' and the 'home front'. During the Crimean War, and in the campaigns in Bohemia in 1866 and Eastern France in 1870, the home provided troops and sustenance, but it was not in itself a 'front'. Now the military vocabulary aptly applied to domestic affairs. In Germany, civil authority capitulated to military. Under the Hindenburg Programme, the 'home front' came under military rule, with the Kaiser in his civil as well as his political function, his civil ministers and the Reichstag, for all practical purposes, pushed aside. The theoretical benefits were not, in the event, realised. Ludendorff's political sensitivity was inversely proportional to his military capacity. In France and Britain, civil authority was maintained, though not without difficulty and at the expense of a well-coordinated policy. Leading generals frequently regarded cabinet ministers with suspicion and contempt, which was as often reciprocated. Personalities apart, the machinery for coordinating policies had to adapt itself to a strategy which in the course of hostilities broke out of the European confines in which it had been originally conceived to become worldwide. The problems which presented themselves were unprecedented in complexity and scale – which explains, if it does not excuse, the fumbling and duplication which marked the administration of the war among all the combatants.

However, just as the *coup d'oeuil* was no longer sufficient on the battlefield, so decisions about policy could no longer be summed up by generals or foreign ministry officials. The relationship between military and foreign policy was expressed – often fought out – in committees and boards – the characteristic apparatus of bureaucracy. The military in all states may have distrusted or hated the civilians but they had to bow to their methods. The difference, compared with 1914, was not only of scale but of composition. Industrialists and representatives of organised labour were admitted to the formulation of policy, since they were indispensable to carrying it out. Industry was now intrinsic to the relationship between what was thought desirable and what could, in fact, be done.

The corollaries shaped the relationship between industry and the state. The state could not allow industry either to come under foreign control or go bankrupt – two vital breaches of the liberal economic order. Furthermore, the state as such could not permit the private establishments of individual industrialists to be the unsupervised repository of technical progress: it demanded a hand of some kind in the development of technique. To a degree, this demand implied subsidy or guaranteed prices for output. Concern for technique was parallelled by care for the national reserves of skills: the state could not be indifferent to the range of skills available or to the education and training which produced them, in view of their demon-strable contribution to national survival.

None of these changes meant that the distinctions between 'peace' and 'war' had been erased or that the industry indispensable to the prosecution of war was, by that fact alone, on a war footing. Time remained an essential ingredient in policy. Plant, except for the production of some gases, could not be converted to war purposes overnight. But the experience of industrialised war enabled the state to tighten its grip on society and make industry more responsive to its demands.

The extent and complexity of the change appears from comparisons with previous wars, within the lifetime of men who lived through the years from 1914 to 1918. For some, the Crimea was part of their experience. Hindenburg, who during the War achieved the status of a somewhat synthetic *pater patriae*, had received his first decoration for gallantry under fire at Sadowa. Clemenceau had been mayor of Montmartre during the siege of 1870/71. These earlier wars had encouraged reform of the military forces, or of the political order of society, at most; they had no further ramifications. The military was the military; politics was politics and industry was industry. They combined reciprocally but otherwise were segregated.

By 1918, it was apparent to both victors and vanquished that a war effort conducted in terms of limited professional manpower, over a relatively restricted terrain and relying on the inventiveness which a few industrialists might provide through their firms was no longer adequate to the ends of foreign policy. Henceforward, war had to be 'total': it would draw on the potentialities of the economy to the point of exhaustion, and would, as the experience of Germany showed, carry with it the risk of making defeat equally total.

PART V

1919–1939

'In war, the confidence ... which a victorious army contracts ... and the dejection of spirit which a subdued party undergoes ... is not at an end when the war is determined, but hath its effects very long after; and the tenderness of nature and the integrity of manners which are driven away ... by war are not quickly recovered: but instead thereof a roughness, jealousy and distrust introduced that makes conversation unpleasant and uneasy, and the weeds which grow up ... can hardly be pulled up ... without a long and unsuspected peace.'

Lord Clarendon, 1670

1. New states – new conflicts – new definitions

The First World War began as a limited dispute over spheres of influence among dynastic powers; it ended as a crusade for democracy, as defined by President Wilson. It was, for many, 'the war to end war' – a slogan expressing an ideal which ruled out compromise. As such, it set in motion a comprehensive reassessment of the values applied to international behaviour. War had ceased to be an honourable exercise or the ultimate arbitrament and had become a squalid and protracted butchery, and one moreover, of which the results were wholly disproportionate to the efforts and sacrifices involved. Article 231 of the Treaty of Versailles, ascribing guilt for the holocaust exclusively to Imperial Germany, demonstrated this new attitude towards war – if war is honourable in itself, guilt can only attach to breaking its laws, not to engaging in war as such – at the price of making the treaties as a whole unacceptable to large and influential bodies of opinion inside Germany and outside.

In contrast to the genuine enthusiasm for war which prevailed in 1914, war itself came to be widely considered to be a repudiation of the moral order. The ease with which German policy at successively crucial turns had been determined by purely pragmatic considerations – the original violation of the neutrality of Belgium, the introduction of gas and of unrestricted submarine warfare – seemed to prove the contention. The attempts of German jurists to prove that 'neutral' did not mean 'inviolable' when applied to Belgium, though it did when applied to Switzerland, and that resort to gas was justified because the Hague Convention only banned gas shells, not the practice of releasing gas from stationary cylinders, were taken as evidence that even German legal judgement had been corrupted by the unrestrained reliance on technique. Allied responses which went beyond the acknowledged right to retaliate only furnished further evidence that the contagion was universal, and that embattled states no longer subscribed to a common code which could mitigate the harshness of war. The technology of war had defeated the morality of war, as understood in 1914. War was, simply, evil.

The reaction in these terms was so extreme that in many quarters any attempt to examine war objectively as a form of human behaviour was excoriated as 'militarism' and 'war-mongering'. This revulsion helped, paradoxically, to limit the rational negotiation of claims at the peace settlement, since it was almost universally held to be monstrous that the dead had died and the maimed been crippled for life, in numbers totalling millions, merely for frontier rectifications in Central Europe and the Balkans. The Wilsonian principle of self-determination was expected to usher in an era of peace and freedom but it was applied in an atmosphere of hatred inseparable from a crusade and limited by considerations of strategy. So in spite of the creditable attempts by the major powers to reorganise Europe on a defensible basis of nationality, the territorial arrangements finally arrived at were a jumble of principle and expediency, which wrecked whatever chances the principle may have had of being generally accepted. National self-determination could not be allowed to work to the benefit of Germany (in Upper Silesia) or Austria (in the Tyrol) or Hungary (in Transylvania) for reasons of security, real or alleged. Europe was henceforward divided into two categories of states, 'satisfied' and 'revisionist'.

These terms did not entirely coincide with 'victors' and 'vanquished'. D'Annunzio coined the phase 'mutilated victory' for Italy, but it applied to France and to all states to which the treaties gave less than a combination of strategy and nationalism demanded.

The terms of the Peace Treaties themselves expressed this paradoxical situation. Through the Covenant of the League of Nations they canalised the widespread revulsion against war, but through their territorial clauses they recognised the existence of seven new states, Poland, Czechoslovakia, Estonia, Latvia, Lithuania, Finland, and the 'Kingdom of Serbs, Croats, and Slovenes', and the enlargement of Romania into what was virtually a new state – all of which automatically increased the potential for armed conflict. In the case of Poland and Czechoslovakia (over the Teschen district) Poland and Lithuania (over Vilna) and Italy and Jugoslavia (over Fiume), the potentiality was soon realised.

These clashes demonstrate that the new states did not enter a pristine Wilsonian world but into the time-honoured competition. Their first task was to create armies and para-military forces for defence, or to exert leverage in confused postwar situations. So although, as creations of the League, the new states tended to use it as a forum for foreign policy rather more readily than the older powers, they were, as their practice soon showed, only conditionally prepared to be pacific, in the League's sense, and acquired weapons for their forces, either from the states under whose patronage they had emerged, or from the vast surplus which remained after the Armistice. This situation was used by France in pursuit of its own security, which was defined in terms of frontier defence (a demili-tarised Rhineland and what became the Maginot Line), a large army, inter-national pacts, and a system of alliances with the territorial beneficiaries of the Peace Treaties, (Poland, Czechoslovakia and Romania). All these demanded or were underwritten by armaments.

The fact of creating new states endowed with sovereign authority would by itself have militated against the pacific intentions of the framers of the treaties. What turned an implicit tendency into a dominant actuality of European politics was the Treaties' provisions for frontiers. About 7,000 miles of new frontiers in Central Europe converted prewar tensions between minorities into postwar hostility between states. The minorities became sovereign and the metamorphosis gave their leaders the recognised military option which they formerly lacked. Additionally, these national sovereignties were democracies, at least in the minimum sense that their governments had at least to appear to attend to the *vox populi* from time to time through elections. But these same electorates, by definition, were the beneficiaries or victims of the frontier settlements, so that their political leaders could not 'write off' the frontier dissatisfactions, in the interest of peace and stability, even if they wished. To that degree their foreign and, by implication, military, policy was inflexible.

Italy offers a useful, but by no means unique, case in point. The frontier adjustments in Italy's favour envisaged by the Treaty of London in 1915, represented the maximum concessions the *Entente* was prepared to make – and even then with some reservations on the part of Britain. But the disaster of Caporetto supervened, and Italian leaders galvanised the nation into recovery by whipping up an unyielding nationalism. Thus, by 1918, the maximum conditions at the time of signature became the minimum conditions which Orlando considered he could convey to the Italian people to justify the sacrifices of their participation in the war. The argument was accepted by President Wilson, even at the expense of the principle of national self-determination. Italy thus acquired a disaffected German-speaking minority and an irredentist problem in the north, and a series of inflammable disputes with Jugoslavia along the coast of Dalmatia. Neither problem discouraged the thought of resort to arms to settle it.

The treaties, by committing League members to seeking non-violent solutions to problems of foreign policy, contemplated a break with the inheritance of inter-state war, but by creating new states they in fact multiplied the possibilities of its taking place and, through the residue of unsolved nationalist feuds, provided the issues. Vendettas between minorities fostered the hopes and actions of those who saw in embittered nationalism a means of overthrowing the established order completely. The *Freikorps* in Germany, *Squadristi* in Italy and Communist groups in Munich, Budapest and elsewhere, advocated violence as a means of national or social renewal. Peaceful solutions were inadmissible, or irrelevant.

Similarly, the economic order of postwar Europe was more closely related to wartime developments than was generally supposed. Liberal capitalism proved incompatible with prolonged industrialised conflict. Prudence and the long view in expenditures were sacrificed to expansion regardless of cost and to short-term expedients. Concentration and scale were the hallmarks of the new industrial patterns and were brought about by the initiative and pressure of the state. The war elevated standardisation and technique and, as a concomitant, the bureaucracy to control the process. The central bureau and the classification system were the necessary counterpart to the production of standardised goods. The state itself became an entrepreneur, or at least an investor, and entered the field of business management.

In this development, property rights, from which liberal economic reasoning flowed, were conscripted for war. Assets were expropriated or compulsorily purchased; the rights to manage were divorced from the rights of ownership; owners of foreign securities were required to surrender them to allow the state to pay its overseas debts. These actions proved not a suspension of liberalism but a fundamental breach of its principles; and they applied not only within states but also to their external economic relations. The peace treaties provided for the expropriation without compensation of specified German assets seized as a special indemnity for France and Belgium, or on account of reparations. Those who summarily lost their property had to look to the German Government for any satisfaction of their claims: the governments where the assets were located disclaimed all responsibility. Such non-recognition of the private property of enemy nationals was a new principle in the international economy and demonstrates how decisively the premises of economic liberalism had succumbed to the stress of war. Economic liberalism could not be restored, not because of the destruction of physical assets or the disruption of established trading patterns but because the basic philosophical premises on which it rested were regarded as no longer valid.

The war strengthened the hold of the state over the economic process. Expanded production during wartime was demonstrably uneconomic in peacetime; should it be destroyed or subsidised? The demands of national security as well as the promptings of unionised labour suggested the latter. In the new countries of Central and Eastern Europe, the state itself was the main or even the only source of capital for reconstruction. Additionally, currencies were unstable and non-convertible. The state therefore involved itself in investment and trade. The pan-European economy of 1914 was broken up and 'the international market' became the aggregate of national markets.

Thus, from about 1916 onwards, the main variables in this argument, the 'state', the 'economy' and 'industry' took on a new meaning. The postwar state expected to play a more positive, directing role even in a country like Britain, where conditions before 1914 continued to provide a potent image of perfection. There is no convenient descriptive label for the configurations of the economy at this time. 'War socialism' was partly dismantled but the economic disruption of Europe consequent on the war inhibited a return to the economy of 1914. Production units in heavy industry and chemicals increased in size and range of product during the war: rather than split up the assets, managements, encouraged by government, preferred to merge and rationalise their undertakings. The firms which survived were more in the hands of managers than of shareholders. The profile of industry changed, since many smaller or family-based firms were squeezed out. In Europe, the major producers re-established or extended cartels and other combined arrangements to introduce some stability into their operations and offset some of the more glaring economic irrationalities of the Versailles settlements. Concentration and organisation of production to meet unstable market conditions worked in favour of government which, for social and economic reasons, wished to furnish subsidies to industry and required easy accountability in return. In fact, after the war, it became very difficult to establish where officialdom ended and private enterprise began. To call the resultant *mélange* 'capitalism' is misleading, if the term connotes a clear distinction between the private and the public sectors. What happened during the years of attempted recovery and even before the Depression, was that the relationship between the state and industry which, before the war, had been devised for weapons production, was extended more generally throughout industry as a whole.

2. 'Aggression', its prevention and costs: the lessons of world war

The war produced a literature of enquiry into its origins. Much of the writing is so polemical as to be of psychological rather than analytical interest, particularly in regard to the curious inversion of values it demonstrates. What had, in 1910, been considered natural, intelligent cooperation between French and German banks, became in 1920 treasonable collusion with the enemy: the German achievement in history, philosophy and science which had been the admiration of Europe in 1914 was widely considered, five years later, to have been merely the mask of a brutal 'Prussianism' which had destroyed the Library of Louvain as a reprisal. The easy prewar cosmopolitanism of the mind was among the casualties. The enquiry, however, went beyond the real or assumed characteristics of the world before 1914 into the causes of war as such. Widely blamed, in this category, were 'the international anarchy' and the system of privately-owned manufacturing enterprise. To compress the various criticisms: it was confidently asserted that Armageddon had come because narrowly egotistical dynastic states, run by militarist oligarchies encouraged by bourgeois enterprise, had clashed in pursuit of hegemony; additionally or alternately, it had been deliberately promoted by armament manufacturers in the search for profits.

The League of Nations underwrote both sets of arguments. Its very existence challenged the assumptions of the pre-war international order, which its policies aimed to replace. The Versailles Treaty introduced into the international vocabulary a new category of war, 'aggressive war', which was different from war as hitherto understood and which was held to merit particular retribution. In the Treaty, the new concept was used to justify the demand for reparations, on the premise that the war had been imposed on the Allies by Germany's long-premeditated attack in 1914. This thesis was the easier to sustain in that one party to the events of that summer, Tsarist Russia, had disappeared. 'Aggression', therefore, related to the invasion of France via Belgium and Luxembourg, not to the invasion of East Prussia by France's ally. Ludendorff complained in his memoirs that it had been impossible to convince the German public that the attack in the west in the summer of 1914 was a *defensive* strategy. The publics of France, Belgium and Britain were equally unconvinced, and assumed that the attacker was the aggressor.

This assumption was afterwards much debated by the League of Nations, with no conclusive result. It proved impossible to define an 'aggressor' for the purpose of international action.

Even so, the debates produced general agreement that aggression could not be defined as straightforwardly as had appeared in 1919, that it encompassed not simply violation of territory but included violation of accepted political preconditions. Unilaterally closing an area already publicly notified as vital by another state, or cutting off access to its customary sources of supply, could constitute aggression even if no troops moved at all. Conversely, a military attack could be a legitimate *response* to an act of aggression in the political sense – in which case the attacker was not the aggressor, even if his forces moved first. Aggression, in fact, was not a military but a political concept, which became vaguer as it was applied to legal or economic affairs. Its core was military, and aggression retained a military connotation, since aggressive behaviour was likely to invoke military action at some stage or other.

The debates tried to define aggression in other ways, as, for example, armed action flouting a general resolution of the League, or by examining the characteristics and use of weapons, in order to discriminate between those which were designed to facilitate aggression ('offensive') and those intended to deter or repel it ('defensive'). The distinction proved as elusive as the definition of aggression itself, and many man hours were spent in trying to square these concepts with the requirements of individual sovereign states.

Irrespective of the approach adopted, the public debates about aggressive war as a concept of international politics necessarily took in the industrialised basis of warfare. The answers to aggressive war were twofold: sanctions, to hamstring military operations by concerted denial of their material requirements, and disarmament, which was intended ultimately to rule out offensive operations altogether. Sanctions were to be embodied in agreements to deprive any state disregarding the League procedure for the pacific settlement of disputes by means of a collective rupture of trade and financial relationships, to be backed by collective force. Obvious items of international trade which came into question were raw materials, particularly fuels and non-ferrous metals, in which no state was self-sufficient. In the 1920s even the United States, in other respects the best-endowed industrial state, relied on imports for such essential minerals as manganese, nickel, antimony and tungsten. Sanctions could only be successful if deprivation was automatic and total. The relevant article of the Covenant (XVI), however, diminished the potentialities of sanctions by limiting the Council of the League to *suggesting* to members what action should be taken, and even a suggestion had to proceed from a *unanimous* decision. Experts and publicists examined the range and type of prohibitive measure, concentrating their attention on the lessons of German capitulation to blockade. They paid less regard to the equally pertinent question as to how a state lacking natural nitrates, rubber and mercury, and with virtually no chrome or nickel had managed to hold out for so long. Their analyses tended to stress the consequences of deprivation at the expense of the reserves which the mobilisation of resources could disclose and the devising of substitutes could provide. It was also assumed that the imposition of sanctions would 'cost' the sanctioning states little or nothing, though it was recognised that in special cases the continued operation of their industries might well depend on finding substitute sources of supply or alternative markets; in these contingencies, the flexibility of the international economy could be relied upon to ease any short-term difficulties.

The course of international politics in the inter-war years showed, precisely, that problems of finding alternative outlets or suppliers, and the administrative lacunae in the League scheme, gave plenty of scope to individual states hesitant or unwilling to apply sanctions. The possibilities of concerted deprivation, however, promoted theories of warfare designed to avoid its adverse consequences; if resources were likely to be finite or to be cut down, even by half-hearted international action, then it was necessary to devise means of destroying an enemy quickly, before accumulated stocks were exhausted. The paradox of the sanctions debate was, therefore, that it fostered the *Blitzkrieg*.

Disarmament, similarly, failed to fulfil the hopes of its advocates. Before 1914, it had been sporadically discussed in multilateral conferences, as at The Hague in 1899 and 1907, or in bilateral negotiations, as in the attempts to slow down the Anglo-German naval race; but the League put disarmament consistently on the international agenda from 1919 to 1934, on the grounds that the maintenance of peace required control over national armaments which was enforceable by common action. Disarmament was interpreted in two ways; 'reduction', which implied cutting down overall numbers of men or classes of weapons over a specified period, and 'limitation', by which numbers or classes of weapons could not be increased above negotiated levels. Both reduction and limitation divided into various sub-categories which occupied negotiators at Geneva and elsewhere till rearmament became general, following the Japanese occupation of Manchuria and the advent of the Hitler regime in Germany. Apart from the scope which the glosses of the subject allowed to negotiators to protect specific national interests, disarmament was not achieved because it played a different role in the policies of the different states. To France and her allies, disarmament was one aspect of the overriding consideration of security, and was acceptable only in forms which preserved the *status quo* established at Versailles. For other states, notably Germany (even before Hitler), Italy, Turkey and Japan, disarmament was an opportunity to achieve equality of status with other states in the international competition. This disparity alone frustrated ultimate international agreement.

The League had slightly more success over the private manufacture of armaments. The signatories of the Covenant had to recognise that private manufacture was open to 'grave objections'. They accordingly attempted to control the activity at its marketing end, by taking powers to supervise and control arms traffic. Between 1919 and 1935, negotiations under one rubric or another of manufacture and trade were almost continuously in progress: they achieved much by way of clarification and definition; little or nothing as regards the ultimate objective. This outcome merely testifies to the fact that the supply of arms was (and is) sustained by the system of sovereign states, compared with which a manufacturer's or trader's pursuit of profit is almost an epiphenomenon!

By implication, however, the League favoured a new relationship between industry and the state: manufacture should be nationalised or under such control that trading should take place between governments only, to eliminate 'the competitive zeal of private arms firms,' which 'promoted' war. The verb chosen was important. By its use, the League carefully suggested that private competition furthered the development of war but was only one factor among others. Many contemporaries missed this nuance. They read 'promote' as meaning that peace could be maintained when, and only when, the manufacture and trade in arms was carried on by the state. This was the vital but all-sufficient condition. This conclusion was shared by pacifist and socialist opinion (when they did not otherwise overlap). Socialists argued that the weapons industries, by reason of their 'advanced' character, offered the most suitable means to their doctrinally-defined end of controlling the economy as a whole.

Pacifist and socialist accusations against private manufacture were prominent in the general attack on the pre-war system. The case, which was elaborated as a whole, involved maintaining, variously, that 'socialist' or 'democratic' states were inherently more pacific than 'capitalist' or 'monarchist'; that new states were peaceable in a way in which old states, corrupted by centuries of power politics, were not; that national states were morally superior to multinational empires, and, at a different level of argument, that Krupp before 1914 was engaged in a peculiarly nefarious activity, while Schneider was not. That such arguments were intellectually *simpliste* when they were not merely tendentious or dishonest, merely increased their political appeal.

They did, however, betray the realisation that command of raw materials and of engineering capacity were indispensable to the waging of modern war, that the concept of 'the nation in arms' was true in a more comprehensive sense than envisaged in the rhetoric of revolution. Military strength was to be assessed no longer solely by reference to armament, trained manpower and their related expenditures, but more fundamentally, by the industrial and economic power of the state. By 1938, Neville Chamberlain was suggesting in the House of Commons that economic power by itself was a deterrent – a view which proved erroneous, since it left out of consideration the type of war and the rapidity of industrial mobilisation. But the nexus between raw materials and engineering and the capacity to resort to war as an option of policy was firmly established. It became common ground between the supporters of 'the system' and their critics.

The extent to which engineering impressed itself on the imagination was demonstrated by the various apologias and critiques of the events of July 1914 which began to be published. They dwelt predominantly on the mechanisms by which the two alliances went to war and not on the psychological or administrative pressures on the politicians and bureaucrats who had been involved in trying to manage the crisis. But perhaps the most telling demonstration of the speed with which what was regarded as the basic lesson of the war (that it was won by superior industrial capacity) was assimilated, was the stream of publications in which the characteristics of any new conflict were analysed, both by those who in some sense or other thought it necessary and by those who abhorred the very idea. Like their pre-war predecessors, the analysts compared and contrasted the demographic factors (which the allied policy of repeated offensives on the Western Front had shifted in favour of Germany), but they now went beyond population trends to cover the entire economies of the contending states sector by sector. The economy as a whole had to be mobilised, not merely men in certain age groups. Material of the right quality was all-important, which called for the organisation of manufacture and distribution throughout the entire economy. Skills were as indispensable as machinery. Technological advance in the form of aerial and chemical warfare, separately and in combination, now extended the battlefront behind the fighting line.

The logical conclusions from these arguments were disturbing. If war was to be 'total', the civilian lost his hallowed status; he could no longer claim exemption from attack, and the entire structure of nineteenth-century assumptions about relations between the civil and military aspects of society was called in question. If the means of war came from the factories of industry as a whole and not just from identifiable state arsenals, and if the factories were located in towns, were towns 'civil' or 'military' objectives?* At what point did a workman, *en route* from his home to his job in a factory cease to be a non-combatant, particularly if he had been exempted from conscription into the armed forces on the ground of his skills? The answers in each case favoured the military interpretation. Much of the argument about

---

*In 1918, the King of Spain attempted to negotiate an arrangement by which the Germans and the Allies mutually undertook to refrain from bombing towns. He failed, but in the same year, Sir Hugh Trenchard was forbidden to undertake bombing operations on the festival of Corpus Christi. Was this the last vestige of 'the Truce of God'?

the bombing of cities in the Second World War ignores the fact that from 1919 onwards, cities were categorised as 'military'.

The industrial implications of war began to break down the accepted categories of law and international relations. Their traditional terms took on new meanings: war construed as aggression (and all wars became aggressions) required special counter-measures beyond those which had ruled hitherto; civilians no longer stood in unequivocal contrast to the military, exempt from the sanctions applicable to military personnel and installations: arms manufacture no longer related to the production of weapons only, but reached into the industrial structure of the nation and its import and export policies; neutrals, as we have seen, were no longer outside the conflict by definition, but were simply non-combatant participants.

Henceforward, the industrial analysis of war comprised two distinct series of problems – the potential for and preparation of war as an act of state (which was traditional), and the behaviour of the economy during wartime (which was novel). Since planning for war affected the possibilities of peace, the first series of problems received the greater public attention. 'War potential' entered into negotiations on disarmament, the acquisition of raw materials and the regulation of international industry. The second series had no similar impact: it remained the province of a few specialists. If, however, war was to be total and likely to be prolonged, then the essential task was to relate means which were finite to ends which were competing with one another. Put in this form, the analysis of war involved economists and statisticians. The initial work appeared in the memoirs of those who, as administrators or managers, had had to tackle the new economic challenges between 1914 and 1918. Subsequently, a few academics not wholly preoccupied with the trade cycle began to discuss the lessons of wartime experience and their implications for the future. Professional concern, however, took in not just the economic factors permitting or sustaining war as one option in a range of policies open to the state but also the practice of war itself. Analysis of weapons and their capabilities itself suggested that some combinations of weapons were to be preferred to others in relation to the foreign policy intentions and economic strength of the state. The implication of this discovery was that economic policy began, not with conventional economic factors as set out in the textbooks, but with military theory and the characteristics of weapons. 'Total war' by itself meant very little, and referred to the mobilisation of effort (rather than its effect on the enemy) but, even so, it did not indicate priorities. What the economy would be required to do during wartime depended directly on the type of war the state proposed to wage, which in turn depended on theories, that is, unproved general propositions, as to the destructive or deterrent effect of specific weapons or combinations of weapons. The latter involved some grasp of trends in technology. In this way, theory suggested the tasks the economy was required to perform.

This approach was elaborated piecemeal in some of the technical literature of the inter-war period but was systematically explored only in 1938 by Stephen Possony in *Tomorrow's War, Its Planning, Management and Cost*. Possony set out 'to give an exact, that is a numerical, basis to the discussion of the organisation of the economy for war,' on the assumption that there was a reciprocal relationship between the duty of the economy 'to further the defence of the country' and the duty of the army 'to keep its demands within the bounds of possibility and to adapt the principles of defence to reality.' War could no longer be planned in the expectation of limitless drafts on the national capital. The emphasis was new, and had a disturbing corollary for planners. If the economy was not a cornucopia of military supply, then it was necessary to establish just what kind of war it would allow them to wage. Which weapons and combinations of weapons were 'within the bounds of possibility' but would at the same time further the foreign policy aims of the state? In seeking an answer to this question, all states ran up against economic and industrial limits.

A statistical examination of the evidence available in 1938 from the Great War, the Italian operations in Ethiopia and the Civil War in Spain showed that the requirements of modern war were so vast that no state (not even the US) had in fact in a serious war covered them from its own resources, even though the degree of that cover varied, and that no country's volume of production was in the least sufficient to cover its envisaged wartime requirements. Governments were thus forced into strategic compromises, based on a 'mixture' of weapons, the preferences for which could be suggested by a statistical demonstration of their effectiveness. Strategies based on aerial bombing, for example, needed to take into account that it was less economical than artillery bombardment – in terms of explosions delivered on target, the ratio was about 1:10. If infantry was to be the main arm, then the past evidence of casualty rates in attack and defence suggested that its primary strength was defensive 'for no rational person can regard as "decisive" a weapon whose only problem consists . . . in how to get it over the last three hundred metres.' Comparative studies of tank attacks respectively supported and unsupported by artillery demonstrated that the two arms must cooperate to stand a chance of achieving their objectives. Fashionable general theories as to the value of strategic bombing as the quick decisive weapon* also failed to stand up to statistical enquiry into the various elements of which air attacks were composed: the aircraft as a means of delivery which was unstable, affected by weather and navigational hazards, the bomb as a free-falling method of conveying an explosion, and active and passive measures of anti-aircraft defence.

Possony concluded that the effects of modern warfare remained far

---

*see below, pages 201ff.

behind the expenditure involved: therefore states had to adopt the criterion of the 'profitableness' of various types of warfare, in evaluating their strategic options. That would suggest the related tasks for the economy. In Part II of his book, he enters into the familiar topics of organising the economy discussed by theorists of 'total war' since 1919.

Possony has obvious affinities with Bloch, even though not engaged in the same type of enquiry. Bloch deduced the logical effects of an unprecedented increase in firepower on the likelihood of achieving a decision in war: Possony analysed the entailments of choices between weapons – hence between strategies – and their respective demands on the economy. He argued that in the end states must choose the strategy they can afford. He denied that he was writing a prescription for military planners: he and they were dealing with fundamental uncertainty. *'The* modus pugnandi *of the next war is completely uncertain. It is equally uncertain which weapons will be superfluous or necessary and which will need to be redesigned.** At the present stage . . . each weapon has its prophet. Which prophet will turn out to be right nobody knows, and . . . no-one engaged in organising the economy for war knows either'.

Some of Possony's inferences were shown to be invalid by the war which broke out in Europe the year after his book was published. He overestimated the importance of blockade in disrupting production: he underestimated the effects of technological improvements such as bomb sights (though, as experience showed, the effects were late in coming): he concluded that strategies of attrition were to be preferred to strategies of destruction. But his views about tank warfare, that tanks had to be used together in large numbers (not dispersed among infantry formations) supported by auxiliary weapons and 'vertical artillery' quickly translated into the Panzer divisions with dive bombers which were effectively used by the German army in the summer of 1940; his criticisms of strategic bombing theories were generally substantiated by enquiry after the war (though this is still a contentious issue).** The importance of *Tomorrow's War* lies not so much in its detailed conclusions as in its approach. Possible strategies were broken down into the weapons on which they would rely: the weapons themselves were examined as complex units in relation to the conditions and the environments in which it would be 'profitable' to use them. Decisions on these questions yielded a hierarchy of tasks for industry and bridged the gap between what the military wanted to achieve and what the economy could deliver.

Possony's approach has become standard to the point of being commonplace – the hallmark of successful pioneering. Contemporary analysts

---

*Italics in original.
**see below, pages 234ff.

have redefined 'profitableness' as 'cost-effectiveness' and have elaborated a whole technique of military planning on this concept. However, he had no official standing and addressed the military defensively, disclaiming any intention to interfere in their professional concerns. He offered a series of conditional judgements deriving from the fact that questions of war, in some aspects, could be reduced to numbers and were therefore open to discussion by anyone capable of drawing logical conclusions. His successors are employed in ministries and institutes funded by governments for the express purpose of shaping decisions on strategy.

That statistical inference should determine which weapons forces received, and which not, might have affronted service chiefs the more had they not been embattled over their own assessments of the consequences of industrialisation for their trade. Those who accepted its lessons most radically argued that the internal combustion engine had created a new set of relationships between force and time, and therefore marked a new era in strategy. On land the mobility and range characteristic of the tank and the aircraft made warfare a matter of areas rather than fronts. The patterns of future combat were indicated by the last phase of the war on both sides. All experience prior to that phase of operations was to be jettisoned, or considered only in the light of what *not* to do. If the tactics in vogue till then were taken as a model, then forces would get bloodily and uselessly bogged down, as between 1915 and 1917, with no hope of meeting chosen strategic or political objectives. These propositions were vehemently denied by the more conservative leaders who drew from the war a conception of warfare which relied on static positions combined with infantry combats in pre-selected areas. 'Fronts' were where the battle took place and the issue decided. All other arms and techniques were useful but ancillary. Infantry remained the primary arm, and the traditional role of cavalry had not been invalidated by technical developments – a view which, as critics pointed out, depended on the invention of a bulletproof horse.

At sea, the staples of a similar debate were the aircraft and the submarine, and the battleship. One school of thought held that the larger the ship, the easier the target for aircraft armed with bombs or torpedoes. The old adage that navies were only as effective as their facilities were secure from attack needed to be reinterpreted in the light of the air weapon. Smaller, dispersed facilities implied smaller ships: battleships were vulnerable at sea and in harbour; they tied up too many resources at too great a risk: their construction should be discontinued. More orthodox opinion considered that war at sea would require concentrations of firepower which only a battleship could carry; the air could provide reconnaissance and protection, if naval aviation were under the firm control of the navy and not of an independent air force. Within air forces, the upper echelons of command were agreed on the supreme importance of the air, but debated fiercely the priorities to be given to its strategic and tactical roles respectively, and the modes of cooperation with earth-bound forces.

The debates were inconclusive because the lessons which could have provided the clinching arguments were from battles which had not taken place. The action off Jutland on 31 May–1 June 1916 was not the grand clash between two line-of-battle fleets which the Royal Navy and the Imperial German Navy had for years believed was their *raison d'être*; it was a running action, marked by the successful escape of the numerically weaker from the numerically stronger. The dreadnoughts on which so much money and propaganda had been spent were not fully engaged. After the war, therefore, no-one was able to *prove* from experience that the line-of-battle ship was a clumsy, expensive and ineffective way of exercising power at sea since it put too many resources at risk. The evidence from Jutland could be read either way – to justify continued reliance on battleships or not.

It was similarly the case with tanks.

A frontage of ninety miles should be selected . . . then the area lying between the lines connecting up the . . . Army Headquarters and those linking their Divisional Headquarters will form the zone of the primary tactical objective . . . Without any warning whatsoever, fleets of . . . tanks should proceed at top speed by day, or possibly by night, directly on the the various Headquarters lying in the primary tactical zone, . . . these targets can be marked by aeroplanes. . . . Every available bombing machine should concentrate on the various supply and road centres. The signal communications should not be destroyed, for it is important that the confusion resulting from the dual attack carried out by . . . tanks and aeroplanes should be circulated by the enemy. Bad news confuses, confusion stimulates panic. . . . Directly penetration has been effected, pursuit should follow, the pursuing force consisting of . . . tanks and lorry-carried infantry. To render this force doubly powerful, it should be preceded by squadrons of tanks which will secure all centres of communication, break up hostile Army Group Headquarters and disperse all formed bodies of troops met with. The . . . GHQ should be dealt with by dropping several hundred tons of explosives on it; that at least will neutralise clear thinking.[1]

This reads like a loosely translated extract from an early draft of a plan for a Panzer division in the attack on France in 1940: in fact, it is taken (with necessary excisions) from a paper written in the spring of 1918 about the next year's decisive invasion of Germany. The campaign of 1919 did not take place, so there was no test which could have provided conclusive evidence as to the merits of using tanks and aircraft combined in this way, rather than in smaller formations as ancillaries to infantry. After the summer of 1940, no one was left in any doubt.

The debate about strategic bombing was slightly more realistic in that some long-range attacks had taken place. Most aircraft, however, had been used tactically in cooperation with armies or navies, and advocates of independent air forces as war-winners found themselves arguing from too slender a basis of experience; their main arguments were more abstract and had to rely on the characteristics of the weapon itself – flexibility, ease of concentration and offensive capabilities – all of which together, it was maintained, demanded that bombers should be used as a combined and therefore independent force and not dissipated in small numbers under the tactical command of non-airmen. This reasoning was true, if at all, only through assumptions and not through the proofs made available by experience. In the world of action, the strength and validity of an assumption depend in part at least on who is making it.

These were not merely controversies between professionals about technical matters and of concern only to the participants. Their conclusions bore directly on state policy. How the forces were composed, and in regard to what contingencies, were questions which affected what the state could do or contemplate in its foreign relations. The relationship had always existed, in the sense that a company of archers was useless for assaulting a fortress. What was new in the 1920s and 1930s was that the relationship became more complex and decisions more difficult to arrive at, because national preparedness raised problems about resources on a wholly new scale. Investment in one strategy began to infringe on the scope of others.

Before 1914, France, Germany and Britain had all been rich enough to afford what technique had made available. Now their governments began to discover that, impoverished by the war and constrained by increasing popular demands for welfare, they were no longer able to cover all the options equally. It was necessary to select. The outcome to that process, however, as shown in the share-out of military budgets, depended not on calm deliberation but on inter-service politics. These were embittered by the introduction of air forces, which cut across traditional loyalties and upset established priorities. How could the air weapon be fitted in to the traditional structure of forces? Or was it a 'superforce' of its own, which in view of its unique capacity to destroy and terrorise, logically merited an absolute priority? Basic disagreement about what air power could or could not accomplish obstructed the formulation of settled policies for all forces, and therefore of the foreign policy to which they could apply.

In Britain, the debate about the type of forces was related to the question of whether Britain would take a major part in continental operations or whether available resources should be channelled into sea and air forces, leaving the army suitable only for ancillary operations in Europe. The nature and extent of the alliances and other undertakings which Britain could offer followed from the answers. In France, the dominant preference for a large land army supported by its own aviation and operating in relation to fixed defences dictated the nature of the country's relations with Belgium. The military restrictions of the Versailles Treaty, even though partly evaded, narrowed the debate in Germany. Fixed defences were out of the question; the planners had to choose mobility, and did so in the forms of the aircraft and the tank. This decision, once translated into forces and a doctrine for their use, gave Germany a series of rapid successes in foreign policy from the mid-thirties onwards. In Britain, the debate yielded no clear, unequivocal answers, and their absence compounded the errors of a political leadership which was able to give no clear direction from its side either. Those in the services or in diplomacy or politics who drew the conclusions which subsequent experience showed to be correct, tended to damage their careers by their advocacy. Total indecision among the experts ensured that the politicians were never forced to consider a unified strategy and were given every excuse for not deciding about its related social and industrial components. Reciprocal unclarity accounted for the confusion and muddle of British defence policy virtually up to 1939.

These were the longterm reassessments of war in an industrial age which were engendered by the First World War among soldiers and diplomats, their political masters or accomplices, and the professional commentators of the newspapers and the new medium, the radio. But for policy-makers after Versailles, the industrial implications of victory and defeat were immediate and straightforward. For the Western Allies, to restrict German military power, it was not enough to deny the Rhineland to German troops, German military industry had to be controlled as well, through commissions of inspection. Conversely, the strengthening of Italian security meant consciously building up Italian industry, as well as insisting on a defensible frontier on the Brenner. The German authorities recognised the relationship between warfare and industry by sub-contracting, in Belgium, Switzerland, Sweden,* Spain and the Soviet Union, the manufacture of weapons forbidden by the Versailles Treaty to German industry. Research and development, being the more easily concealed, could be carried out at home, but its costs were met by maximising exports of arms, munitions permitted by the Treaty and plant to Latin America, the Balkans and the Soviet Union.**

There was, however, a wider implication. War now demanded too many resources on too large a scale to be satisfied from the international exchange of commodities. Germany had invented 'autarchy' as a wartime measure in an effort to offset the allied superiority in raw materials, but its theories entered into the post-war contingency planning of all states. From 1919 military and diplomatic thinking registered the nexus between raw materials and industry on the one side and the options for war and negotiation on the other. The break with the pre-war era is expressed most vividly by the contrast between the younger Moltke's abrupt dismissal in 1914 of advice about organising production and supply and the German generals' reluctant recognition in October 1918, as evinced by the Reichstag's Committee of

---

*The first 'Stuka' dive bombers were designed and built in Sweden in 1928 by Junkers' associate company, AB Flygindustrie.
**The Russian Government provided factories for a *Luftwaffe* training school at Lipetsk from 1924 and for tank training at Kazan from 1930.

Enquiry, that allied superiority in manufacture, as well as manpower, spelled defeat.

If the practice of the war revised the operative concepts of warfare, the results of the war brought about a similar revision of the accepted axioms of diplomacy. The politics of Russia, Italy and, later, Germany brought into existence regimes which, if they accepted the idea of diplomacy at all, totally rejected the rules by which it had hitherto been conducted. These were condemned as 'bourgeois'; they were, in fact, aristocratic in origin, and for that reason were obnoxious to another emergent power, the United States of America. The Old Diplomacy was held uniquely responsible for the catastrophe. President Wilson's remedy of 'open covenants, openly arrived at' demonstrated merely his inability to grasp the distinction between foreign policy and negotiation, as well as the Manicheanism which informed American attitudes to Europe. The United States and the Soviet Union withdrew from Europe during the twenties, Germany still contrived to follow the old codes, and it was left to Mussolini to pour public contempt on them.

The coexistence of two philosophies of diplomacy spread confusion as well as distrust. To diplomats trained in the old school, the idea that Mussolini *must* be seeking an accommodation, that his violence was only verbal, died hard. It was difficult to believe that he signed treaties not with any particular intention of abiding by them, but only for their news value, or that the much vaunted leadership principle which 'proved' Italy superior to the effete democracies could in practice produce so much uncoordinated, contradictory action. Mussolini was unperturbed by such trifles, but he did not in any case think that the function of diplomacy was to reconcile and reassure, and that confidence was its essence. In this he was quite logical. If, as he so frequently proclaimed, war is not a distressing necessity but the ultimate means whereby the regime can work out its ideological *raison d'être*, then diplomacy ceases to be concerned with reconciling opposites; its primary task is to exploit them. Hence its goals are set by ideology and trumpeted by propaganda – both of which are indifferent to the formal truth of any points at issue, or to the dignity of negotiation, or to maintaining confidence through consistency.

The Old Diplomacy had the virtue of attempting to convince: the New addressed itself to the fears of peoples. The change was registered inside the institutions concerned with foreign policy; the patient analysis of difficulties gave place to the intuitions and snap judgements of leaders. The original Fascist programme, drawn up in 1919, called for the abolition of secret diplomacy. Mussolini, in power, denied the competence of the League of Nations which designedly had replaced it. The change in the tone and temper in the transaction of international business may be illustrated by the decline from Contarini to Ciano in the Italian Foreign Office, and later in Germany from Stresemann to Ribbentrop. The first-named in each case stood for the intellectual appraisal of aims and for careful competence in execution: the second, in comparison, were facile hacks, but their appointment as minions of their respective dictators did demonstrate that 'total war' demanded 'total diplomacy'; that if, as Mussolini put it, 'violence is more moral than compromise,' then the old forms and practices had to go. Diplomacy could no longer be an alternative method of pursuing the ends of the state: it had to be integrated with, and in practice subordinated to, considerations of military power.

The proposition that warfare was not about cavalry charges and the heroism of individuals but about raw materials and rates of output soon became commonplace – the more easily since it appeared to substantiate Marxist theories as to the nature of the capitalist system and the causes of war. The notion that war derived uniquely or ultimately from the clashing interests of states whose capitalists were struggling for supremacy in the world's markets, especially for raw materials, enjoyed wider than Marxist support and was readily adopted by American historians and publicists seeking to expose the 'old' diplomacy and to discredit American participation in the war. Only the more sophisticated minds recalled that access to raw materials was not a pre-war problem, or a generally dominant motive for the war. The Marxists and their American allies read the frictions occasioned by economic policies or aspirations, not as empirical facts, but as confirming a prior ideological axiom for which there was no empirical evidence. Hence, their analyses concentrated on the state (which could be attacked) instead of on the trading area which was the relevant analytical category, and which was the more amorphous target. They also overlooked how often the pre-war conflicts, to which they ascribed a determining role, had been settled by compromise.

Only those analysts who watched technology, as distinct from concentrating almost exclusively on finance, realised that the industrial system had generated some of its own alternatives. A culture which could produce a Fritz Haber did not need a military attack on Chile to assure itself of nitrates, while the researches of a Bergius into synthesising gasoline from coal released a state from dependence on the world market. Bergius' hydrogenation techniques applied to indigenous coal deposits could provide aviation fuels which could not be subjected to sanctions. It appeared that inventiveness and systematic access to the international corpus of research were as necessary to the capacity to make war as access to raw materials. The problem for governments was to ensure that the results of invention accrued only to themselves, or to other states only by permission. Science had to cease to be international – which could be achieved only by putting scientists into uniform or under a militarised discipline in special institutes. This had to be done in advance of war itself as a normal feature of state policy.

The opportunity to develop along these lines did not wait on war or even the preparation for one: it arose from the collapse of the world economy which marked the Depression. Governments in all countries were induced to resort to measures of control and protection which had the effect of putting their economies on something very like a wartime footing. The economic pattern of Europe during the thirties resembled the wartime economies of 1916–19. The hallmarks were intervention and planning. Currencies were managed by central banks according to state requirements: the need to save convertible foreign currencies encouraged the production of substitute materials – a process which was justified also in that it improved national employment statistics. Access to raw materials was determined by centrally-directed import programmes. Industrial control schemes were deliberately modelled on wartime experience. Key industries such as shipbuilding, iron and steel, which employed large numbers of workers, were subsidised and rationalised to maintain a given level of employment. The measures adopted to protect national economic life also served to prevent the collapse of industries vital to any war effort. Recourse to such measures was not an explicit preparation for war, but helped those preparations when the trends of international politics made them seem desirable. The states of Europe entered the Second World War without the institutional shock of 1914.

3. Security in the air age: reassessments of 'civil' and 'military'

The defeat of Germany and her allies and the withdrawal of Russia from 1920 changed the configuration of power in the European polity. As they went into abeyance, two other states which had been staple elements in European diplomacy, Austria-Hungary and the Ottoman Empire, disappeared altogether. The field was left to Britain and France, but, as events made clear, the two governments had divergent views about the role and reorganisation of Europe. Additionally, Britain was the more preoccupied by extra-European problems. So postwar Europe was very much the Europe of France – as much by derogation as by the undoubted prestige and military strength of the Third Republic. The traditional enemy, Austria, had been eliminated as a power; Germany was disarmed and partly occupied and in the throes of domestic turmoil; Italy, although a competitor in the international scene, could not offer the kind of rivalry which Germany had done before the war. French military opinion took it as an axiom that there were only two armies in Europe which could fight – the German and the French. The Germany army was to be kept in a position of inferiority as the penalty of defeat; the Italian army was *hors concours* and the British little better than a colonial police force, it could not be relied upon. France and the French army would be the unrelenting guardians of the Versailles settlements. Poincaré was reputed to know the Treaty of Versailles by heart: he certainly quoted from it on every possible occasion, and, in this, he reflected the sentiments of the vast majority of Frenchmen, who regarded the Treaty provisions as a means of repayment for damage and as an insurance against its reoccurring.

During the first years after the war, European politics revolved round the efforts of France to turn the victory of 1918 – which public opinion thought of as exclusively French – into long-term security. The search implied establishing a military presence in areas considered vital to French foreign policy. Of these, the Rhineland was easily the first in importance. French generals, during the Versailles' negotiations, pressed for it to be detached from Germany and permanently occupied by French troops. They were, in fact, appealing for the agreement reached by France and Tsarist Russia in 1917 (and not communicated to their British ally) to be implemented: France was to occupy the Rhineland and the Saarland, and Russia was to acquire the Straits from the Ottoman Empire. Gabriel Hanotaux, the distinguished historian, went even further than the generals and publicly demanded the occupation of German territory as far as the Elbe – to, roughly, the limits of direct French rule in the time of Napoleon I. The reasoning behind these demands was the mirror image of arguments put forward by the German generals for the annexation of Alsace and Lorraine in 1871 and could reasonably have been expected to create the same effect.

The French military arguments were not adopted; the government abandoned its demand for security in that extreme form under the persuasion of Wilson and Lloyd George in return for an occupation of the Rhineland for fifteen years and an Anglo-American guarantee of France's frontiers. For reasons of American domestic politics, Wilson was unable to ratify the agreement;* it thereby became void, since by its terms withdrawal by one signatory automatically invalidated the responsibilties of the other. Britain alone was in no position to give efficacious guarantees to France since the war had demonstrated beyond doubt that cooperation with the American navy in the Atlantic was the *sine qua non* of British military intervention on the continent against Germany. French governments of all parties failed to grasp this reasoning and thereafter harboured a grievance against their western partners. In consequence, they devoted even greater energies to an alternative strategy, already embarked upon before the Peace Conference, of establishing a military presence, either French or French-trained and supported, to the east of Germany. Hence a battalion of *chasseurs* found itself quartered in Memel** and French officers appeared as advisers in Warsaw, Prague, Bucharest and Belgrade. The armed forces of the emergent states in central and eastern Europe were equipped by France and their costs subsidised by the French taxpayer. Some 400 million gold francs a year went to Poland alone on this account (and diminished the force of French Governments' pleas to their wartime allies that France was too impoverished to pay its war debts).

The collegial links between the military forces were paralleled by links between French and allied military manufacture in Poland and Czecho-slovakia. The key to both was the assumption by Schneider of a share interest in Skoda, the engineering firm in Plzen (Bohemia), the output of which had been the mainstay of Austrian forces during the war. The Skoda works, as other enterprises in Bohemia and Moravia, had to be transferred to Czech ownership in consequence of the setting up of the new Czechoslovak

---

*This was, perhaps, the first experience by Europeans of the American constitutional arrangement whereby the President can promise but not necessarily deliver. The rejection by the Senate of the Versailles Treaty underlined the point even more forcibly.

**They stayed till January 1923, when Memel was seized by Lithuania in order to forestall the creation of an independent territory, under the League of Nations, on the model of Danzig. From the French point of view, the seizure was satisfactorily anti-German.

state; the restructuring of the shareholding provided the opportunity for Schneider to participate. The question was opened soon after the ceasefire on the Western Front and the terms of the transfer negotiated through Benes' bureau in Paris during the winter of 1918–19, before the Peace Conference convened. The deal was neither private, in the strict sense, nor commercial in motive, though formally both participants were private entities and the expectation of profit played a part in the transaction. It was an inter-state deal, prompted and regulated by governments pursuing their own interest as they saw it, during the administrative chaos attendant on converting Hapsburg Bohemia into the Czechoslovak Republic, and as one item on the agenda of a postwar alliance aimed at Germany.

Since France had been the first to recognise the Czech National Council as the interim government of the new Czech state, even before hostilities ceased, Czechoslovakia emerged into international politics under French patronage, and its governments under Masaryk and Benes maintained the French connection as fundamental. The relationship was construed in straightforward military terms, but suggested by the new technology of aerial warfare. Bohemia was about as far from Berlin as Paris from the German frontier; its position offered a means to overcome the restricted range of contemporary aircraft. Berlin could more easily, and more regularly, be bombed from Bohemia than from France itself. The aircraft relieved France from the necessity to maintain troops in Czechoslovakia, as a threat to Germany. It also absolved France from having to send an army to fight there if Germany were to cross the Bohemian frontier, since French troops could best be employed on their familiar terrain in the Rhineland. Hitler subsequently recognised the basis of this two-fold strategy when he stigmatised Czechoslovakia as an 'aircraft carrier' in Central Europe.

The strategy also implied that Czechoslovakia would be able to defend itself. The nucleus of the Czech army was the Czech Legion, which, formed during the war for both military and political ends, had received its first regular equipment and uniforms from France. But the army was supported by a weapons' manufacturing industry which fell to the nascent Czech state as part of its Hapsburg inheritance – the Skoda Works at Plzen and the Zbrojovka firm at Brno. The existing chemical industry guaranteed a supply of poisonous gases and the political leadership took note of the latest technology to begin the construction of military aircraft early in 1919, as one of the first ventures of the new state. The engines were imported from France.

This capacity to manufacture advanced weapons as well as small arms of the highest quality underwrote Czechoslovakia's alliances. In this respect, Czechoslovakia exercised an influence disproportionate to its size. But export sales of arms took on a new justification in that they secured for Czechoslovakia not simply a money income but an income in currency, which, unlike the Czech crown, was convertible on the international money market. In consequence, the kind of money earned was as important, to the balance of payments, as the destination of the weapons from a political point of view. This had not been a motive for the governments of the pre-war exporting states, Britain, France and Germany, whose transactions were related to an accepted gold standard.

The Czech state, as responsible manager of the national currency, developed a special care for the performance of its major export items, and through that, a day-to-day concern with the weapons industry, unrelated to the immediate needs of national defence. The concern expressed itself in the form of financial subventions against losses, and in subsidies to make the Czech firms more competitive in their pricing.

These incentives to export were vigorously exploited. Within ten years of the foundation of the state, Czechoslovakia claimed about ten per cent of the world market; Czech arms in due course appeared in large quantities in China, Japan, Ethiopia and on both sides in the Civil War in Spain.

Supplies of Czech origin were not the only pattern available on the market; they competed with the output of the traditional suppliers in Western Europe, notably French and Belgian, and with the huge surplus of weapons thrown up by the war, 'second-hand' perhaps, but in good order. The mood induced by the war and the vehicle offered by the League permitted *part* of the trading possibilities to be embargoed, or at least monitored. In May 1919, eleven states subscribed to the China Arms Embargo, whereby no arms should be sent to China until there was a recognised government in that country. It is customarily criticised as a failure or as hypocritical. The definition of 'arms' was limited – it did not include aircraft, for example, and Czechoslovakia was a conspicuous absentee, with Germany and Russia, among the signatories. There was a great deal of smuggling. For these reasons, the embargo was anything but complete, but was maintained until April 1929, in conformity with its intent, when the Nationalist Government had been recognised as the legitimate government of the country. As it worked out, the embargo put some limits on the competition among suppliers, rather than inhibiting conflict in China. But from the suppliers' point of view, their policy was conditional from the outset; when a recognised sovereign authority could be defined, the restriction could be dispensed with – as it was. Control measures had to recognise the relationship between sovereignty and the option to go to war.

For all states, the exercise of that option had ceased to be a matter of two dimensions, land and sea. The ascribed role of Czechoslovakia as an 'aircraft carrier' points to a new factor in international relations – and therefore in the assessments of power – aviation. The progress in the air enforced by the war turned military flying from a private enthusiasm, usually deprecated by higher commands, into a recognised branch of the profession of arms. Air forces had demonstrated that they had an important part to play in a nation's defence and had built up an identity and an *esprit de corps* of their own. Their aircraft were no longer the general purpose vehicles which had gone to war in 1914 but were designed for specific uses. The uses themselves were the subject of intense professional controversy.

Inter-service rivalry took on a new aspect: armies and navies now confronted a third party, an air force, which complicated command problems and was another contender for a share of government funds. In the inter-service conflicts, the claims of the air force inevitably brought into question its anticipated role. Was it to operate tactically, providing reconnaisance and airborne artillery for the older services and therefore under their aegis, or was it to act in full independence – in which case, the air force would be primarily employed on long-range strategic bombing of the enemy? If so, the answer implied that air power was not an adjunct to the older arms but inherently superior to them. It alone could break the battlefield defensive and destroy the enemy's sources of supply and manufacture.

These issues were vehemently discussed in all states. The case for independence was formulated most coherently by Giulio Douhet in Rome, in 1921. Douhet originally trained as an artillery officer, became a proponent of motorised transport for armies and then of the use of aircraft, 'to destroy nations from the air.' During the war, his untimely and critical memoranda about general staff policy earned him a court-martial and imprisonment. In 1918, he was reinstated, as head of the Central Aeronautical Bureau, and three years later published his first comprehensive exposition of the role of air power, *Il Dominio dell' Aria*; *saggio sul' arte della guerra aerea*, in which he propounded two basic assumptions (i) that the bomber was an offensive weapon against which no effective defence was possible, and (ii) that it should be used to attack centres of population to disrupt production and destroy civilian morale, thus directly causing a revulsion against the war.

Acceptance of these assumptions logically implied that the air force should be an independent arm of policy, and that its primary target was not the military but the civil aspect of society. Stalemates between armies could only be broken by destroying the apparatus which supported them, namely the industries and the will of the people to work in them. So the targets must not be fortifications but cities, attacks on which, properly carried out, would generate a demand for peace even before the armies had time to mobilise!

Much of the detail of Douhet's analysis was faulty, particularly where it involved problems of aeronautical engineering. He thought, for example, that transport aircraft and bombers had the same basic functional character and therefore progress in civil aeronautics was directly related to military potential in the air. His general doctrine, however, became the core of professional discussion stimulated by the appearance of his books and articles in translation in military journals. Moreover, the basic message was discussed in the popular press, even by those who had no opportunity to identify it with Douhet's name.*

Fear of intensive mass bombardment dissolved the practical distinction between the soldier and the civilian and created a new constraint on policy. With the advent of the bombing aircraft, planners had to contemplate the possibilities of induced panic on the 'home' front and the disruption of the ability to make war. Moreover, for this to result, it might not be necessary to experience the attacks, the mere threat might be enough to paralyse the popular will. In consequence, such air bombardments as did occur strengthened the feeling that civilians were completely vulnerable. The object of policy was no longer to convince ministers and officials that war was too hazardous in the given circumstances but to induce populations in an 'enemy' state to demand peaceful solutions of their own governments. The effect of the change was demonstrated by Douhet in his book *La Guerra de 19...* in which popular pressure under the threat of air bombardment brings a new Franco-German war to an end in forty-eight hours.

This outcome, as Stephen Possony pointed out, became a kind of military *Weltanschauung*, which jeopardised the objectivity of discussions of the strategy. In *Tomorrow's War* he took issue with the partisans of air warfare. By analysing the arithmetic of Douhet's two-day war he showed that a clash between a power with land forces to which air was an auxiliary (France) and an adversary armed only with a Douhet-style air force (Germany) would by no means necessarily conclude in favour of the latter, partly by reason of the likely loss rates in aircraft, partly because enquiry into the effects of bombing on cities demonstrated that air raids were relatively ineffective. Examination of materials on the raids on Paris and London in the Great War showed that only small numbers of aircraft actually reached the target area and that the dispersed nature of the cities themselves – Paris and London being only thirty-five per cent and twenty-five per cent built over, respectively, kept casualties down. The losses per ton of bombs dropped worked out at 8 dead and 21.7 wounded in Paris and 9.1 dead and 21.7 wounded in London. Such results were hardly likely to promote the panic demand for the cessation of hostilities which Douhet supposed, even less so when account was taken of the improved measures of active and passive defence which Douhet did not allow for.

Statistical evidence also cast doubt on another of his main suppositions, namely the ability of aircraft to stop troop movements by destroying communications. Bridges were difficult targets to hit, in the given state of

---

*A translation of *Il Dominio dell' Aria* (2nd ed.) was published as *The Command of the Air* in Britain in 1943. Similar ideas about the role of strategic bombing derived from the Independent Air Force of 1918 and the views of its commander, Sir Hugh Trenchard, who became Chief of Staff of the RAF in 1919 and kept it in being as a separate arm throughout its crucial early years in the teeth of opposition from the other two services. The RAF was a strategic bombing force from the beginning.

aiming, and the lower the aircraft flew, the more vulnerable they were. The bombs they carried would be inadequate to demolish bridges unless dropped in large numbers – a requirement which entailed massive bombing fleets for this task alone. The same arguments applied to more spread-out targets such as railway junctions.

These criticisms, apart from revealing the falsity of Douhet-type arguments, had two important implications for policy; that civilian populations were able to withstand aerial bombardments and that strategic bombing by itself was not a war-winning strategy. The first was proved correct by the experience of civil populations in the Second World War, so long as bombs were filled with conventional explosives; the second is still a contentious issue. If we neglect Douhet's figures and consider only his general proposition, then his predicted outcome *might* have been verified by experience if, say, either side in the autumn of 1939 had been able to field the numbers and quality of air forces available to the western allies in the spring of 1945, or if the destruction meted out to Hamburg at the end of July 1943 had been visited on Berlin, Paris or London at the beginning of September 1939. The debate goes on, but the issue has been closed by the advent of nuclear warfare using rockets rather than aircraft.

In the international politics of the twenties and thirties however, the air provided a new dimension from which political opponents could be threatened and induced to comply, and at speeds hitherto unexperienced. The time-honoured components of strategy, time, space and force, took on new meaning. The effect was like that of the railways in the previous century, but in an element where the international rules had yet to be elaborated. In contrast to the railways, there had been no time to accommodate the new technique: practice preceded theory, so that the military and diplomatic implications of the use of 'air space' had to be worked out before a public which had already experienced its destructive possibilities during the war. Attempts to convince the public that it was not helpless were tardy and unavailing. The public 'knew' otherwise. Moltke in using the dominant technique of his generation could work in private and was not responsible to public opinion. The theorists of the air age could not, and were accountable to governments which themselves responded to the public will, or had to take it into consideration. Some theorists thought that air bombardment was so overwhelming that the concept of 'air defence' was a myth: the only remedy was total internationalisation of air transport and the abolition of bombers. Others reacted more cautiously; but for all, the key question was 'how much bombardment can the public be expected to stand, and under what conditions?' The answer generally given was 'very little, if any.' The available evidence about the behaviour of civil populations demonstrated their liability to panic on a scale wholly disproportionate to the tonnage of explosives dropped. The experience was limited but memories of it were not allowed to die. Air bombardment made admirable, that is harrowing, material for the cinema, which became a mass entertainment during this period. Newsreels recorded disasters more vividly than newspapers, and pictures of the shattered structures and human victims induced in audiences not so much a rational fear but an irrational panic.

There was another important corollary to Douhet's doctrine: the ability to make aircraft (which in his time still used wood as a basic material for airframes) demanded complex skills but not the extensive amounts of industrial materials used by other weapons such as ships or fortifications. Consequently, acquiring the most modern weapon, in the shape of an air force, was an option open to states deficient in raw materials of their own or in heavy engineering. The postwar status of Italy in the international political order was enhanced by its pioneering developments in the production and use of aircraft. Italy demonstrated that the possession of massive coal, iron and steel industries was no longer absolutely essential to the claim to be a first-class power.

The industrial basis for the development of Italian aviation had not matched the dash of its early aviators or the ingenuity of its designers. The factories which produced for the Allies during the war were allowed to run down, the market for their products to contract. But the inauguration of the government of Mussolini, in October 1922, brought into Italian politics the issue of the modernisation and re-equipment of the armed forces – especially the air arm. Douhet provided the doctrine, Italo Balbo, the dynamic leadership, with Mussolini's support. Italy became the second power, after Britain, to have an independent air force, under an Air Ministry established in 1925. The pre-eminence of the air force was reflected in its role in Fascist theories – the appeal to youth and to Italy's glorious technological future. 'Italian aviation,' proclaimed Mussolini, 'must be on such a scale and so powerful that the noise of its engines must surpass any other noise and the area of the wings of our aeroplanes must obscure the sun.' To translate the rhetoric into reality, the share of aviation in military budgets was increased from about two per cent when Mussolini took over to about twenty per cent at the time of the Ethiopian campaign in 1936.

The Italian air force did not embody Douhet's teachings *tout court*. It was part of a balanced force, with the army and navy, and was designed partly to operate as a tactical air force, not as the single supreme arm which Douhet had envisaged. Notwithstanding this limitation, the propaganda about the air force as an irresistible striking force accorded with Italy's strategic position and the aims of Italian diplomacy in Africa and Central Europe. The discrepancy between propaganda and reality was only to be forced into the open nearly twenty years after the force was re-founded. Until that time Italian air power was taken very seriously by planners and commentators as a new factor in the politics of southern Europe and the Middle East.

Although in the long term the nexus between military and civil aviation was not, as Douhet thought, in the characteristics of the aircraft, there was a relationship between the two. Its nature was much debated, particularly in 1919 and 1920 when, if the defeated states were to be denied 'military' but allowed 'civil' aviation, it became an immediate practical necessity to discriminate between the categories. Furthermore, the initial definitions of the problem were military: after the war, the planes used on passenger traffic were simply converted bombers, piloted by men who had received their flying instruction for military purposes. This phase passed as comfort and operational economy, especially in fuel, became dominant considerations, but for roughly a decade, the 'convertibility' of airliners for bombing or other military uses became a virulent issue among professionals, in parliaments and between services. The administrative counterpart of this debate was the transference of responsibility for the development of aviation from war ministries to departments which were more plainly civilian. Through such agencies government controlled the terms on which aircraft were constructed and operated. The ministries, however, were never wholly severed from military responsibilities – a fact which became apparent to contemporaries in the politics of establishing international air routes and in domestic debates about subsidies for manufacturers and operators.

International routes were governed by the 'Convention for the Regulation of Aerial Navigation' signed in Paris in October 1919 by the main states assembled there for the peace conference. The Convention was established before the participants had any large scale commercial aviation interests to protect; but, in implementing it, governments showed themselves remarkably sensitive to the opportunities which civil traffic in peacetime allowed for the identification of targets in wartime. The French government found that its cherished ambition of using air transport as a sinew of the French Empire could not be realised, in view of the ranges of existing aircraft, without a treaty with the Spanish Government permitting use of air space and landing fields and the establishment of facilities. The routes that were agreed had to avoid specific zones, notably Cartagena, Carroca, Cadiz and the island of Leon, the first two being the sites of arsenals, and the last two, naval bases. Such prohibitions became common practice in the bargaining between states.

France also took the lead in subsidising the purchase and operation of aircraft, directly after the war, in 1919; to be followed by Belgium, in the same year, Germany in 1920, the Netherlands and Britain (to meet competition from French subsidised cross-Channel traffic) in 1921 and Italy in 1924. Their example was emulated by other states, as they moved into the air age. The subsidies took different forms – bounties for the purchase of aircraft of a certain specification or with certain equipment such as radio, the financing of airfields by central or local authorities, the right to accelerate rates of depreciation for tax purposes and so on – but, irrespective of the method, subsidies for civil aviation were justified on the grounds that they provided for national security through bringing into existence the basic facilities required for training and operation. An airfield could be used indifferently by military and civil aircraft. Civil aircraft, even if not as convertible as the enthusiasts advocated, helped to keep in being the facilities and manufacturing skills from which military needs could be satisfied. In both respects, civil aviation offered the advantage of offsetting the costs of purely military necessities. Using these arguments, the French Government achieved the *tour de force* of persuading the 'Little *Entente*' governments to subsidise the operation of French airlines in their territories. At home, it gave special subsidies for the manufacture and operation of small, fast machines, carrying, at a maximum, four passengers, which could be converted easily to reconnaissance or fighter purposes. The military use was built into the design and specification, and, logically, these aircraft were reckoned as part of the air force reserve. Similarly, designers and manufacturers were encouraged to support the national engine industry by bounties, which the use of a foreign engine forfeited. In Italy, an operating airline qualified for a special subsidy if it could guarantee that at least fity per cent of its aircraft would be ready to fly, if suddenly requisitioned by the Commissioner for Aviation. In all states, subsidies were employed to encourage manufacturers to experiment, with a view to establishing results which could be applied militarily. Aviation, in all its aspect, confused the 'civil' and 'military' categories from the beginning, and the development of the first never lost sight of the advantage of the second, even where the two were not explicitly related – as they were in Weimar Germany.

Under the Versailles Treaty, Germany was forbidden an air force. As the German Government subsequently failed to persuade the Allies that the police should be allowed aircraft, development in the air had to be ostensibly, if not ostentatiously, 'civil'. The German authorities thus had an incentive to expand airlines to provide the training and operational experience necessary for building a cadre of pilots and ground staff. To evade allied control of construction, the Ministry of Defence negotiated a secret agreement with the Soviet Union whereby Professor Junkers established a plant for warplanes at Fili, near Moscow. Restrictions on the speed, altitude and payload of civil transports were lifted in May 1922 – which allowed the embryonic airlines to become fully operational and the state to use its power to subsidise to enforce them into one company, Deutsche Lufthansa, in 1925.

The Reich subscribed 10 million marks: state and municipal governments, a like sum. Junkers was included as an airline operator but not as a manufacturer. Lufthansa concentrated on passenger and freight traffic, and fast mails, which respectively could yield troop transporting facilities or fighter or reconnaissance aircraft in case of need. The company had a virtual monopoly of German airspace, since Germany, as an ex-enemy state, was not a party to the international convention of 1919 on international air traffic. Until it was admitted into the League of Nations in 1926, and therefore automatically to the convention, Germany forbade flights by aircraft of the *Entente* countries over German territory. Aircraft which inadvertently trespassed were confiscated on landing – a practice which caused continual friction with France in the Rhineland.

Lufthansa, however, did more than give operational experience to personnel. To German policy-makers, it was the sole means of keeping the design and manufacture of aircraft going in Germany, for which reason it had to accept wider diversity in types of aircraft and engines than its competitors. For similar reasons, Lufthansa aircraft provided working laboratories for new types of radio or navigation equipment and for experiments with synthetic gasoline.

In other states, not under the restrictions of Weimar Germany, the distinction between 'military' and 'civil' aviation could be maintained somewhat more easily, and aircraft could be designed and developed to specifically 'civil' requirements. In Germany, military objectives could only be served by civil means, until a government could negotiate or assert the country's military independence.

Nevertheless, even though its range of choice was wider than Germany's, Britain had a similar problem of keeping design and production capacity in being and usefully employed for military projects. The Government, faced with pacifist, or at least pacific, opinion and with the need to limit government expenditures, planned all activities on the assumption, adopted by the Cabinet on 15 August 1919, that there would be no major war for ten years. The 'ten year rule' was intended as a basis for estimates. It made strategic planning impossible and reinforced the psychological preferences of postwar commanders who thought of warfare in terms of cavalry in the colonies rather than tanks in Europe. It cut the ground from under the feet of the enlightened few who wished to rethink war after the mechanised experience of the Western Front. The 'rule' was progressively in force until March 1932. Under its influence, the Royal Air Force, which had 185 squadrons at the Armistice, was reduced to three, for home defence, by 1923. Reductions of this size necessarily cut the demand for engines and airframes, and therefore the work available for an industry which, built virtually from scratch in the war, included firms which had few civil alternatives, or none at all.

It soon became apparent that manufacturers of aircraft engines were much more dependent on the production of aircraft than, say, heavy engineering firms were on siege guns. Hence for any equipment but the lightest of aircraft, the Air Ministry became the prop and stay of the manufacturers. Government required a capacity to be kept in being but having drastically cut its own demand was forced to select those firms it wished to support, and then support them. Fifteen firms were 'approved' in airframes and four in engines. New entrants were officially discouraged, on the grounds that it was pointless to invest in plant for which a work-load could not be guaranteed. Under such a regime, progress in design and development was not rapid: it was not intended to be. The object was to keep work teams in existence and facilities employed in those firms granted official recognition.

The relation of government to industry was expressed not merely through the distribution of contracts, but through the ultimate control of the future. In this, the strength of the Air Ministry lay not in its being the sole purchaser, but in the fact that it could furnish the major orders and could encourage the development of the new types. This latter function was vested in the state-owned Royal Aircraft Establishment which during the war, replaced the Royal Aircraft Factory. The RAE was the central research institute of the industry and supervised the work of research teams in private firms and approved the use of specific plant. In this way, the state exercised control but did not itself manufacture. Development contracts were placed with individual firms on terms intended to ensure that the firm incurred no loss, while earning no profit. Prices for prototypes were fixed so as to enable the manufacturers to write off the costs of development, but only after satisfying officials of the Air Ministry that they were validly incurred. In principle, profits could only be made under production contracts.

The costs of tests and evaluations were met by the state, since prototypes were tried out by the RAF. Private ventures by individual firms were not forbidden – the need to spread the overhead costs of facilities ruled that out – but neither were they officially encouraged, since private orders, from the government's viewpoint, might generate excess capacity.

Though the individual firms competed in terms of their techniques and 'know how', they were not competing in the same sense as firms producing civil goods. The normal practice was for the Air Ministry to chose one firm, or a group, to develop a new design, and then negotiate the production with one firm, whose costs were closely scrutinised. Competitive tendering was, ordinarily, avoided; so was competitive selling. Moreover the Air Ministry reserved the right to ban sales to all other potential customers. All these characteristics of Britain's air policy followed from the 'ten year rule'. In the absence of any agreed political or strategic objective which could determine a series of priorities, military aviation suffered from slow rates of innovation, marked by postponements and drift.

In France, the situation was equally lamentable, but for different reasons. The professional debate over the role of the air arm was not formally decided till 1933. Till then, air forces were strictly subordinate to army and naval command and as such were used in purely auxiliary roles, giving protection to army and naval units during operations, and carrying out reconnaissance on their behalf. The aircraft was simply a flying camera or an airborne gun; it was deprived of all offensive possibilities. This fixation on support roles survived the constitution, in 1933, of the French Air Force as an independent unit. In contrast to the RAF, however, it was not to carry out a strategy based on strategic bombing. It might be separate, but it was merely an aggregate of small units combined for administrative and command purposes in peacetime. On the outbreak of war, nearly all the squadrons were to revert to service with the land forces, for either reconnaissance or for tactical support of the army, but in either role under army command. For this reason the French aircraft industry virtually dispensed with developing heavy bombers and tried instead to design an all-purpose fighter-bomber. Success even in this limited aim was frustrated by the dispersal of production facilities among too many under-capitalised firms – a factor which prompted their transfer to state ownership in 1936. Concentration of control with an assured capital supply proved to have been brought about too late in the day, and France entered the Second World War with an air force which was a conglomeration of prototypes, backed by series production which can properly said to have begun only in 1938/9. French production of all types was running at about 500 aircraft a year, while Germany's was five times as large. The disparity related not only to the timing and defined scope of air rearmament but to the quality of the aircraft. French observers were inclined to be scornful of German production as crude and badly finished. The prevalence of handwork methods in France gave more finely finished products, but kept the making of aircraft one of the luxury trades.

In France, the aircraft industry might be nationalised but in the other two states, relationships were not markedly different. The conditions of aircraft production after the war extended the wartime relationship between the government and industry. Neither in Germany, where the state's influence in technology was already strong, nor in Britain, where the tradition of economic liberalism was still influential, was the design and production of aircraft carried on with the government acting only as a referee in the public interest. Constructors were not allowed an unimpeded right to design and develop their own types; their progress in each was financed and monitored by the state. There were residual differences between the two countries, largely ascribable to the difference of meaning attaching to the word 'state', but in industrial terms, the necessities of production in the given circumstances, and the reliance of manufacturers on the state as the dominant customer, brought about a recognisable degree of convergence. *Laisser faire* never applied.

In aircraft, the state *began* to enter into the research for weapons which were intended to match certain contingencies of foreign policy. It was no longer the case that, say, Krupp or Armstrong designed and produced a bigger gun, which then allowed the military to contemplate specific options, or even, as with the mortars which destroyed the forts of Liège, that the weapon was made for a specific target as part of an overall military plan devised in pursuit of a particular foreign policy. The situation was now reversed. Developments in aeronautics even in the 1920s demanded solutions to practical problems which could be arrived at only through research into fundamentals. The state began to finance and direct the process itself. Contracting firms were by no means passive. Design and entrepreneurial talent remained vital to the future, but henceforward the initiative for the development of the industry was shared between the firms, state-owned establishments and university departments and polytechnics. In France and Britain, however, the links were very loose. Much depended on the acumen of the individual firm.* Production facilities were in small units; production runs were limited and slow; directors of research in ministries responsible for aviation had so little authority that they were effectively precluded from tightening the links between theoretical knowledge and strategy, even if they saw the need to do so.

These beginnings apart, theory was peripheral to strategic calculation, at best. When at the end of the first decade of peace, the Inter-Parliamentary Union sponsored an enquiry into the character of a new war[2], the panel of eminent experts addressed itself to the time-honoured problems of mobilisation and resources, the mechanisation of warfare and the air weapon. Contributions also dealt with wider but still essential matters, such as the economic role of forces as consumers who do not produce and the adaptation of industry to wartime needs. The essays all reveal stimulating, if occasionally ironical, insights. The French contributor, General Requin, concluded: 'the general military character of a future war would largely resemble that which the war of 1914-1918 assumed in its last phase,' and italicised the last four words to make his point. But there the enquiry reached its speculative limits. No one advanced the need for any systematic exploitation of pure science by the state. It was assumed that laboratories would provide what was needed, on demand. The military would define the need, and the scientist would respond with ideas.

---

*The classic case in the inception of the 'Spitfire': Sir Robert McLean, Chairman of Vickers Aviation and Supermarine decided 'after unfruitful discussions with the Air Ministry' to build, in conjunction with Rolls Royce, 'a killer fighter.' He noted: 'The Air Ministry was informed of this decision and were told that in no circumstances would any technical member of the Air Ministry be consulted or allowed to interfere with the designer.' (The terminal illness of the designer made some official cooperation necessary.) See J. D. Scott, *Vickers: A History*, London, 1962, ch. 18.

4. Strategy as public works: Maginot

The French concept of security comprised not only military alliances with the other beneficiaries of the Versailles settlements but also protection from a repetition of the invasion of 1914. The debate about the means by which protection should be assured was dominated by the specifically French experience of the war, when reliance on *l'offensive à outrance'* in the frontier battles of 1914 contributed 600,000 to a total casualty list, over the four years, of about 1.5 millions. In reaction to this, the successful epic of Verdun the next year was taken to justify the superiority of the defensive. It was fondly concluded that, in spite of all pressures throughout the years of travail, the French line had never broken; the front had remained 'inviolable'. In consequence, security meant doing deliberately what in 1914 had been a response to circumstance, that is to construct a 'continuous front' covering the frontier with Germany in the form of a defensive system embodying the lessons of Verdun in 1915 and the Germans' Hindenburg Line in 1917.

The decision to build a defensive line rested on more than the tactical lessons drawn from the War; it was also an attempt to use engineering to overcome deficiencies in manpower deriving from a falling birthrate. The offensive tactics adopted by the French army in 1914 demanded a fixed number of soldiers per kilometre of front: now the numbers available had declined, and by 1935–1940 would be at their lowest, but the distances remained the same. Therefore it was necessary to conserve manpower behind concrete and steel.

In January 1930, the French Assembly voted the first instalment – 3 milliard francs – to cover the construction of a fortified defensive zone stretching from the Swiss frontier to Longwy in Lorraine. The 'line' subsequently named after the War Minister, André Maginot, was to ensure that Alsace and Lorraine should be closed to an attack from across the Rhine. The French field army would then be able to concentrate on the north-eastern frontier, protecting the vital industrial area of Tourcoing, Roubaix and Valenciennes (of which France had been deprived in the war) by advancing into Belgium and fighting there. The line was not intended to be a complete substitute for manpower, but merely a means of making France's diminishing resources go further: construction had to be finished in four years, since in 1935 France was obliged to withdraw all troops from the Rhineland.

These premises were rapidly overtaken by politics. French forces left Germany, not in 1935, but in June 1930, as a *quid pro quo* for Germany's acceptance of her reparations responsibilities as settled in the Young Plan. Belgium also changed its status. At the time the Maginot Line was first mooted, Belgium was an ally, having in 1920 abandoned its neutrality in favour of an agreement between the respective general staffs (never ratified by the Belgian parliament) providing for Franco-Belgian cooperation in the event of a German attack. Under its terms, Belgium was bound to be a manoeuvring ground for the left wing of a French army, on the basic assumption that French and Belgian forces would be attacking eastwards. In that contingency, Belgium itself would suffer only minimal and transitory physical damage.

The building of the Maginot Line made it more likely, however, that the fighting would take place in Belgium itself. At one stage, the idea was canvassed that the line should be extended along the border between Belgium and Germany, with French financial assistance. Pétain opposed the idea. In 1934, the British Chancellor of the Exchequer, Neville Chamberlain, raised the possibility of Britain's contributing towards the construction of defensive works along the Belgian frontier with Germany, but the idea was not adopted. Belgium was thus a designated battlefield again. This prospect suggested to the Belgian Government other means of ensuring the country's security, as distinct from having France as the senior partner in a military arrangement, with whom plans could be coordinated (but were, in fact, not). The Maginot Line made the Military Agreement a liability for Belgium, which might be drawn into a devastating war on its own soil as a partner of France. The German reoccupation of the Rhineland in 1936 helped the Belgian Government to make up its mind, and revert to its traditional policy of neutrality.*

This response automatically called in question the defence of north-west France. The French High Command decided on the construction of light field works on the terrain along the vulnerable frontier. The flats from Dunkirk to Montmédy were easily floodable, and the Ardennes were impassable from Montmédy to Mézières, where the line began. Marshall Pétain pointed out to the Senate Army Committee in March 1934, that 'certain dispositions of forces' were necessary to make the assumption about the Ardennes true, but his *caveat* was ignored. Everyone agreed that defence further back inside France would have to cut through the heavily

---

*The reversion to neutrality postponed or alleviated certain difficulties in Belgium's internal politics: the net result militarily was that no conversations took place between the French and Belgian staffs from 1936 till September 1939. Belgium thus became an almost unknown quantity for French planners.

industrialised area the chosen strategy was designed to protect.

Thus it was that, by the time that the postulates which the Maginot Line presupposed, namely fortifications and a field army, had been falsified by politics, construction was well under way, and the original appropriation of 3 milliard francs had stretched to 7 milliard – an early example of the phenomenon now familiar as 'cost overrun'. The excess was not due to increases in material costs, since the prices of steel and concrete were relatively stable. It resulted from a decision to eliminate the gaps in the system, intended originally to force the Germans to fight on ground of French choosing, in deference to the inhabitants of Lorraine, who objected to being a designated battlefield and insisted that the line should be continuous. This was done, but only by making it too 'thin'. Even so, its construction monopolised the French military budget, to the detriment of investment in weapons related to other possible strategies (particularly the use of armoured corps) as well as to the detriment of the dominant psychology of command.

However, the extra expenditure was not considered wasted since the Maginot Line was viewed as a massive public works project which stimulated the economy and employment during the Depression, the full severity of which was experienced in France somewhat later than in Britain and Germany. The argument that the project would create jobs was specifically used by André Maginot to deputies of the Left when soliciting support for his original bill in the Chamber of Deputies. It was no fault of his that only half the labour eventually employed was French, the rest being Russian, Czech, Hungarian, Polish and German.* Maginot and his successors were offering a specific strategy, deriving from an equally specific foreign policy, as a way out of the nation's economic difficulties. French employers and workers engaged on the contracts to construct and supply, and the deputies and local government officials in the areas through which the line passed did not dissent from the strategic assumptions on which construction was based, and indeed formed a bloc of opinion in its support. This development as such was not new, but hitherto it had been confined to limited sections of the population, such as shipyard workers, or for limited periods of time, for instance during the war when the population was generally presumed to approve the ends of foreign policy. The novel feature about the Maginot project was that it accomplished this effect in peacetime, for a range of industries and over an entire region of the country. The line itself became an inflexible element in military policy; other projects had to be fitted to it or receive the funds it did not consume. But its grounding

---

*The hiring of Germans, perhaps, explains why details of the construction soon appeared in the German press; as does reliance on German sub-contractors, whose tenders were far lower than their competitors. Maginot tried but failed to stop the practice of accepting German offers.

in popular support also worked against any changes to a more flexible strategy, had the General Staff wished to make them.

Policy-makers in democratic states had created a new problem for themselves. In 1914 the strategy embodied in Plan XVII did not depend on more than conventional fortified strong points, and was not publicly debated beforehand. There was no large social group in its favour whose prospects of employment or income depended on the adoption of *that* particular strategy and no other. Seventeen years later the chosen strategy was advocated as an economic stabiliser in which many people had a direct interest, apart from their general concern as citizens with the security of the nation.

The progress of construction of the line was extensively publicised, not just to reassure the population of Alsace and Lorraine and the taxpayers of France, but to let the Germans know that an attack on France through the Rhine provinces would inflict losses wholly incommensurate with any gains it might make. The German High Command took the point. In January 1935, an appreciation of the *Truppenamt* reported that the construction so far had increased French defensive strength by about three times. Five years later, the deterrent was still working on the minds of the generals comprising the General Staff (*Oberkommando des Heeres*) who were prepared to settle for a decisive battle in Belgium and Holland, that is, beyond the French frontier defences. It did not have the same effect on three other generals, von Manstein, von Rundstedt and Guderian, whose plan for breaking the frontier defence at the point where the line proper joined the extension towards the north-east, between Mézières and Dinant, eventually carried the day with Hitler and destroyed France in May 1940. This *débâcle,* on the French side, stemmed not from the line but from the foreign policies associated with its construction. French military officers and diplomats failed to overcome non-cooperation on the part of the Belgian Government, virtually up to the day the country was invaded.

The 'civil' justification for the Maginot Line, that it generated employment, was later in the thirties advanced in support of rearmament programmes generally, as the most easily implemented of the 'public works' advocated by many progressive economists as a way out of the Depression. The national defence was an objective which allowed government to inject capital into privately owned undertakings, and create jobs, without appearing to discriminate between industries, as would have otherwise been necessary. But in the conditions of the time rearmament operated, with the protection of national markets and devaluation of currencies, as a technique for increasing employment. In the particular case of France the effect on employment and incomes of increasing armament expenditures was offset by large-scale private hoarding and endemic flights of capital. It is, therefore, misleading to take rearmament as a uniquely regenerative force in the economy. As a much-needed inflow of capital into industry, rearmament helped, nonetheless, and could be easily justified politically. It promoted the psychological mobilisation of civilians, and in this sense reinforced contemporary debates about aerial bombardment in which the civilian was a legitimate target because the industrialised work force was essential to sustaining a war. Governments implicitly accepted the point by announcing that the worker was to be a conscious beneficiary of investment in weapons' production. Both lines of argument further eroded the distinction between 'civil' and 'military' which had been commonplace till 1914.

5. Options and the industrial system: air rearmament in Germany and Britain

While the French forces drew on their terrible experience at Verdun as the primary source of experience for any new war, the Germans paid more attention to the tactical benefits of infiltration, as practised in the Spring Offensive in 1918, and to the offensive options given by the tank and the aircraft. To an extent, the Versailles restrictions on fortifications (which could not of their nature be hidden from inspection) automatically reinforced the consideration of other methods to rectify what German opinion generally regarded as the 'injustices' of the peace treaties. But however much study the *Reichswehr* could carry on, legally or illegally, and whatever the arrangements made to build tanks and manufacture poison gas in the Soviet Union, the basis of the activity was hypothetical. There was, in Weimar Germany, no foreign policy in which the military force could be employed, or which it could be overtly used to support. Stresemann's policy towards the west expressly rejected military solutions, while in the east, the army was designated only a defensive role in the event of a Soviet invasion following the collapse of a politically invertebrate Poland. But Stresemann never commanded the full support of his party, and was excoriated by extremists on both Right and Left. After his death in October 1929, his successors discarded his formal limits, and war was widely envisaged among the diplomats as well as the military as the only means of recovering the Corridor and West Prussia, lost to Poland in 1919.

The political manoeuvres by which Hitler became Chancellor of Germany brought into office someone who was determined to rectify the losses suffered by Germany in consequence of the war and who was happily pre-pared to consider initiating a war as a means to this end, and to exploit the threat of war on an international scale. His effective consolidation of personal power by the summer of 1934 left him free to tear up the Ver-sailles Treaties, against which he had campaigned since they were signed. This aspiration was shared by many Germans, but for Hitler it meant more than putting back the frontiers to where they were in 1914; it implied reducing France to permanent political impotence – and France was universally considered to be the foremost military power on the continent, in spite of internal scandals and the effects of the Depression. German rearmament, therefore, was not just to assert claims to parity but had to be on a range and scale which would allow Germany comprehensively to defeat France – and its allies.

The evidence published after the Second World War shows that progress was not as rapid nor as well coordinated as contemporaries feared, but rearmament was consciously geared to the type of war which would avoid Germany being ruined through prolonged attrition or sanctions, namely the *Blitzkrieg*. In this concept the quintessential weapons were the tank and the aircraft used in conjunction, not to besiege towns or conquer territory, but to annihilate the enemy forces. This choice of strategy was built round the internal combustion engine and the freedom of movement it could confer. Highly mobile firepower would lead to quick, crushing solutions.

The complementary role of air in German strategy was implicit in the design of the *Luftwaffe* from 9 February 1933, when, ten days after Hitler was sworn in as Chancellor, the initial sum of RM 40 million was set aside for the construction of an air fleet and the basic studies commissioned for 1,000 aircraft (Britain's firstline strength was less than 500). The *Luftwaffe* personnel emerged from their flying schools in the Soviet Union and the sports clubs in Germany, but the organisation of the industrial facilities presented more difficult problems.

The German aviation industry comprised fourteen plants – which in the years 1933 to 1935 were expanded to thirty-six. Design talent existed in the persons of Willy Messerschmitt, Ernst Heinkel and, the doyen of the profession, Hugo Junkers. Work on airframes had never been seriously interrupted during the years of allied supervision but engine building had proved easier to control, and in 1933 the German engine industry lacked continuous experience of development, for which the adoption by BMW of American Pratt and Whitney engines, under licence, was no adequate substitute.

The expansion of the manufacturing facilities was financed by specially invented short-term bills guaranteed by the state to be exchangable against cash at the Reichsbank and accepted by industrialists and contractors accordingly. This system had the added advantage that it escaped public scrutiny. The Air Ministry also insisted that the manufacturers put their own money into rebuilding the air power of Germany, but assisted them in raising finance through the banks. The average annual cost of this programme till September 1939 was three milliard RM.

The money was invested in airfields, plant for manufacture and testing, machine tools and equipment. The compliance of any industrialist who, like Hugo Junkers, might have demurred on grounds of principle was ensured by the fact that the Reich was the sole provider of contracts to firms to whom exports were denied, and by the personal fate of Junkers itself. He, at seventy-four, was first systematically intimidated into transferring his personal design patents to his companies and then into divesting himself of any control by ceding his shareholdings to the Reich under duress.

From the outset, the Reich Air Ministry was effectively in charge of all aspects of German aeronautics. Its task was the easier since the Versailles Treaty restrictions, even though only applied in part, had prevented the emergence of entrenched interests comparable to those in Britain and France. The Ministry's primacy was also buttressed by the status and prestige of Goering in the Nazi hierarchy and the structures of government. The Air Ministry was never reluctant to use the initiative it possessed. In recruiting expertise, it consistently put scientific competence before Party affiliation or demonstrated ideological enthusiasm. It refused to make compromises with private manufacturers over research and development (which its army counterpart accepted) and in particular did not tolerate company's claims to secrecy for innovations made in their laboratories. The Ministry commanded overriding priority in the procurement of raw materials and facilities for the research programme on which government depended absolutely in order to bring an up-to-date air force into being. Under its aegis, research was confined to nine major establishments, of which the institutes grouped together as the *Technische Akademie der Luftwaffe* were first and foremost. The TAL carried out research into basic theory as well as the problems relating to the design and development of weapons and their ancillaries. It was central to the organisation of air research, directing the work of laboratories and institutes nominally in private hands, and of the *Technische Hochschulen*. The TAL and its associates received generous, even lavish, funds for their tasks. Their primacy endured, so that even when, early in 1942, German research and production came under the control of Albert Speer, 'Air' remained a separate and privileged category virtually till the end of the war.

The essence of air rearmament was secrecy and speed; the first, to ensure that foreign powers could form no clear picture of what was going on, and therefore could not prove any violation by Germany of its international obligations; the second to minimise the period of vulnerability, if by chance they did piece together what was going on sufficiently to make out a case and take pre-emptive action. The official declaration on 1 March 1935 that the *Luftwaffe* had been brought into existence demonstrated that German policy had succeeded in both respects. The emphasis on speed, however, had three crucial corollaries for the composition for the air force and its envisaged role in German policy. The number of types of aircraft was restricted and their individual characteristics closely defined: Heinkel, and to a lesser extent, Junkers and Dornier, bombers, Junkers dive-bombers and transports and Messerschmitt fighters. This was in complete contrast to French policy, which, as we have seen, encompassed too many experiments for roles which were too generalised. In Germany, the imperative of rapid progress, taken in conjunction with the intended operational object of the air force, meant that certain types of aircraft, such as those for naval aviation, were not produced at all or, like four-engined long-range heavy bombers* were soon abandoned. These options were discarded in advance. The third corollary was that concentration on the mass production of a few types made the best use of existing labour and materials but, in the longer term, was to a degree inflexible towards the innovations which the stresses of war suggested. Inventiveness could not be easily translated into products.

The intentions and practice of 1935, however, put the *Luftwaffe* technically further ahead and on a larger scale than the air force of any other power. It was the perfect instrument, alike for the type of diplomacy which Hitler practised till 1939, and for *Blitzkrieg* thereafter. As a threat it played on widespread fears of aerial bombardment – which the news reels of Shanghai and Spain reinforced – among the populations of Germany's opponents. In its designed combat use, it destroyed centres of resistance throughout Poland Western Europe and the Balkans. Thereafter, German policy was committed to ends which the *Luftwaffe* had not been designed to serve, while its industrial base was under intense bombardment. It ran out of aircraft, fuel, materials and time. Nevertheless, its history till 1941 remains instructive.

The political objective (tearing up Versailles) was translated into a specific military instrument (the *Luftwaffe*) with a specific character. Its development was put under a high-powered ministry, which was given all the priorities it needed to mobilise research and design and extend production facilities. The ministry was equipped with adequate powers to break bottlenecks and impose solutions where necessary. As the representative of the state, it did not accept what industry could or wanted to provide as a datum, but brought about the configurations it wanted. Government financed the whole operation by special means. The connection between the state's political aims, the chosen strategy, the industrial system and the national research effort was direct and complete.

Hitler's overt reassertions of German power caused the British Government to reassess the assumptions and priorities of its defence policy. The 'ten year rule' had been abandoned in response to Japanese actions in Manchuria, while Brüning was still Chancellor. Now the private information which was filtering through put a rather more menacing gloss on Germany's intentions than the public statements of its representatives and reopened the old suspicion, as in the days of Tirpitz, that the public statements could not be relied upon. The British Government found itself having to consider the possibility of a war on two fronts – in the Far East against Japan, and in Europe, against Germany. After the disruption of relationships with Italy in 1935–36 over the latter's attack on Ethiopia, it appeared likely that a hostile state might straddle the main route between the two fronts.

---

*Goering, when told that in terms of cost, two four-engined bombers were equivalent to three two-engined bombers plumped for the latter: 'The Führer will ask how many aircraft we have, not how big they will be.'

The Germans had declared themselves prepared for an arms race, but attempting to match their policies involved the British Government in difficulties for which there was no German counterpart. Public opinion had to be taken into account, and public opinion was fiercely pacifist, as by-election results, public debates and the excoriation of the few advocates of rearmament showed. (The German public was not given an opportunity to express its views on the Peace Ballot). Finance was also a problem. In the aftermath of the Depression, the British Government, largely at the insistence of Neville Chamberlain as Chancellor of the Exchequer, considered that it had to provide for the 'amount' of defence the country could afford – a view in which it was eventually supported by the Opposition on the assumption that the country could or should not afford much. (The extreme Left opposed any rearmament on the grounds that it was a device to enable a 'fascist' government to subdue the working class). This approach to policy was in direct contrast to Germany, whose rulers could put military needs first, at least in their planning assumptions, and make the general economic development of the society follow.

Again in contrast to Germany, the British Government could not finance rearmament in secret: the funds had to be voted by Parliament after debate. Neither could the relationship with the industry be as smoothly managed. Fourteen firms made airframes and five, engines, but their directors and managers by no means saw eye to eye with the Air Ministry about the aircraft it was desirable or necessary to produce, and through their association, the Society of British Aircraft Constructors, insisted on rates of profit and conditions of security which the Treasury condemned as excessive.* The British Government had to relearn the lesson that if through negligence or neglect, or through suddenly being forced to revise its strategic assumptions, a government has to undertake a crash programme, then all routine practices are no longer valid, and the bargaining position of those who can meet the requirements is immensely strengthened. The German Government coped with this problem by 'strong arm' methods, but the British Government had neither the power nor the will to bring industry to order as the German Government had dealt with Professor Junkers. The British Government had no construction capacity of its own, since the RAE had divested itself of all manufacture. Finally, Britain was not setting out to design from scratch an air force with a specific pre-determined role.

---

*In the absence of materials from the SBAC, the published accounts rely heavily on the Treasury papers. The authors, Shay and Middlemas respectively, underrate the suspicion of, if not outright hostility to private industry among Treasury officials (not necessarily because they are socialists but because they are mandarins) who failed to grasp that what they regarded as exorbitant demands from industry were, from the latter's standpoint, merely a premium for renovation and security after years of inadequate state funding. Shay's account shows how officials took a Cobdenite view of defence spending and how, through a naive and erroneous analysis of German policy, they hoped that rearmament could be made unnecessary.

Britain had a force in being – which was disadvantageous in that it contained a high proportion of obsolescent machines or aircraft designed for uses other than war in Europe. There was not even basic agreement on the type of war to be waged and on the corresponding breakdown of effort between fighters and bombers.* So there was no objective which automatically suggested an order of priorities in construction and calls on resources.

In the absence of agreement on strategic objectives, there was no incentive to change the system, and as that, for fourteen years, had contented itself with keeping an aircraft industry in being, the system of procurement was geared to very leisurely schedules in which the largest single period of time was spent on the manufacture and testing of prototypes. Unkind critics suggested that this was the main reason why the aircraft were obsolete by the time they arrived in squadron service.**

Hence, for Britain, 'rearmament' in the air took on quite another meaning. In contrast to Germany, no clear thread could be discerned between the chosen end of policy and the techniques in science and organisation for producing the weapons which policy required. The British Government took a long time to sort out priorities. But in 1935 when rearmament formally began, there were certain more positive features. Aircraft manufacturers could draw on the new light industries which had not been so badly hit by the Depression as shipbuilding and heavy engineering. The motor-car industry offered a reservoir of transferable skills. Further, although the funds had to be voted by Parliament, there was nothing to prevent an individual firm from experimenting with its own money and facilities – however much the Ministry might deplore it – and then trying to convince the air procurement authorities to write their specifications round the experimental results. By this process, the RAF was weaned from biplanes made of wood to monoplanes made of metal.† Technical progress issued from vigorous debate, in which no situation was ruled out in advance.††

---

*Eventually, fighters were given priority, but not as a result of deep strategic analysis; they were cheaper to make and their operating cycle costs were far lower than those of bombers. They therefore offered 'more' security per unit of expenditure. Fighters could prevent Britain from being knocked out and would give time for the creation of a force of bombers. This argument meant that if there were no war, the manufacture of bombers need not be funded, but that if war did break out, then Germany would not be under threat from the air.

**One of Lord Swinton's first measures, as Air Minister, was to stop the elaboration of prototypes and to insist that modifications be carried out during (not before) the production stage.

†This much-needed development put Britain at a disadvantage: aluminium production in 1935 was 15,000 tons: in Germany and Austria it totalled 200,000 tons.

††It also helped that those who became involved in air rearmament whether they were in the services, in the aircraft industry or in universities and technical institutes formed a select, unofficial club, whose members were well known to each other. In this way, eg, the aeronautical department at Cambridge developed new ideas about aerodynamics which affected the design of aircraft in the 1930s.

In the long run, this was the vital distinction between the revival of the RAF and of the *Luftwaffe*, since the RAF was not hamstrung by having the wrong types of aircraft when the conditions of war diverged from those for which it was designed. But the *Luftwaffe* was ready for action far more quickly than any other air force and exerted a decisive influence on the politics of Europe during 1937 and 1939, when it provided the overwhelming physical threat behind the foreign policy moves of the Third Reich.

In comparison, the uncertain aims of British air planning (in 1936 the Chief of the Imperial General Staff was arguing in favour of a tactical air force and in the following year the navy tried strenuously to regain control of naval aviation) and the fragmented industrial base crippled rearmament in the air. The 1935 target was 3,800 aircraft in twenty-one months, without disrupting the production of civil aircraft or components. This qualification made even more acute the shortage of skilled labour, since operatives could not be released from the civil sector without damage to current output and to exports. In the vital machine-tool sector, for example, some twenty-five per cent of current output in 1935-1937 was finding its way abroad, to the benefit of the balance of payments. Here was an immediate constraint on the building programme: should policy aim at training new operatives – which would take a minimum of six months out of the twenty-one of the planning period – or should policy concentrate on using the existing force on the work to which it was best accustomed, namely producing aircraft built to the usual specifications? If the latter course were adopted, then the aircraft which emerged would be obsolescent and no match for the *Luftwaffe*. They might be in greater numbers than would result from, say, gearing production to new types, but greater numbers would hardly deter the opposition and inferior performance was a positive invitation.

Such problems of choice arose because there was no clear, universally accepted idea as to how 'the defence of the realm' translated into specific forces, land, sea or air, or into specific weapons. Everyone concerned agreed that Nazi Germany posed some kind of threat; no-one agreed how to 'weigh' its constituent elements, with the result that at the time of the Sudeten crisis – September 1938 – Britain had only about 1,600 front-line aircraft, approximating half the size of the *Luftwaffe* and mostly inferior to it in performance. Of the fighters available, less than 100 were Hurricanes and only six were Spitfires.* In the event, the *Anschluss* and the Sudeten crisis concentrated minds and revised programmes. Britain concentrated on

---

*The Sudeten crisis shows most acutely that the criterion of power was not potential capacity but the time taken to design, develop and produce weapons and associated systems in sufficient quantities to make some impact on balances of *deployable* power, and hence on the options open to foreign policy. Properly coordinated innovations yield political dividends.

producing the Hurricane and the Spitfire,* in greater numbers than any other fighters. They were integrated operationally with radar to make them more certain of intercepting the enemy. But the Battle of Britain** showed that the numbers were only just sufficient – and then to the detriment of the bomber programme.

The stipulation to rearm without disturbing necessary peacetime production was met by the creation of 'shadow factories'. These were plants owned by firms which would automatically be drawn into the war effort after the outbreak of hostilities. Such firms were asked by government to equip part of their facilities or add to them, to produce materials for the rearmament programme and to train their managements and operatives in the techniques concerned. In return, the plant and productive equipment thus made available were paid for by the state which also bought the output and paid a management fee. By this means, the government ensured a certain contribution to current rearmament needs and created the basis for expansion in wartime, when the entire plant would be committed to war production. In Britain this was a new type of relationship between government and industry in peacetime. It was a compromise forced on government by the need to serve civil and military 'markets' at the same time, by the shortage of skills, the existing structures of industry, and by the policy conflicts at the highest levels.

Limited improvisation in industry was matched by equally restricted moves to exploit natural science for the purposes of national defence. 'Science' was still regarded as a source of ingenious gadgets, designed to improve the performance of the fighting forces and frustrate the knavish tricks of the enemy. It was an adjunct to strategy – and the application of scientific talent in the thirties was commensurate with this opinion. True, the British Government had at its disposal the National Physical Laboratory and the Royal Aeronautical Establishment at Farnborough, but they worked to restricted budgets and were not used to organise and manage a comprehensive national research effort over a wide spectrum of activity. Instead, British policy relied on a number of individuals, recruited to defence research through personal friendship and professional connection, who initiated and conducted experiments on such problems as came their way. Of these, the most famous, subsequently, was the enquiry into detecting and locating aircraft by using radio waves.

---

*The Spitfire proved the more difficult to manufacture initially through the complexity of its structure and the problems of sub-contracting the manufacture of the wings. So on 3 September 1939, 299 Spitfires, involving some twenty-four million man hours had been built, as against 578 Hurricanes, representing some twenty million man hours.

**The outcome has been taken to indicate that, in the last analysis, the military and political leadership got its priorities right, but it may be argued that a British army, fully trained and equipped to deal with *Blitzkrieg* would have made the Battle of Britain unnecessary, by confining the *Luftwaffe* to bases in the Rhineland, and giving it other targets.

The work revolved round a small group of academic scientists of whom two, Henry Tizard, Rector of Imperial College, London, and F. A. Lindemann, Professor of Experimental Philosophy and Head of the Clarendon Laboratory at Oxford, achieved public notoriety when their professional feud was presented by Sir Charles Snow in 1960 as 'a cautionary story' about science and government. The publicity has tended to polarise the discussion and obscure the contributions of others. Tizard and Lindemann met as research students in Berlin in 1908. Six years later, they each became involved in applying scientific analysis to improve the combat performance of aircraft – Tizard in the Royal Flying Corps and Lindemann at Farnborough. Both qualified as pilots. Although they returned to civil employments, both retained a military dimension to their thinking, along with friendships with former colleagues and active memberships of professional bodies and advisory bodies especially the Aeronautical Research Committee.''

In December 1934, Tizard became Chairman of an Air Ministry Committee for the Scientific Study of Air Defence. Lindemann's *point d'appui* was his long-standing association with Winston Churchill. By the 1930s both Tizard and Lindemann had long since ceased to publish any experimental work of their own, but, as directors of important institutions in the world of science, were acquainted with the tasks of administering research and were in the best position to recruit promising students to explore the needs of defence. Hence, the British variant of a full-funded institute working on possible strategies and the relationships they entailed with science and technology was a network of connections between individuals, whose interactions took place at a number of disparate locations, official and otherwise, and included luncheons at the Athenaeum and country house weekends. These arrangements had the advantage of obscurity and cheapness; in the nature of things, they could not be comprehensive. The job of Tizard's committee was to spot winners.

The experiments in radio location were successful and were accepted by serving officers who were only too acutely aware of how inferior their equipment was to that of the *Luftwaffe*. But they were exceptional at the time, even in the RAF which was perhaps the most technologically–minded of the services. The dominant opinion doubted whether scientists as such could have anything to say on matters of strategy and tactics: their job was to find new ways of improving the working efficiency of engines or of the mountings of guns, when requested to do so. It was out of the question that they should initiate purely theoretical enquiries which would impinge on the deliberations of the high commands. Officers of Bomber Command rejected conclusions stemming from work done under Tizard's auspices since they were convinced that only they could know all there was to be known about the accuracy of bombing. A naval authority informed Tizard that radio location, as it was then called (it became 'radar' in 1942) would never be used at sea because ships had too many aerials already. (The designers of the *Graf Spee* did not share that view.)

Such reactions cannot wholly be credited to professional obscurantism. The services had been kept short of funds for ordinary day-to-day working – a constraint which enhanced the attractions of the tried and tested. An accepted, comprehensive view, jointly worked out by or imposed by government on the navy, army and air force, as to just how Britain, the Commonwealth and Empire were to be defended would have suggested priorities, and perhaps made commanders more receptive to innovations initiated by the scientific community. It is significant that the only coherent view which did emerge was that the defence of Britain meant primarily the RAF and, within the RAF, Fighter Command, and *that* not for strategic but for financial reasons. It was cheaper than the alternatives.

The idea of radio detection was worked out and put into operation just in time for the outbreak of war: the major chain of stations was completed and handed over to the RAF in May 1939. It was vital to the margin of success in the air battles of the summer of the next year. Radar was, however, the only prewar achievement in Britain in the use of theoretical science to devise new techniques for war. It was relatively straightforward, in that the phenomenon that aircraft could disturb radio reception was known, if only to a few, that a member of Tizard's committee (Professor Edward Appleton) had done virtually all the basic theoretical work necessary and that the additional research was minimal and could be carried out with existing facilities. Most important of all, the whole operation did not raise those fundamental questions of getting enough machine tools and finding or creating suitable industrial skills which hamstrung industrial preparations for war.

With radar, the nature of the problem was such that *ad hoc* relationships and minimal investment sufficed, but the development served notice that state policy could no longer afford to ignore the advantages offered by the conscious and systematic exploitation of theoretical science. Government had to sponsor experiments directly, through appropriate committees, and incorporate their results into its chosen strategy and even into the training and command structures of those who were to implement the strategy in time of war. In this process, the experimental results affected the choice of strategy and of the weapons needed to give it effect. Had the radar experiments failed, Britain, unable to put up an effective defence against the *Luftwaffe*, might well have had to change its basic strategy into one of retaliation and therefore pressed on with the construction of bombers. As it was, the near certainty of a high rate of interception, which radar made possible, was coupled with a weapon which could make the best use of the 'information' on the radar screen to destroy the enemy. It would be useless to match radar with the old, slow under-gunned biplanes. Equally, it would be unavailing to combine radar with Hurricanes and Spitfires without habituating the pilots to the discipline of being ordered about the sky from the ground. Pilot, aircraft and radar had to be integrated into a system. Moreover, in terms of the national resources as a whole, radar-directed combat released squadrons from patrol duties and yielded the same 'amount' of defence coverage with fewer aircraft, thus releasing more resources for the development of other types. All these options followed from the initial investment in radio physics.

These, it must be stressed, were only the initial steps in the involvement of government in fundamental natural science. On the eve of the Second World War, the capacity to make war tied together design, engineering, certain types of skills, access to raw materials, the 'right' balance between enlistments and reserved industrial manpower and, for all this, government control of the relevant sectors of the economy. The origins of these links lay in 1916.

PART VI

1939–

'Dire combustion and confused events
New-hatched to the woeful time.'
Macbeth

1. The conscription of pure science: methods and operations

The Second World War opened in a way recognisably similar to the First, with an attack across a frontier – the German-Polish – following an ultimatum. This time, however, the German command did not wait for the time-limit to expire. (There were no ceremonial leave-takings, either.) As in 1914, though with determination rather than enthusiasm, France and Britain became involved through their alliances with the attacked state.

In all the forces engaged, vestiges of the techniques of the First World War remained. The German invaders used horse-drawn transport, the British sent two squadrons of biplanes to France and the French army occupied its steel and concrete version of the Verdun forts. The succeeding months conclusively proved the inadequacy or irrelevance of these techniques in the face of *Blitzkrieg*. The technology of the victors in the campaigns in Western Europe in 1940 was not intrinsically new, nor was it vastly superior, but it was employed with a consistency and on a scale which was overwhelming. The German forces were performing a task which they had been specifically designed to do. Their opponents had no accepted and up-to-date doctrine about how to employ their technology or how to counter the Germans, who used tank and aircraft in combination to achieve specific political and military objectives.

Six countries were overrun in a matter of weeks. From the attack on Poland on 1 September 1939 to the surrender of French forces on 25 June 1940, the *Wehrmacht* was in action for a total of ninety-six days. Battles aiming at the annihilation of the opposing forces paved the way, after each campaign, for the revision of the European order. The political dividends fell to the state which had most systematically examined the possibilities held out by technological advance and applied them. The German Government won the opportunity to reshape the European polity as it wished. It promptly squandered the opportunity by invading the Soviet Union for political objectives which were not thought through and were unrelated to the forces involved. Army and air force were presented with exactly the war of attrition they had been designed to avoid. *Blitzkrieg* was not an all-purpose method of waging war.

From the summer of 1940 onwards, the war took on an increasingly technological character. Britain attempted by superior use of technology to make up for its deficiencies in manpower. After December 1941, the entry of the United States brought into the hostilities a nation which, as it were, instinctively ran to technological solutions. In both Britain and the United States, finding solutions to problems took the state into pure as well as applied research. The prosecution of war depended not just on engineers and a stock of equipment reasonably secure from attack, but on the efforts of scientists in laboratories and in operations rooms, both in the analysis of the data which combat generated and in the devising of measures and countermeasures. Radar established the link. Its introduction showed 'science' to the military in its traditional character, that is as a store of esoteric knowledge which could provide inventions useful in the search for strategic or tactical advantage; but in consequence of the operation of radar, 'science' took on another meaning, as a method by which the tactical problems disclosed by combat could be evaluated and overcome. This use of scientific method came to be known as Operational Research.

It had in fact been devised and practised during the First World War when A.V. Hill, a Cambridge scientist in uniform as an infantry major, was asked to apply himself to the problems disclosed by using conventional artillery against air attack, taking for his initial data the six-pounder gun with which the navy was attempting to defend London against Zeppelins, from the roof of the Admiralty. Hill's investigation led to the formation of what would now be called an Operational Research Group, which carried out systematic experiments among anti-aircraft units in Britain and France to improve their performance. Hill's group had to analyse not just the weapon and its performance under conditions for which it had not been designed, but the manning requirements and the flows of information in the entire operation of sighting an aircraft, laying and firing the gun; in today's terms, he had to consider the operation as a system.* The results were eventually crystallised in the official handbook but the technique of submitting operational problems to scientific scrutiny was among the many lessons jettisoned after the war.

Operational Research had to be 're-invented' some twenty years later. It was not concerned with discovering knowledge for its own sake but with translating knowledge into action by structuring and measuring the problems presented by battle as if they were problems in natural science. This required minute analysis of the whole cycle of an operation, to establish which particular factor or set of variables needed to be changed and what the effect of changing one element would be on the whole. The traditional

---

*Hill had to overcome the hostility of regular artillery officers whose professional convictions led them to question what a mere infantryman could know about gunnery. After 1918, Hill returned to Cambridge but kept up his connection with service problems as a civilian member of the Naval Anti-Aircraft Committee, and was, from 1934, a member of Tizard's Committee. By that time, he had been awarded a Nobel prize.

approach of 'going back to first principles' was dismissed on the ground that it merely replaced one *a priori* concept with another. The justification of the new technique was twofold: it improved performance and it helped 'to avoid running the war with gusts of emotion'.*

The first OR units were formed to follow up RAF Fighter Command's use of radar interception, but the paradigmatic case arose out of antisubmarine operations. One of the techniques adopted by Britain to counter attacks on convoys by German submarines from bases in the Bay of Biscay was to attack the submarines by depth charges dropped from aircraft. The charges, of necessity, had to be set to explode at a pre-arranged depth, which was, in fact, 100 or 150 feet. That was thought to present the greatest possible chance of destroying the enemy vessel since that depth offered the best compromise between a shallower setting, which would cause most of the explosive force to be lost into the air, and a deeper one, which would cause it to be muffled and therefore neutralised by the pressure of water. Experience showed that the rate of destruction was sporadic and unsatisfactory.

Scientists began flying with RAF Coastal Command to observe minutely the sequence of events and operations in hunting submarines over a large number of sorties. The observations were then correlated and analysed to establish which factors were present in successful actions (when the submarine was sunk) and in unsuccessful actions, respectively. Possible solutions in terms of varying the height, speed and course of the aircraft were explored, as well as technical improvements in the radar location systems to detect the submarine. None of the solutions stood up in practice. Then attention turned to the behaviour of the submarine under attack and the depth at which the charge exploded; where was the submarine at that point? Systematic analysis of the data from the flight observations showed that in nearly all instances, the submarine *had not had time* to submerge to anywhere like the depth at which the depth charge was pre-set to explode with maximum effect. Furthermore, if the submarines were operating in packs, the nearer they were to the surface at the time the depth charges were dropped, the closer together they would be, since they would not have had time to scatter. Conversely, the more time available before the charge exploded, the more widespread they would be under water. On both counts – improving the chances of destroying individual submarines and of catching packs of submarines before they had time to disperse – the *nearer* the surface the explosion could be timed to take place the better; 100 feet was far too deep.

This conclusion was tried out in practice; the settings were altered to twenty-five and thirty-three feet, and the rate of successes improved. The German authorities concluded that their enemy must have a new secret weapon. In fact, the results rested on the strictly scientific analysis of what

---

*The stipulation was made by Professor Blackett – a physicist in charge of Operational Research at the Admiralty and Coastal Command.

was to hand. The 'secret' lay in evaluating a series of events not by reference to the axioms of military experience but to the assumptions and procedures of a separate discipline. Neither the military problem nor the technique of scientific analysis was new; the novelty was in relating the two for practical ends.

When scientists went on operations they ceased to be just purveyors of laboratory results to the military but participated directly in the making of tactical decisions. Authority derived from knowledge, viewed as a disqualification from the higher direction of affairs only fifty years before, entered into military planning at all levels. With their new techniques the scientists brought, however, a different ethos which competed with that of the military. Effective command depends, to an extent, on the ability to discount inconvenient evidence. This is not entirely a question of personality. Commanders work against time as well as against the enemy, and he who is too open to evidence will fail to achieve anything. The practice of systematic doubt, moreover, has a bad effect on morale. Military hierarchies are, by definition, authoritarian, in the literal sense of the term: by reason of the need for discipline and loyalty under stress, they are also tribal. The net effect is to confuse truth with status.

Scientists do not work to these rules. Their authority rests on the results of applying a self-correcting method to their initial ideas and on the results having survived a degree and range of criticism from colleagues which no general on active service could tolerate. For this reason, they tended to function best as civilians, who donned uniform, if at all, only for temporary assignments or for representational purposes. Civilian status was advantageous inasmuch as it kept them out of the formal hierarchies but it made them vulnerable if they were not consistently backed by someone at or near the top of the regular hierarchy. Their success rested, ultimately, not only on their being able to deliver the results but on the persuasiveness with which they could urge them on to commands working to different principles. Finally, there was the overriding problem that the operational facts with which the scientists had to deal comprised a number of variables, some of which at least could not be measured. So in solving problems, recourse to theory and to numerical thinking could only be effective within limits and competed with judgements deriving from authority.

The enrolment of scientists in the operational side of war introduced a different relationship between knowledge and action. As long as the scientist stayed in his laboratory, he could work to the traditional norms and axioms of his trade; experiments were repeatable. Outside, in the world of action, they were not, and there, success only came to those who could adapt the methods of exact science to inexact situations. For this, they had to feel intellectually comfortable across the hallowed boundaries of their specialisations. Scientists also had to be able to translate their own private language of mathematics into terms which commanders responsible for operations could understand and apply. The tart observation that wars were won by weapons and not by slide-rules ignored the fact that war had got to the point at which it could be lost by not using them.

On the side of the military, accepting and using gadgets no longer sufficed: what was required of them was participation in the processes of control and verification – which in itself presupposed some informed acquaintance with scientific techniques somewhere in the chain of command. Since high-ranking officers immersed in the problems of combat are expected to do other things than sit back and appraise scientific techniques, they had to rely on the conclusions reached by experts on grounds for which commonsense,* routine service procedures, the exercise of will or intuition provided no basis. The decisive factor in judgement was whether the commander was willing to follow where the evidence led or, put another way, what reasons he had for disregarding the evidence or saying it was not applicable.

Conclusions arrived at by mathematical reasoning were not automatically conclusive. Mathematics is a technique; if the premises or assumptions to which it relates are 'wrong', then mathematics as such is of no use: the way the problem is defined has also to be taken into account. Operational researchers defined their problems by experiment and verification, to the extent that conditions allowed. Others, say, using mathematical techniques to hone down deductions from *a priori* assumptions could produce quite different conclusions, although the methods and calculations used in each case were equally rigorous. The difference between the two approaches was merely that scientific method did permit putting theoretical deductions to an empirical test, when reaching decisions on the options open to policy. The alternate method of working by logical deductions from *a priori* assumptions is the older-established method of inquiry, which can yield weighty practical judgements as to what to do. It is one which accommodated itself more easily to the command structures through which operational problems were articulated and decisions carried out (at the crudest evaluation, because the initial *a priori* assumption was what the commander felt ought to be done – which is beyond measurement).

It is difficult now, when the military have a deep professional interest in innovation and when research is welcomed as an indispensable part of operations, to convey the difficulty and animosity which the attempt to incorporate scientific conclusions into practical judgements could evoke during the Second World War. The resultant tensions are conveniently illustrated by the controversy in 1942 over what the bombing policy of the RAF should be.

---

*Eg, 'commonsense' would suggest that the bigger the bomb, the more effective it is as a producer of casualties. Scientific analysis showed that the conclusion was false, under the operational circumstances, and that, ton for ton, 50 kg bombs yielded more casualties than 250 kg bombs.

Tizard,* in a lecture to an audience of makers of strategic policies in February 1942 summed up 'the strategy of pure science as applied to war' as being 'to attack the point where dividends are greatest in results in relation to effort.' The problem, as Tizard knew only too well from experience, was to identify that point from among the competing claims of the services in relation to the resources immediately available and probably achievable, and from among the competing strategies for which those immediate or realisable resources could be used. From the standpoint of British strategy at the time at which Tizard spoke, it was extremely important to establish whether the area bombing of cities was having the effects claimed for it, as against competing strategies of destroying specific industrial targets or communications systems, or using the RAF for some other purpose.

Since 1939, the rationale of area bombing had shifted from attacking cities as the locations of factories and their indispensable workers (who, by definition, had forfeited their civilian status) to one of breaking the Germans' will to resist by 'de-housing' the population. Experience had shown only too clearly that Bomber Command were not too skilled at finding pinpoint targets, let alone hitting them. So cities themselves became the targets. It would have been possible to have concentrated attacks on those associated with particular manufacturing firms such as Bosch at Stuttgart and Heinkel at Rostock, on the grounds that even if the factories escaped, the workforce would suffer casualties and would be less inclined to work efficiently after prolonged bombardment. This possibility was rejected in favour of a general sociological argument about the behaviour of human beings in cities, submitted to acute stress.

Did the argument stand up to empirical analysis? The question was put by Solly Zuckerman** in a high table conversation at Christ Church, Oxford. Lindemann, now enobled as Lord Cherwell, agreed that the only empirical evidence came from the surveys of the reactions of British populations to bombardment by the *Luftwaffe*. These were given to his office in the form of statistical analyses of the experience in Hull and Birmingham, chosen because they were a typical port and industrial town respectively. The results showed that there was no evidence of breakdown of morale at the intensity of bombardment experienced (which was comparable with what the RAF was at the time capable of inflicting on Germany), and that losses in production occurred not because workers were deprived of their homes but because the places where they worked were damaged or destroyed.[1] Lord Cherwell's Minute,[2] submitted to the Prime Minister on 30th March 1942 took the opposite view:

---

*By now semi-official adviser to the Minister of Aircraft Production.

**Formally, Professor of Anatomy at Birmingham University: in practice, Director of the Bombing Survey.

Investigation seems to show that having one's house demolished is most damaging to morale. People seem to mind it more than having their friends and relatives killed. At Hull signs of strain were very evident, though only one-tenth of the houses were demolished ... we should be able to do ten times as much harm to each of the principal fifty-eight German towns. There seems to be little doubt that this would break the spirit of the people.

Lord Cherwell derived this conclusion from a number of assumptions as to the output and availability of bombing aircraft by 1943, the number of sorties which could be flown, the tonnage of bombs dropped during the period in which, statistically, the bomber could operate before being shot down or damaged beyond further use, and the degree of accuracy achievable, ie that one half of the bombs dropped fell in built-up areas.

Other scientific advisers to government, particularly Tizard and Blackett, questioned these assumptions, and thereby cast doubt on the policy; aerial bombardment was a feasible strategy but not under the circumstances postulated and could not be decisive by the middle of 1943 (which was Cherwell's contention). The ensuing row has been well-documented and still excites partisan comment. It helped to bring about Tizard's retirement from public service in the middle of the war, though it was not a proximate cause. The war effort was thus deprived of a superior scientific intelligence. Evidence examined after the war proved that all parties to the dispute were wrong, but that the dissentients' case was far nearer the empirical truth of the matter than Lord Cherwell's had been. On the figures and arguments advanced in 1942 Tizard and Blackett suggested a more rational use of the available resources, which, instead, were devoted to missions that conspicuously failed to produce the breakdown of will they were intended to promote.

The adoption of area bombing automatically closed down the other options: it meant, for example, tolerating a higher degree of risk for longer in the Battle of the Atlantic, as the price for continuing the air offensive against Germany at that juncture; it meant devoting to bombers manufacturing resources which otherwise could have been used to build up armoured divisions. It did, however, produce a number of valuable if costly lessons for the RAF which Bomber Command was able to apply in 1944 on something like the scale and intensity the theorists had said was necessary. Area bombing attacks also forced the *Luftwaffe* to change from being a tactical bombing force to being a fighter defence force, which was very significant in relation to the Reich's use of its dwindling resources. But area bombing did *not* destroy the Germans' will to resist by 'de-housing' the population.

What remains puzzling is how Lord Cherwell, on the evidence presented to him, ever thought that it would. The published materials and the unpublished Cherwell papers do not disclose how he came to use the evidence from Hull and Birmingham in an exactly opposite sense from that originally given to him. Lord Zuckerman prints in his memoirs the conclusions of the Hull and Birmingham surveys which were given to Lord Cherwell's office. Among the Cherwell papers, there is a detailed break-down, dated 12 February 1942, of the effects of the attacks on dwelling houses in Birmingham as well as a note summarising discussions with Zuckerman about the results of his bombing surveys – both of which tend to support the case the dissentients subsequently made. There is also a curious remark in a letter to Tizard, dated 22 April 1942, commenting on his figures; 'even on your figures, the weight of attack on all the proposed German cities would be three or four times as great as Birmingham or Hull. From those who have studied the effect on these towns, I gather that even this intensity of bombing spread over the whole country would be catastrophic.' If by 'those who have studied the effects' Lord Cherwell meant his own staff, then he was, apparently, receiving some oddly calculated evidence: if he meant Zuckerman's survey results, then he was ignoring it. These are conjectures; what actually happened to the analyses between the gathering of the materials and the submission of the Minute is uncertain. Lord Zuckerman later talked of Lord Cherwell's 'vigorous extrapolations', but they were carried to the point of contradiction.

Eventually, 'de-housing' dropped out of the rationales of bombing policy, and area bombing came to be justified in terms of what were originally thought to be its by-products.* In 1942, however, bombing Germany was about the only offensive action which British forces could take, and possibly, that concern underlay Lord Cherwell's thinking. Although the debate was between scientists, they were not debating in a scientific environment. The processes of publication, criticism and rebuttal which are customary in, say, the Royal Society, were not being applied in this instance. Criticism was mutual but not free; it was constrained by institutions and the need to act. It was also secret and not public, although the number of participants was greater than those mentioned here. But whether a freer debate would have affected the outcome remains doubtful, since the argument was about doing something, rather than explaining it. In science, it is not enough to be 'right' for the 'wrong' reasons; in the world of action, that frequently has to suffice.

The idea of area bombing did not originate in the Minute, but Lord Cherwell crystallised thinking about it and gave it the necessary status. The Minute determined action, since resources had to be committed for the policy it advocated, and that very act of commitment implied the denial of other objectives. The paradox of war in the industrial age is that necessity may spur invention but it is very difficult to do anything new, quickly and on a scale adequate to the task. The main hindrance is not the hierarchy – though that may be considerable – but the weight of accumulated knowledge on which the hierarchy can rely in situations in which no-one knows the final

---

*A commonplace in the world of action.

answers. Scientists are used to systematically destroying accretions of past knowledge: others codify them as 'experience' or 'tradition'; in military operations the equivalent of the scientist's experiments, as a method of invalidating the past, is defeat.

The whole episode has been treated as a contest between enlightenment and dogmatism, between the scientific and the *engagé* intelligence or between a latter-day Galileo and a Cremonini (Professor of Philosophy at Padua) refusing to look through Galileo's telescope to observe the satellites of Jupiter which reason told him could not be there. The well-advertised personal factors in the case lend colour to this view. In what concerns this enquiry, it illustrates vividly the limitations of applying scientific method to action in the early days, even under the compulsions of war. Those responsible for carrying out policies had been accustomed to think of scientists as providers of solutions to set problems. In this guise, scientists were acceptable. They ceased to be so when they concluded that policy was fundamentally unjustifiable on the terms stated. For this reason, the criticisms of Tizard and Blackett provoked feelings of outrage which dispelled any chances they had of being considered on their merits. From the nature of the case, the chances were not very high: in the area bombing proposals, far more hung on the conclusions than the likelihood of the survival of a number of German towns.

At the time of Lord Cherwell's Minute, Sir Arthur Harris had been in charge of Bomber Command for just five weeks. He had arrived at a critical moment in its history, since the navy was clamouring for the diversion of bombers to anti-submarine patrols and for setting up a series of 'Coastal Commands' in the various sea areas; the army was attributing its setbacks in the Western Desert, partly, to the failure of the RAF to block supplies and reinforcements to Rommel: in the Far East, the triumphant advance on the Japanese, in the absence of ground forces in sufficient numbers and quality, could only be halted by systematic bombing. Complying with these demands would mean the reduction of the RAF to a residual role in strategy and the denial of its *raison d'être* as an independent arm, so persistently asserted since 1919. Throughout his career, Harris had been convinced that aerial bombing on the right scale could win wars,* destroying the enemy to the point at which operations by ground forces became mere police actions: to use an army without first destroying an enemy from the air was a guaranteed formula for failure. (He interpreted Dunkirk in this sense.) In this belief he had personally carried out and later supervised experiments to improve bombing techniques. To this professional conviction, Harris brought to his

---

*In April 1978, Sir Arthur Harris in a documentary broadcast on the BBC repeated his conviction that 'strategic bombers won the biggest land battle of the war, the biggest air battle of the war and the biggest naval battle of the war.' His judgement specifically included the American contribution.

task, in the words of the Official Historians, 'a facility for concentrating on one side of a question and regarding the other as mere obstruction' – a characteristic not without its uses in other spheres of action. So even if Cherwell and Tizard had respected each other's judgement, if Blackett had not been written off as a partisan of the Admiralty, if Harris could have brought himself to consider the whole issue dispassionately, there was no way in which he could admit the critics' case, except at the cost of resigning or of presiding over the partition of his service among its older rivals. He was not the man to do either. Indeed, anyone intellectually prepared to do that would not be judged suitable for command in the world of action.

Harris' personal characteristics may, perhaps, have had little or no effect, had he not stood for an organisation which considered itself under threat of dissolution. He took care to establish and keep in trim direct contacts with the Prime Minister, who was temperamentally averse to getting rid of anyone who was or appeared to be doing something to hit the enemy: that quality was especially helpful to Harris at a time when Bomber Command offered the only positive prospect of doing so. Secure in his institution and buttressed by the political authority, Harris was freed for almost another three years from arguing about ends, and could concentrate solely on means.* His own Operational Research Branch followed suit.

The admission of scientific method into professional debates over operations was novel, and it is not surprising that commanders who admitted its necessity were nonetheless reluctant to pay the price of sharing their traditional prerogatives with newcomers whose criteria and convictions were different, if not alien. Under the pressure of combat, a working relationship between knowledge and action was arrived at – the more easily, perhaps, because the research staffs and facilities required were on a small scale. No formal high-level negotiations were necessary. Much depended on personality and the ratio of success between prediction and outcome.

---

*He later had fierce arguments with his counterparts in the USAAF, but not about the validity of strategic bombing; if anything they had to be even more single-minded about it than Harris himself, since the USAAF had still only a qualified promise of independent status after the war; its leaders therefore had reason to insist, in and out of season, that wars could be won by bombing alone. The US Strategic Bombing Survey was deliberately drawn up, after the war, to prove that this had been the case, as an unassailable argument for Air Force independence. It is far from valueless, but is an *ex parte* document, not a dispassionate, scientific assessment of the results.

2. 'War' and 'Peace' at the limits of knowledge: nuclear war

In Operational Research the dimensions of the problem and the techniques relevant to solving it, if not actually applicable, were both known. The essential research task, whether it related to land, sea, or air or combined forces, was to isolate the key factors in an operation considered as a system, and see what would happen if one or other were changed. During the same war years, 1939 to 1945, however, war broke out of the limits of the known into the realm of what could only be guessed to be knowable; it required the sustained exploration of pure theory, for ends which could not themselves be defined except in the most general way, and demanding the use of techniques which still had to be researched and developed. War thus entered the most esoteric realms of human knowledge.

For what 'lay to hand' in 1939 was a dispersed quantity of international research into the nature and structure of the atom, and, more specifically, of the energy which could be released by 'splitting' its nucleus. Experimental results appeared to show that under certain conditions, splitting (fission) reactions could be self-sustaining. These conclusions had been established through the work of a number of scientists in Europe and the United States. In January 1939, a small group of initiates was aware that nuclear fission might be usable to produce explosions for which volcanic eruptions and meteorites offered the only known precedent. Other initiates disagreed with this interpretation of the research results. The dispute was about matters of theory, and participation in it restricted to those who spoke the language of nuclear physics and physical chemistry. If nuclear fission was to be used at all, for any purpose, their esoteric dissensions would first have to be resolved, the outcome experimentally verified and then translated into terms of engineering.

Even then the strategic implications could only be considered in the vaguest terms: was the explosion to be effected by bombing or by loading a ship, as it were, with the means of producing a nuclear reaction? The answer in part depended on the critical mass of uranium needed. Alternatively, would it be better to use the self-sustaining characteristic of the fission process to provide fuel for an engine for submarines, which would then be able to travel under the Polar ice-cap? The answers could not possibly be formulated till experimental research into the means of producing the explosion had been verified. The theoretical debate had to be resolved first.

Furthermore, the individuals taking part in the debate were all civilians, formally speaking, although for reasons of security, they were supervised by military personnel. The military could not have produced the weapon themselves: they were totally dependant on civilian effort. This would have been the case whether the bomb was produced, as was widely feared, in Nazi Germany, or, as it was in fact, in the USA. In neither type of society are professors of advanced theoretical physics found in the ranks of the military; the pre-suppositions and working conditions of the two are wholly different.* The dependence of the military on the civil resulted not only from the professional background of each but from the fragmentation of knowledge. In former ages, the military tradition in engineering sufficed to allow the military to produce weapons, if need be or at least to supervise their design and production. This no longer applied. Moreover the neccessary range and variety of knowledge not only separated the scientific specialists from the user but also the specialists from one another. They had to be brought together. The atomic bomb was the result of intense professional debate among *teams* of experts, with differing approaches, although they were lumped together as 'scientists'.

The teams were assembled from distinctly civilian institutions, within which their expertise had been developed – technical institutes and universities dedicated to the disinterested pursuit of knowledge. All the necessary preliminary research into the structure of atoms, including the pioneer experiments in fission, took place in the traditional places for the traditional reasons. Rutherford, one of the crucial investigators, maintained till his death in 1937 that nuclear fission would have no practical use. Yet only two years later other research scientists, whose work owed much to Rutherford's, were fearful that a controlled reaction might be added to the armoury of a scientifically-endowed state. Such a state was Nazi Germany, and among the initiates was a number of distinguished researchers who had already contributed to the 'atom debate' and were refugees from Germany or Fascist Italy. Italy lacked the industrial resources to translate laboratory theories into military practice; Germany, by contrast, had the resources and a political organisation to develop them. Even before the Second World War broke out, the fear that a state with the *Weltanschauung* and capabilities of Nazi Germany might discover how to make military use of the energy released by the atom prompted natural scientists to make representations to the American Government, in the form of a letter dated 2 August 1939 over

---

*This is not to suggest that scientists, as such, cannot work in militarised or totalitarian societies, but they need access to the corpus of international research and effective freedom to experiment, irrespective of the ruling dogmas.

the signature of Albert Einstein and addressed to President Roosevelt. The letter was not delivered to the President until October, and then not by a physicist but by a banker – an episode which illuminates the relationship between science and government at that time. The scientists in the United States were behindhand, had they known it, for on 24 April previously, a German physicist, Paul Harteck, had written a letter in similar terms to the German Ministry of War, drawing its attention to the most recent developments in nuclear physics, which suggested the possibility of producing an explosive more effective, by many orders of magnitude, than those in use. The Ministry responded immediately and began to create the organisation necessary to take the enquiry further. That it was ultimately unsuccessful did not invalidate the fears which prompted the letter to President Roosevelt.

Although the United States remained out of the hostilities for the next two years the sense of crisis which the scientists felt, was in no way dispelled although the administrative and committee structure imposed delays. The decisive experiments between 1939 and 1941 were not inspired by disinterested scientific curiosity or even a professional desire to win the Nobel Prize, but reflected the urgency of war. The results soon demonstrated that private funds and agencies could not finance the work or command the raw materials, especially uranium. As the emphasis moved from research to engineering, the role of government enlarged. The final bill for the whole project was some 2,000 million dollars.

Expense on this scale included the cost of overlapping and nugatory research as well as such necessary construction as building a new town for over 40,000 people at Oak Ridge, Tennessee. It signified that the United States was now in a class by itself. Expenditure of that order called in question the absolute size of the economy, for making war or for any other purpose. It submitted a new criterion for the analysis of power. The lesson was that, while a moderately endowed state could easily finance laboratory research, finding out how to make an atomic bomb and then producing it required a commitment of funds beyond the capability of other states. The distinction became clear in practice after the war, when the United States embargoed the exchange of information on grounds of security. For the length of time that America had a monopoly of the knowledge and the manufacturing facilities in being, it had options in foreign policy not open to any other state. For a variety of reasons these options were not acted upon, and their range was abruptly diminished in September 1949 when it was announced that the Soviet Union had also exploded a nuclear device. The Soviet Union was able to emulate the United States because it could mobilise the resources of society for that purpose and possessed, or acquired, the expertise in advanced natural science which the project demanded. As nuclear explosions became allied to developments in missiles, so the United States and the Soviet Union became 'superpowers' whose interactions bear on or determine the politics of the rest of the world.

In the production of the atomic bomb, war reached into the last remaining 'civil' domain – pure research. Individual scientists from Archimedes onwards had offered their findings to government for military purposes. The process was now much more problematical. Government systematically sponsored research into the pure unknown in the hope that the results would be useful in connection with an end which could be supposed but could not be defined until the research results were known. In January 1942 United States authorities had set out a schedule whereby a means of delivering a nuclear explosion was to be manufactured and ready in three years, notwithstanding the fact that many of the theoretical problems were unresolved and that the facilities for manufacture existed only as blueprints. No-one at that time could be certain that the schedules would be met, that all the theoretical problems which had to be solved had even at that stage been identified or that solutions could be ready for use. Many eminent scientists doubted whether a practicable nuclear explosion could be produced in time to be used in the war, but the Manhattan Project established, for the first time, a direct connection between a state's options in foreign policy and explorations in the domain of theoretical knowledge. The military required entrance to the ivory tower.

Furthermore, the project showed that, at its most advanced levels, war could no longer be identified with one firm or one predominant industry; its demands were dispersed throughout the entire industrial structure. It entailed a day-by-day working partnership between government and industrial firms in which the distinction between 'civil' and 'military', already eroded, became simply irrelevant. The nature of planning for war also changed. Traditional 'step-by-step' methods arguing to the future from the present were shown to be of no use; the future had first to be imagined and the objective decided regardless of any ignorance about the means of achieving it. Men had to ask themselves, 'Where do we want to be in 19—?' and, from their answer, work back to the present; identifying at each stage in the regression the problems which would have to be solved. In this way, they arrived at an idea of their immediate tasks. Only those states whose educational systems produced not only the natural scientists but also advanced mathematicians and others skilled in abstract intellectual analysis were henceforth capable of advanced war.

The atomic bomb forged the last link in the chain between pure theory and practical policy. It was known by the researchers at Los Alamos as 'the gadget', but in fact it was the end-product of theoretical analysis and systematic engineering, far removed from the practice-based gadgets applied to war only a hundred years earlier. The link between theory and policy involved the investigators of theory in the public debate about the relationship between values and technique, let loose by moral shock at the bombing of Hiroshima and Nagasaki. In 1945, as in 1919, condemnation was not universal. In some quarters, including the military, but by no means confined to them, the bomb was simply a more economic means of delivering explosions to cities – more economic not in the production costs but in the delivery vehicle – one aircraft – and in the weapon itself – one bomb. It had not revolutionised war, negating all previous experience, and therefore the traditional rules about war and peace still applied. But among some natural scientists engaged on the project and in many sections of the general public, horror at the fate of the two cities stimulated a revaluation of 'war' and 'peace' which continues to this day.

It was charged that obsession with purely technical considerations had anaesthetised if not destroyed, the moral sense of both those who made the bomb possible* and those who authorised its use. The Manhattan Project was represented as the final betrayal of science for the ends of the state; the 'white-coated saviours of civilisation' were transmogrified into 'mad scientists': the political and military authorities were not even permitted the excuse of insanity – they were stigmatised as the sinister minions of a technological Moloch, who had opened up the possibility of universal destruction. 'War' and 'peace' had taken on new connotations; the atomic bomb was not merely a tidier method of delivering explosions but a weapon with the power to make the planet uninhabitable. No conceivable political objective could justify running that risk; hence war could no longer serve its traditional purpose, and peace required to be defined more comprehensively than the mere absence of war, since the technology which sustained war was inherently unstable.

In 1919, scientists as such had not been condemned generally in the revulsion against war (though there were plans to bring Fritz Haber to trial as a war criminal). In 1945 they were. The published record soon showed that for the vast majority of scientists and engineers engaged in the project, technical success had exercised its own professional fascination, at least until the test at Alamogordo in New Mexico on 16 July 1945. That set in train much questioning about 'what have we done?' one outcome of which was an attempt to intervene in the political decisions about the use of the new weapon in action. The failure merely inflamed the subsequent row, since it was held to demonstrate that the 'scientists' had had the whip hand over the 'politicians' (because they alone had the knowledge) but had failed to use it.** However accurate this contention may or may not be, it does show that

---

*The opportunity to investigate the limits of knowledge, backed by sufficient funds, made Los Alamos the most intellectually exciting place for a physicist. It was the centre of world physics. The average age of the scientific staff was twenty-six.

**The critics' case also rests on the conclusions of the US Strategic Bombing Survey that 'air supremacy over Japan could have exerted sufficient pressure to bring about unconditional surrender and obviate the need for invasion.' The conclusion may, of course, be right, but the politics behind the Survey must cast doubt on the methods by which it was reached.

the relationship between knowledge and action had become so close that the furnishers of knowledge could no longer count themselves detached from the use which was made of it; that they could no longer defend themselves against their critics by reasoning that they were merely instruments of a national purpose defined for them by the constitutionally recognised authorities. If the state relied upon pure theory, then the theorists could not take refuge in their purity.

This embittered debate has been conducted mostly in the United States, where the bomb was manufactured and used in war, and has naturally demonstrated American presuppositions about power, and also a peculiarly American feeling for guilt. In other societies, with different traditions about the principles which govern the use of power, the accepted presuppositions would hardly allow the issues to be formulated: that pure science should be at the command of the state is regarded as so elementary as to require no particular comment, far less justification.

3. 'Civil' and 'military' in the nuclear age: the state as researcher, producer and user

The outcome of the new style of planning became evident in August 1945 when the two Japanese cities were destroyed by nuclear explosions from bombs carried by aircraft.* These attacks demonstrated that warfare had entered a new dimension of destructiveness and changed the body of received ideas about war. From being, successively, an honourable arbitrament and a protracted massacre, it had now become the likelihood of suicide for the human race. In 1945 the conclusion was premature, but only because there were too few bombs and the means of delivery was itself vulnerable. Both limitations have since been overcome, and the proliferation of nuclear weapons now justifies the conclusion advanced in 1945. Even then, however, the extent of the change could be measured by reference to the change in the use of air power since 1939. The attacks on Germany by the RAF and the US Army Air Force varied in effectiveness and cost in aircraft to the attackers. Hiroshima and Nagasaki each showed that instant obliteration and delayed death could be inflicted on large populations with the use of only one aircraft and only one bomb. After that demonstration, what would be the future role of force as an instrument of policy in the world political order?

It soon appeared that there were two kinds of war: 'nuclear', which could 'pay' only in restricted circumstances, and 'conventional' for which the scope was somewhat wider. They have not remained entirely distinct. Policy-makers have been much exercised by the problem (so far argued theoretically) of contemplating or of actually waging a conventional war without its escalating into a nuclear one, either on the battlefield itself or through the threatened use of strategic weapons as an inducement to desist. Present policy-makers, in contrast to their nineteenth-century predecessors, have to pursue their interests without relying on their main weapon. The possibilities of nuclear annihilation have not, so far, removed war as a recognised option in foreign policy. They have merely set limits to its

---

*The two bombs released a total explosive power equivalent to 35,000 tons of conventional TNT. For comparison: between 1939 and 1945, the total of bombs of all kinds dropped on Germany equalled 1.3 million tons.

exercise, and put a premium on terrorist campaigns or on war by proxy through client states.

The destruction of Hiroshima and Nagasaki marked a turning point in the preparations for war. Nuclear physics and the associated engineering were not the only spheres of the unknown which had to be explored. The use of the jet engine for aviation and experiments with rocketry took warfare into new environments, the nature of which was largely unknown. Pressing home an attack at 300 mph in 1940 did not pose problems of an essentially different order from operating at 100 mph in 1918; flying and fighting at speeds expressed as proportions of the speed of sound did. Controlling weapons at such speeds or at greater altitudes presented complex problems to which the answers could not be reached by taking previous experience as a datum; they had to be investigated from the beginning. In consequence, basic research entered into the production of even conventional weapons to a degree which had not been previously experienced. Nor was it possible to restrict enquiry to applied research only; questions of fundamental theory were involved and on a large scale.

The shift to the systematic exploration of theory has affected the entire cycle of production. Research is followed by development, in which the research results are engineered into pilot plants or prototype products so that officials responsible for policy can evaluate the basic requirements for manufacture. Changes in the scope and depth of what has to be accomplished, even before manufacture can begin, have caused a qualitative change in the demands made by warfare on industrial societies.

Research into the unknowns of natural science has demanded time and incurred costs beyond the resources of individual firms or laboratories. It has become too hazardous to be financed by the banks. Consequently, the costs have had to be met or underwritten by the state. The need for more intensive research and development has dictated the systematic organisation of the existing resources of manpower and of facilities available to the community, in universities and specialised institutes. Cost and the quality of expertise required have brought the production of weapons intrinsically under state control and management in all industrial states, irrespective of the social system, or the scale of their armed forces. It has not happened only in the United States and the Soviet Union. Their possession of the means of nuclear manufacture on the scale they command makes them 'superpowers' but, in producing weapons related to threats from each other, they have defined the problems of policy and technology which other states have to face. So the qualitative change does not only affect the superpowers *vis à vis* each other: *all* states electing to stay in the international competition, at some level or other, have been compelled continuously to organise and exploit their scientific and industrial resources to the greatest possible extent.

In the contemporary world, strategy is a question of managing resources and taking explicit decisions about technology. It reaches into the society as a whole and can no longer be confined to the 'military' aspects of it. 'Civil' and 'military' have become the two sides of the same coin. Typically, pure research is located in universities, applied research in universities and industry, engineering skills and facilities in industry. These distinctions are not hard and fast but indicate roughly the division of labour, which rules regardless of whether the institutions, laboratories, or plant are publicly or privately owned. The demand originates with government, which defrays the costs. Scientists, engineers and industrialists, who in law are civilians, are now intrinsically part of the decision-making process about military policy.

This blurring of time-honoured distinctions concerns also the notion of a 'weapon' itself. A cannon was a cannon and had no civilian use (ceremonies apart) but the same micro-circuit can be put to either civil or military use without modification. Similarly, 'military industry' has ceased to be identifiable as a few firms at the heavy end of iron and steel manufacture; it is now merely the aggregate of activities of a number of firms virtually all of which are engaged in serving the civil market. The practice of subcontracting makes identification even more problematical. The complexity of advanced systems ensures that the design and manufacture is spread throughout industry, not confined to one factory or group of plants. Nowadays it need not even be confined to one country. The cost of advanced weapons in relation to the national tax capacity and the other calls on government funds, as well as considerations of alliance politics, have taken the design and development of weapons across frontiers.

The business of war is not only a more socially comprehensive activity than before, it also reaches further into the future, again for reasons to do with the nature of the technology concerned. Designing and producing an advanced weapon takes some eight to ten years; its working 'life' may be taken as a further ten years. So military and political planners have to work to situations envisaged up to two decades in advance. They are, therefore, driven to base their policies on assumptions about the configuration of the states in the international system during that time and have to employ prediction, conjecture and forecasting to a degree unimaginable, and unnecessary, a hundred years ago.

In the middle of the last century, Napoleon III and Moltke could plan with the confidence that the uncertain factors were confined within reasonably firm limits. The identity of the enemy, the size of the forces to be engaged, their speed over the terrain, were all questions which could be answered with assurance, if not absolute certainty. Generals could inspect the terrain over which they might be called upon to fight. By the middle of the twentieth century, the policy deductions of governments have no such limits. For them it is no longer a question of conjecturing what is going on 'the other side of the hill' – it is a problem of postulating which hill up to twenty years in advance, years during which rapid changes in science and technology are likely to make obsolete the means of getting there. Planners have to make commitments (say, to design particular weapons, establish specific bases or seek certain alliances) long before they can identify the nature and timing of a conflict to which the commitments apply.

Fundamental uncertainty characterises contemporary policy-making and it takes two forms: *technological* uncertainty stemming from the need to investigate questions of pure theory, as well as solve the practical problems of production and *political* uncertainty as to the course and character of world politics over a twenty-year period. The hazards inherent in having to rely on a form of planning which cannot be based on reasonable certainties but, at best, on rather insecure probabilities, may be summarised by reference to recent history. How many American planners – one wonders – *in 1949* took decisions on American foreign and military policy on any assumption but a close and continuing identity of interests between the Soviet Union and the Peoples' Republic of China? Soviet planners, with perhaps a cannier sense of history, might have returned the answer which subsequent history gave, but, at the time, for them, as for the Americans, a break with China could only have been a very remote conjecture. To take an earlier example; the evidence discussed above shows that while numbers of policy-makers in Europe thought about or prepared for a war before 1914, they did not forecast its type and duration, much less that the structure of alliances within which the war originated would be fractured by the Russian Revolution. Under our present conditions, they would be required not only to have forecast these outcomes but to have done so in 1897 and used them as the datum of a policy which they would have had to initiate in the same year.

Political forecasting has become a necessity of foreign and military policy but, apart from the intrinsic difficulty of deciding what the relevant factors are and then weighing them, there is a psychological aspect to be considered. The behaviour of a people at any given time varies with the state of its morale and its particular mood – which by definition are unpredictable. Mass movements, emergent nationalisms, economic conflict – all of which have taken on new importance since the Second World War – have made institutions more vulnerable to change and international politics more responsive to mood, in comparison with, say, European politics of the last century. The public mood was important to Bismarck, but only as an adjunct to policies on which he had already decided, and for short-term ends. Now the mood and morale of the public have to be built into assessments about the more remote future. In open societies, the public itself demands a share in the determination of foreign policy, and its fears and general sense of insecurity are sharpened by its awareness of the speed, range and destructiveness of advanced weapons. Governments can never be certain that fear will not collapse into panic. In this respect, the Cuban crisis of 1962 may prove to be the last, as well as the first, example of 'crisis management'.

The rituals of war declarations can no longer be relied upon to mark the transition from 'peace' to 'war' and the nature of the weapons themselves rules out any conversion of peacetime industry to war production *after* hostilities have broken out. Governments expect to fight with what they have to hand: they will not have an opportunity to develop weapons during hostilities as a result of the experience gained or the tasks presented. Planners accordingly have to rely on the deterrent effect of the number and quality of weapons available to them and hope to cover as many of the forseeable options as they can afford. One consequence of thus accumulating stocks for deterrent purposes is an international arms race.

All states, even the superpowers, have run up against the constraints of mounting costs on what they deem necessary to their security, but the United States and the Soviet Union still retain, by reasons of their resources, a degree of choice which is not open to any other state. Nevertheless, it remains the case that only those states which generate, or have access to, the latest findings in basic natural science and can translate them into processes and products through their command of engineering skills and facilities, can produce advanced weapons. States which cannot have either to buy from those who can or go without. The complexities of technology have thus widened the gap between producers and non-producers. This latter category includes virtually all the states created since the Second World War – a process which, as in Europe after the First, has enlarged the demand. The trade is conducted, exclusively for advanced systems and very largely for other weapons, by governments. The Zaharoffs of this world have been superseded by bureaucrats.

The act of choice forced on governments by the complexities of technology and the hazards of forecasting itself implies weighing expected gains against anticipated costs. War has now run up against the absolute limits of the economy and governments are increasingly driven to begin their analyses of policy by asking not, 'what do we want to defend?' but, 'how much defence can we afford?' and trying to arrive at the 'correct' mixture of means to cover only the major conjectured contingencies. Foreign policy, in this sense, is a residual, not a premise: the 'primacy of foreign policy' has been displaced by technology. In the process, however, the primacy of the General Staff has also suffered. Strategy is no longer the acknowledged realm of purely military considerations. It comprises many civil elements and requires the expertise and judgement of individuals who are not in uniform and are not subject to the traditional codes of discipline. They are nevertheless professionally engaged in identifying the options and weighing them, in relation to one question, 'which strategy (or force, or weapon system) offers the greatest amount of military effectiveness for a given outlay?'. The answers are usually complicated and extensive and in the jargon of the profession have become known as 'cost-effectiveness' studies.

Determining the objectives of policy by relating them to the forces or weapons systems that are the most 'cost-effective' is a new approach to the problems of war and peace. In Moltke's day, steel cannon were undoubtedly more effective for the greater cost, but the only problem was whether the military authorities *wanted* to afford them in relation to their chosen objectives, such as war with Austria or France. It was beyond question that they could order steel, rather than bronze, cannon if they wished. Now, precisely because of their entailed costs, the objectives of the state have to be defined in terms of those systems which cover more of its options more effectively. On this criterion, some objectives, however desirable, have to be discarded because they do not make the 'best' use of the resources available.

Cost effectiveness analyses suggest not only the final choice of strategy but also the decisions about the mixture and range of the weapons or forces by which it is to be implemented. Here the question to be answered is whether the ability to deploy a specific number and type of weapons or group of forces is worth their cost both in money and outlays and in the alternative opportunities which their use automatically forecloses. The typical instance is the decision whether a small percentage of capability is worth a disproportionately large disbursement of funds. Assessing the rival possibilities as to their cost effectiveness points to the decision and to the possibilities of substituting one means for another. The most 'cost effective' solution is not always adopted – there may be political reasons which supervene – but, if applied, the technique does yield criteria for what to do, in situations which are inherently complex and problematical. It is an innovation which in itself testifies to the scope of the demands of war on contemporary industrial society.

The demands are articulated by the state across the whole spectrum of industrial production: consequently, government, in virtue of its role as planner, banker and sole or dominant customer, has brought about a new style of relationship between itself and industry, even in non-socialist societies. Today, government has altogether ceased to be a customer, as defined by classical theory. It does not have to compete with other customers; it makes the laws under which producers operate and taxes their results; it often has superior powers in the courts; it always has superior access to public opinion. As the wielder of the authority of the state, it commands the residual, if not the actual, assent of citizens in their various guises as taxpayers, employees, customers and voters. Governments define the issues. All these qualities condition the relationship between government and manufacturers.

In practice, there are a number of constraints on the exercise of its absolute consumer (ie government) sovereignty. Fear of disorganising production or of alienating a section of the voting public may lead the government not to exercise the initiative it possesses; administration may be incompetent or inadequate; the known or inferred policies of other states may give it pause at home. The net effect of such constraints may well be –

usually is – to enable the producer to exert much more leverage than theory allows but the resultant relationship fits into no traditional textbook account of capitalist industrial enterprise. American theorists have fastened on 'the contract state',[3] or 'the new industrial state'[4] to describe the nexus between government and industry as currently experienced. But, as this book has argued, the nexus causes much more shock in the United States than elsewhere. The basic lineaments of 'the contract state' were first systematically explored by Napoleon III.

Conclusions

This discussion began with the Industrial Revolution in Europe, and therefore covers a span of some hundred and fifty years. During that time, war, as an aspect of state policy, has gone through three broad phases. In the first it was a matter for an élite, essentially landowning in character and values from which its techniques and social composition derived. The landowners relied on their equestrian skills and led armies manned largely by their peasants or labourers. The demands of warfare on society as a whole were minimal. With industrialisation, this simple pattern broke down. In the second phase, war came to imply engineering industry and the command of raw materials necessary for production. Warfare itself was more prolonged, as battles were fought not between peasant armies but industrial systems. It was consequently more devastating. In the third and current phase, war is essentially a matter of theoretical science, as well as of engineering capacity and raw material supply. In its nuclear form, it promises total devastation in which the distinction between 'victor' and 'vanquished' would be obliterated along with the rest. As 'war' has changed, what can be called 'peace' has altered likewise.

The decisive changes in attitude and organisation may be traced to the First World War; they were extended and systematised by the Second. In consequence, as between the first and current phases, 'war' and 'peace' have ceased to be opposite poles of behaviour and have become correlatives. The armed forces are no longer the exclusively war-making part of society, but merely that part professionally trained for combat. Ministries of industry are as vitally concerned in the making of foreign policy as the ministries of foreign affairs. The rituals associated with the transition from 'peace' to 'war' have been largely dispensed with: a nuclear exchange would not be preceded by an ambassador's solemnly asking for his passports. Troops become committed to action as a by-product of civil war, without formal declaration. Nationalist guerillas assume war to be a permanent state, at least until the Liberation or the Revolution (the one is usually construed in terms of the other). Even in societies which regard themselves as being at peace, and whose officials adhere to the traditional dichotomy, the ramifications of industrialised war, whether nuclear or not, have already destroyed the distinction between 'military' and 'civil' in the context of the scientific research necessary to produce advanced weapons. Equally, in these societies, it is no longer automatically true that the military are employed only on warlike pursuits.

The ability to contemplate warfare as an option of policy is now, for industrialised states, a matter not only of theoretical science but also of prediction or conjecture. The fundamental research which goes into the production of weapons is one end of a spectrum, bounded at the other by predictions about the political situations in which they are likely to be used, if used at all. Theory rules at both ends. In the middle, in the world of social facts with which the governments deal, the production of weapons and options open to foreign policy are more closely integrated than before. Weapons are now so complex and costly and make so many demands on the national capacity that any decision in favour of one system rather than another must involve a prior policy decision as to its likely use. This determines the characteristics of the weapon and automatically excludes a whole range of other options which different prior policy conclusions might suggest.

Such integration between the production of weapons and the policy options demands a similar integration between the relevant institutions: the world of research, (which provides the theory), industry, (which engineers the results), and government itself. Government appears in three guises: as overall policy-maker (defining the ends), as the armed forces (which translate the ends into specific demands) and as the national revenue-raiser (which finances the whole process). These links are not only lateral, as between institutions; they must also have depth. 'The world of research' implies the findings of universities and technical institutes and hence the content of education. 'Industry' implies a series of working relationships between industrialists and bureaucrats. 'Government' in its various guises, is central and has to assess and implement priorities for the security of the nation. For these reasons, foreign or defence policy is not a separate activity but one which ramifies into society as a whole. What we are accustomed to consider as purely domestic, such as education or welfare, is directly related to the options open to makers of external policy. It is of no use embarking on a supersonic jet fighter or complex electronic devices if the educational system fails to produce the right kind of engineers at the highest level of professional competence. The problem also has a dimension of time. Failure to include mathematics and physics in secondary education now may well affect the options available to defence policy, say, fifteen years hence, if those options depend upon the use or threatened use of advanced weapons. The curriculum need not be tailored to meet the needs of defence policy but governments have to be aware of its relationship to the future security of their society.

The links have to be established as a matter of deliberate policy and kept in good order. The penalty for getting them 'wrong' is severe, particularly if a state is not rich enough to buy its way out of trouble. The links are indispensable to the production of advanced weapons, and to the options which their possession confers. They make up what, since President Eisenhower's Farewell Address in 1959, has been known as 'the military-industrial complex' but they are common to capitalist and socialist states alike. One suspects that the Soviet Union has experienced less difficulty in creating and monitoring the links than the United States. Whether they are politically obnoxious or not depends on other judgements deriving from the culture as a whole. So in France they raise no particular problem, while in America they are widely stigmatised as undermining the civil order and the quintessential values of American society for militarist ends.

These ends – it is argued – are determined by the 'imperatives' which science and technology generate. On this view, the relationship between knowledge and action is now so close that the first automatically and exclusively determines the second: the rationality of organising resources for specific military ends has taken over or negated all other ends. One can observe that, in practice, 'imperatives' are not self-subsistent entities which can be ostensively defined, but imply a prior belief in the existence of an intrinsic law or system of development which governs the way states behave and allows one to predict how they will behave under certain circumstances. In this context, 'imperatives' are associated with some kind of technological metaphysics, or are ideological deductions masquerading as empirical facts.

The evidence discussed in this book suggests a contrary view: that 'imperative' only means that no-one has hit upon or devised an alternative course of action or has bothered to investigate one. The 'imperatives' of policy, so far from being compulsions, are *choices* (though the language of necessity is frequently used by those who retrospectively want to justify choices which have turned out badly). Over the period covered by this study, the methods of reciprocally matching theory to manufacture to weapons to strategies have made the choices increasingly complex and problematical and have made increasingly sophisticated demands on knowledge, but they have not in themselves produced any greater finality in judgement. In fact, one could plausibly maintain that the tighter and the more comprehensively the links between theory and action have been drawn, the less certain the outcome. The hallmarks of contemporary strategic planning are uncertainty, indeterminacy, choice between the more and the less probable. It is perhaps small comfort to suggest that final nuclear obliteration may come about not because of the working-out of some implacable, occult 'imperative' but because we are incompetent at making choices.

However the logic of the relationship between theory and action may be interpreted, it is undeniable that the contrast between the current relationship of weapons' manufacture to foreign policy and that existing at the beginning of this study could hardly be greater. Then, weapons were for general use and, within classes, not widely differentiated in performance.

Design and development were left largely to the maker. Production was a matter of days or weeks. The right to make foreign policy in either the diplomatic or military sense was reserved to a minority. In its thinking the public at large was no more than the recipient of the beneficial, or the victim of the ill, effects of the courses adopted.

Now the opposite conditions rule. Weapons are tailored to use, because they are designed to meet a specific threat envisaged as being the one of a range of threats most likely to happen, some ten or twenty years hence. Design and development are either a direct interest of government or are supervised by it. The production cycle may well take years. Controlling the successive phases of production and making officials effectively accountable for their actions has proved extremely difficult. Nationalisation of the assets concerned does not dispose of the problem since it arises through differentials in knowledge. At the extremes, politicians with powers of decision have to rely on advice from scientists and technologists which they may well not understand. The experts' arguments, even if understood, may not in themselves be decisive because they are apt to be distorted in the politics of weapons' procurement. Compromises have to be made, but in the process, formal accountability becomes muddied. Decisions themselves have taken on a new meaning. The public, following the dictionary, still thinks that a decision implies the settlement of problems or the will to act conclusively. Those in the business of procurement know from experience that decisions have become 'bets about how to control or influence rather distant futures.'

The need to bet has one dire outcome. Verified facts are so few that policy works to hypotheses. They are based on 'the worst case' – a procedure which appeals to prudence but also dictates the kind of weapons system needed to match the contingency imagined. Hence, with 'worst case' piled on 'worst case', there is a tendency to over-valuation of weaponry – some knowledge of which gets to the opponent and is taken into his calculations and reading of intentions. For this reason, the arms race is not only an aspect of the action and reaction of the Soviet Union and the United States to each other but is also a form of interaction between strategic analysis and scientific know-ledge within each state. This in itself tends to produce inflated qualities and stocks of weapons, apart from the natural tendency of the military to ensure liberal margins of safety in their requirements. At any given period, working to 'worst case' hypotheses may lead a state into running an arms race with itself.

The making of foreign policy may still be carried out by a minority, but it is a much less exclusive minority than before, comprising not only officials of ministries of foreign affairs and defence and their political masters, but pressure groups, publicists, academics assembled in institutes of foreign affairs and departments of international relations, and lay strategists – all of whom may in varying degrees influence the formulation of policy. But apart from these, foreign policy as it emerges in practice is, in Western societies at least, very much the residual of what the public, as voter or taxpayer, will stand. One of the consequences of this reference to the wider public is that the nexus between warfare and welfare is being broken. Historically our present apparatus of social welfare stems as much from the wartime necessity to mobilise resources and subsidise activities as from the writings of theorists and the pleadings of reformers. Among all the main combatants, the two world wars offer numerous examples. Today, however, the preparation for war is permanent and co-extensive with the economy; it thus competes for resources which are needed to meet increasing demands for welfare. (In this context, the security of the realm is not usually regarded as a social good.) The competition has already opened up conflicts, especially evident in Britain and the United States, between those who have to appropriate resources for defence and mass voters primarily concerned with levels of welfare.

The objective of foreign policy, now as in the nineteenth century, is security, but its relationship with weapons is more ambiguous than before. The operative hope is that producing the weapons will 'produce' security, in much the same way that applying the law is intended to produce 'justice'. But 'security' is as protean a concept as 'justice' and leaves open as many questions as to how it is to be achieved. Even if it is accepted that armaments are indispensable (which pacifists deny), then advocates of rival weapon systems can justify their preferences on grounds which are ultimately irrefutable because they have no basis in certainty. Discussions of policy have always involved juggling with assumptions but hitherto the assumptions were easily verifiable; they are no longer, and a nation's security may be no more certain than its forecasting techniques.

A difference between 'war' and 'peace' is still acknowledged but it is not so hard and fast as the nineteenth century was able to assume. The main solvents of the distinction have been ideologies, which provide a series of reasons why war becomes less intolerable than peace (if not actually preferable to it), and the process of state creation which, since the Second World War especially, has multiplied the chances of war by increasing the number of war-making agencies. Both ideology and the desire to create a new state by asserting an old identity have created specific preferences for war, often in its guerilla variant, so that in many areas individuals may legitimately wonder whether 'war' or 'peace' more aptly describes the circumstances in which they live. The consequences of this shift in emphasis may be seen in the United Nations, the majority of whose member states are now less interested in its initial overriding aim of peace-keeping; for them other objectives, dictated by ideology and nationalism, enjoy priority. In that case 'peace' means 'avoiding nuclear war', not, 'seeking to dispense with war as such'.

These changes could, in theory, have taken place without any change in

257

the technology of war, but, in fact, advances in technique, once assimilated into society, have also fudged the distinction between 'war' and 'peace', creating uncertainty about their respective meanings which affects the forming of policy. The world does not grow safer, and both old and new states have an interest in building up their weaponry to the fullest possible extent, irrespective of whether they belong to the Warsaw Pact, or NATO, or are neutralist. Since, as we have seen, military preparedness is related to the society and economy as a whole, and not, as in the last century, to a limited section of both, and since 'war' and 'peace' are no longer clear cut and opposed concepts, new questions are being raised for state policy in the western world. If military orders begin with pure research *and* cover the economy as a whole, can or should government deliberately use its military requirements to increase or stabilise the levels of demand in the society? Put more broadly: does the entire military effort underwrite the economy as a whole and therefore delay the apocalypse of capitalism, which its opponents so confidently predict? Are profits from producing 'defence' goods higher than in comparable civil production – a question which has proved deceptively difficult to answer – and if so, how far does the search for particular rates of profit affect the choice of particular weapons systems and, by that means, influence the choice of foreign policy objectives? Alternately, has not military industry eroded the old categories of 'capitalism' and 'socialism' along with the distinction between 'peace' and 'war', and given rise to a 'new industrial state' which requires a different set of conceptual tools for its analysis? If this is so, what is or should be the role of the technocrats in the making of decisions, and how, especially, can it be reconciled with the requirements of democracy in its various current forms? The fudging of the concepts of 'war' and 'peace' raises an entire range of complex problems. Industrialisation during the last century increased the options open to policy; it has now reached the point of multiplying the ambiguities.

Notes and References

Preface

1. See G. I. A. Draper, 'The New Law of Armed Conflict' in *RUSI Journal*, London, 1979.
2. See the discussion in Landes, Chapter 1.

Part I

1. See Joffre's account in his *Mémoires*, Vol. 1, p. 125.
2. The 'mitrailleuse' was a gun with thirty-two barrels, cranked by hand, designed by a Belgian engineer, Montigny in 1851. It was adopted by Napoleon III and manufactured secretly at the Meudon arsenal. 'Mitrailleuse' afterwards became a generic term for any type of machine gun.
3. See P. Mason, *A Matter of Honour*, London, 1974.
4. See M. Howard, *The Franco-Prussian War*, London 1961, p. 157.
5. The title of a book by Hoffmann, published in translation in London in 1929.
6. On Vickers' move to armaments, see Scott, p. 42.
7. See M. Howard, *op cit* p. 36.

Part II

1. See Cavour's essay of 1846 'Des Chemins de fer en Italie', *Scritti*, Vol. II, pp. 3–50.
2. See G. A. Craig's essay in *War, Politics and Diplomacy*.
3. See H. Vizetelly, *Berlin under the New Empire*, 2 Vols, London, 1879, Vol. 1, Chapter 1.

Part III

1. Five of the component states, Russia, Austria, Prussia, France and Britain were formally allied in 1818: Ottoman Turkey remained outside. Thereafter, disputes which brought the states to the verge of war or to war itself divided them as follows:
   1821 Russia v Turkey (over Greece)

1822   France (on behalf of Russia, Prussia and Austria) v Britain (intervention in Spain)
1827   France, Russia and Britain v Turkey (over Greece)
1833   France and Britain v Russia and Turkey (over Mehemet Ali and the status of Egypt)
1840   Russia, Austria, Prussia v France (over Mehemet Ali)
1849   France, Britain and Turkey v Russia and Austria (over the extradition of Hungarian refugees)
1851   France v Turkey (over the Holy Places in Palestine)
1853   Britain, France and Turkey v Russia (over Russia's occupation of Moldavia and Wallachia)
1854   France and Britain v Russia (Crimean War)
1859   France v Austria (Italian War)
1863   France, Britain and Austria v Russia and Prussia (over the Polish insurrection)
1864   Prussia and Austria v Denmark (war over the Danish duchies)
1866   Prussia v Austria ('Six weeks' war')
1870   France v Prussia (Franco-Prussian War)
Perhaps the last flourish of the flexible system was the Congress of Berlin 1879; otherwise, from 1871–1914, there were only two alignments:
1871   Germany, Russia and Austria v France
1892   Germany, Austria and Turkey v France and Russia, plus Britain eventually.
2. See Tint, *The Decline of French Patriotism*, p. 29.
3. The publicist was Francois Coppée, quoted in Michon, p. 85.
4. See the discussion in Landes, p. 245.
5. In September 1807, Napoleonic France, at war with Britain, demanded that Denmark, hitherto neutral, join the blockade system established the previous year, to exclude British trade from the Continent. Napoleon also initiated discussions for an alliance. From the French point of view, these measures would plug the last loophole for trade and tie up the Continent in an anti-British alliance. The British Government retaliated by making counter-demands, culminating in the bombardment of Copenhagen and the destruction or capture of the Danish fleet to prevent it from falling into French hands or under French control. The Franco-Danish alliance was concluded and French troops occupied islands in the Baltic.
6. See Bethmann's memoirs, *Betrachtungen zum Weltkriege*, Berlin, 1919–1921, Vol. 2, p. 7.
7. The Homburg memorandum is printed in *Erinnerungen, Briefe, Dokumente*, p. 18, ff.

Part IV

1. See *Archiv für Wissenschaft und Sozialpolitik* No. 41, 1916, p. 745.
2. The effectiveness of the submarine, as distinct from other weapons used in the attempt to defeat Britain by cutting her lines of supply, appears from the following statistics of losses of British merchant shipping from August 1914 to November 1918.

Merchant vessels sunk	no.	gross tonnage
Submarines	2,099	6,635,059
Cruisers, torpedo boats, mines, aircraft	380	1,124,031
Total	**2,479**	**7,759,090**

Merchant vessels damaged or molested but not sunk		
Submarines	1,727	7,335,827
Cruisers, torpedo boats, mines, aircraft	158	672,140
Total	**1,885**	**8,007,967**

Fishing vessels sunk		
Submarines	578	57,583
Cruisers, torpedo boats, mines, aircraft	97	14,182
Total	**675**	**71,765**

Source: *Statistical Review of the War against Merchant Shipping*, Admiralty, London, Director of Statistics, 23 December 1918, HMSO, August 1919.

3. Industrial targets bombed October 1917 to November 1918 are listed in H. A. Jones, *The War in the Air; Appendices*, Oxford, 1937.

Part V

1. See J. F. C. Fuller, *Memoirs of an Unconventional Soldier*, London, 1936, pp. 329–30.
2. In asking 'what would be the character of a new war', the Union was seeking an answer or a series of answers, as a method of testing the existing concepts of and arrangements for security. In particular, it addressed itself to the question 'whether the belief that armaments were the first guarantee of security could be sustained in face of the infinite possibilities of mutual destruction created by the development of new methods of warfare'.

Part VI

1. See Zuckerman, *From Apes to Warlords*, Appendix 2.
2. The full text is printed in Webster and Frankland, Vol. 1, pp. 331–332.
3. The subject of Nieburg's *In the Name of Science*.
4. See J. K. Galbraith's book of that title.

Select Bibliography

Adams, R. J. Q. *Arms and the Wizard: Lloyd George and the Ministry of Munitions*, London 1978

Ailleret, C. L. *L'organisation économique de la nation en temps de guerre*, Paris 1935

Aitken, H. G. J. (ed.) *The State and Economic Growth*, New York 1959

Aldcroft, D. H. 'Investment in and utilisation of manpower: Great Britain and her rivals 1870–1914' in Ratcliffe, B. M. (ed) *Great Britain and Her World 1750–1914*, Manchester 1975

(ed) *The Development of British Industry and Foreign Competition 1875–1914*, London 1968

Allen, H. R. *The Legacy of Lord Trenchard*, London 1972

Anderson, P. A. 'Gustav von Schmoller' in Halperin, S. W. (ed) *Essays in Modern European Historiography*, Chicago 1970

Andrezewski, S. *Military Organisation and Society*, London 1954

Angel, N. *Arms and Industry*, London 1915

Armstrong, Whitworth Co Ltd, *The Chilean cruiser, 'Esmerelda' – description of armament*, Newcastle on Tyne n.d.

Babron, J. A. *Les Etablissements imperiaux de la Marine française*, Paris 1868

Backe, H. *Das Ende des Liberalismus in der Wirtschaft*, Berlin 1938

Bacon, R. *From 1900 Onward*, London 1940

Batty, P. *The House of Krupp*, London 1966

Bankutz, P. C. F. *Weygand; Civil-Military Relations in Modern France*, Cambridge, Mass 1967

Bardoux, J. *De Paris á Spa*, Paris 1921

Barkhausen, J. and Springer, H. *Männer gegen Stein und Stahl*, Berlin 1942

Barnett, C. *The Collapse of British Power*, London 1972

Bartlett, C. J. 'The Mid-Victorian Reappraisal of Naval Policy' in Bourne, K. and Watt, D. C. (ed) *Studies in International History*, London 1967

Baxter, J. P. *The Introduction of the Ironclad Warship*, Cambridge, Mass 1933

Beachey, R. W. 'The Arms Trade in East Africa in the late Nineteenth Century', in *Journal of African History*, Vol. 3 No. 3 1962 pp. 451–467

Bell, A. C. *A History of the Blockade of Germany 1914–1918*, London 1937

Belperron, P. *Maginot of the Line*, London 1940

Berdrow, W. (ed) *Letters of Alfred Krupp*, London 1930

Alfred Krupp, Berlin 1937

Berghan, V. *Rüstung und Machtpolitik*, Düsseldorf 1973

Germany and the Approach of War, London 1973

Berkely, G. F. H. *The Campaign of Adowa and the Rise of Menelek* (2nd edition) London 1935

Best, G. and Wheatcroft, A. (ed) *War, Economy and the Military Mind*, London 1976

Bigant, A. *La Nationalisation et le Contrôle des Usines de Guerre*, Paris 1939

Birdsall, P. *Versailles Twenty Years After*, London 1941

Birkenhead, Lord, *The Prof in Two Worlds*, London 1961

Birkhill, R. *Seeds of War*, London 1925

Birnbaum, K. *Peace Moves and U-boat Warfare*, Stockholm 1958

Blackett, P. M. S. *Studies of War*, Edinburgh and London 1962

Bloch, I. S. (also Jean de) *La Guerre*, Paris 1898

Block, H. 'Subcontracting in Germany's Defense Industries', *Social Research* February 1942

Boelcke, W. *Krupp und die Hohenzollern*, Frankfurt a/M 1970

Boggs, M. W. *Attempts to define and limit aggressive armament*, Chicago 1940

Böhme, H. *Deutschlands Weg zur Grossmacht*, Cologne and Berlin 1966

Boon, H. N. *Reve et Realité dans l'oevre économique et sociale de Napoleon III*, Paris 1936

Borbstaedt, A. *Preussens Feldzüge gegen Oesterreich*, Berlin 1867

Boucher, A. *Les Doctrines dans la préparation de la Grande Guerre*, Paris 1925

Boycott, A. G. *The Elements of Imperial Defence* (2nd edition) London 1936

Boyle, A. *Trenchard*, London 1962

Brackenbury, C. B. 'Ironclad Field Artillery' in *The Nineteenth Century*, July 1877

Brandt, O. *Die deutsche Industrie im Kriege 1914–1915*, Berlin 1915

Bravetta, E. *L'Industria della Guerra*, Milan 1916

Brodie, B. *Strategy in the Missile Age*, Oxford 1959
   War and Politics, London 1973

Broms, B. *The definition of aggression in the UN*, Turku 1968

Bruge, R. *Faites Sauter la Ligne Maginot!* Paris 1973
   On a livré la Ligne Maginot, Paris 1975

Bruneau, P. *Le Rôle du Haut Commandement au point de vue Economique de 1914 à 1922*, Paris 1924

Burnham, J. *Total War; the economic theory of a war economy*, Boston 1943

Buxton, N. K. and Aldcroft, D. H. *British Industry Between the Wars*, London 1979

Bywater, H. G. *Navies and Nations*, London 1927

Cameron, R. *France and the Economic Development of Europe*, New Jersey, 1961

Campbell, J. F. *The Foreign Affairs Fudge Factory*, New York 1972

Carroll, E. M. *French Public Opinion and Foreign Affairs 1873–1914*, New York 1931
   Germany and the Great Powers 1866–1914, Hamden, Connecticut 1966

Case, L. M. *French Opinion on War and Diplomacy during the Second Empire*, Philadelphia 1954

Challener, R. D. *The French Theory of the Nation in Arms*, New York 1955

Chapman, G. *Why France Collapsed*, London 1968

Charlton, L. F. O. *War from the Air, Past Present and Future*, London 1935

Chevalier, E. *Histoire de la Marine Française 1815–1870*, Paris 1900

Select Bibliography

Chilston, Viscount. 'Rearmament in Britain and France between the Munich Crisis and the Outbreak of War' in Toynbee A. and Toynbee, V. M. (ed) *The Eve of War 1939*, London 1958
'Political Reasons for Poor Progress in Rearmament', in *Survey of International Affairs 1938*, London 1941–53
Clark, E. (ed) *Boycotts and Peace*, New York 1932
Clark, R. W. *The Rise of the Boffins*, London 1962
Tizard, London 1965
Clarke, I. F. *Voices Prophesying War 1763–1984*, Oxford 1966
Clarkson, J. B. and Cochran, T. C. *War as a Social Institution*, New York 1941
Clough, S. B. *The Economic History of Modern Italy*, New York 1964
France, a History of National Economics, New York 1970
Cobden, R. *The Three Panics*, London 1862
Colin, J. *Les Transformations de la Guerre*, Paris 1912
Collier, B. *The Defence of the United Kingdom*, London 1957
Cosett, M. W. W. P. *The Triumph of Unarmed Forces 1914–1918*, London 1928
Cox, F. J. (ed) and others. *Studies in Modern History in Honour of Frederick Charles Palm*, New York 1956
Craig, G. A. *The Battle of Königgrätz*, London 1965
War, Politics and Diplomacy, New York 1966
Crouzet, F. (ed) *Essays in European Economic History*, London 1969

Danhof, C. *Government Contracting and Technological Change*, Washington DC 1968
Davis, S. C. *The French War Machine*, London 1937
Debeny, M-E. *Sur la Sécurité militaire de la France*, Paris 1930
Deist, W. *Flottenpolitik und Flottenpropaganda*, Stuttgart 1976
Delbrück, C. *Die Wirtschaftliche Mobilmachung in Deutschland*, Munich 1926
Delbrück, H. *Ludendorff, Tirpitz, Falkenhayn*, Berlin 1920
Douglas, D. *The Great Gun-Maker*, Newcastle on Tyne 1970
Doukas, K. A. 'Armaments and the French Experience', in *American Political Science Review*, April 1940
Dredge, J. *The Works of Messrs Schneider and Co*, London 1900
Dunham, A. C. *The Anglo-French Treaty of 1860 and the Progress of the Industrial Revolution in France*, Ann Arbor 1930
Duscha, J. *Arms, Money and Politics*, New York 1964

Earle, E. M. 'The Influence of Air Power' in *The Yale Review*, June 1946
Eastwood, J. *The Maginot and Siegfried Lines*, London 1939
Elliott, W. Y. and others. *International Control in the non-ferrous Materials*, New York 1937
Emery, B. *The Strategy of Raw Materials*, New York 1934
Enock, A. G. *The Problem of Armaments*, London 1923

Fearon, P. 'The Formative Years of the British Aircraft Industry 1913–1924' in *Business History Review*, 1969 No. 43
'The British Airframe Industry and the State 1918–1935' in *Economic History Review*, 1974 (No 27)

Feldman, G. D. *Army, Industry and Labor in Germany 1914-1918*, New Jersey 1966
Fontaine, A. *French Industry during the War*, New Haven 1926
Friedenson, P. *Histoire des Usines Renault*, Paris 1972
and Lecuir, J. *La France et La Grande Bretagne face aux problèmes aeriens 1935-Mai 1940*, Vincennes 1976
Fuller, J. F. C. *War and Western Civilisation*, London 1932
The Dragon's Teeth, London 1932
Memoirs of an Unconventional Soldier, London 1936
Furniss, H. S. *Some Economic Aspects of International Relations*, Birmingham 1917

Gatzke, H. *Stresemann and the Rearmament of Germany*, Baltimore 1954
Gessner, L. *Der Zusammenbruch des Zweiten Reiches; seine politischen und militärischen Lehren*, Munich 1937
Gilkerson, W. *Gilkerson on War; from Rocks to Rockets*, St Louis 1963
Gilpin, R. *France in the Age of the Scientific State*, New Jersey 1968
Golovine, N. *The Russian Campaign of 1914*, Fort Leavenworth, Kansas 1933
Gooch, B. D. *The New Bonapartist Generals in the Crimean War*, The Hague 1959
Gooch, J. *The Plans of War*, London 1974
Gorce, P. M. de la. *The French Army*, London 1963
Gorlitz, W. *Der Deutsche Generalstab*, Frankfurt a/M 1954
Grady, H. F. *British War Finance 1914-1918*, New York 1927
Gray, E. *The Devil's Device*, London 1975
Grey, C. G. *A History of the Air Ministry*, London 1940
Groves, P. R. C. *Behind the Smoke Screen*, London 1934
Grünwald, R. 'Railways and Jewish Enterprise' in *Leo Baeck Year Book*, London 1967
Guardet, R. *La Société Militaire dans la France Contemporaine 1815-1939*, Paris 1953
Gulick, E. V. *Europe's Classical Balance of Power*, New York 1967

Haggie, P. 'The Royal Navy and War Planning in the Fisher Era' in *Journal of Contemporary History*, Vol 8, No 3
Hall, A. R. (ed) *History of Technology*, Oxford
Hallgarten, G. W. F. 'La portée politique et économique de la mission Liman von Sanders' in *Revue historique de la guerre mondiale*, 1935
Halpern, P. G. *The Mediterranean Naval Situation 1908-1914*, Cambridge, Mass 1971
Hantos, E. *L'Europe centrale: une nouvelle organisation économique*, Paris 1932
Hardach, G. 'Französische Rüstungspolitik 1914-1918' in Winkler, H. A. (ed) *Organisierter Kapitalismus, Voraussetzungen und Anfänge*, Göttingen 1974
Harrison, R. J. 'British Armaments and European Industrialisation 1870-1914' in *English Historical Review*, 1974
Hartcup, G. *The Challenge of War, Scientific and Engineering Contributions to World War II*, Newton Abbot 1970
Hartshorne, R. 'The Franco-German Boundary of 1871' in *World Politics*, June 1950
Harvey, D. J. *French Concepts of Military Strategy 1919-1939*, New York 1953
Hawtry, R. G. *Economic Aspects of Sovereignty*, London 1930

Hayes, D. *Conscription Conflict*, London 1949
Helmreich, J. *Belgium and Europe*, The Hague 1976
  'Belgian Concern over Neutrality and British Intervention 1900–1914' in *Journal of Modern History*, December 1964
Henderson, W. O. *The State and the Industrial Revolution in Prussia*, Liverpool 1958
  The Industrial Revolution in the Continent (2nd edition), London 1968
Hermann, C. F. (ed) *International Crises: insights from behavioural research*, New York 1971
Hewlett, R. G. and Anderson, O. E. *The New World, Volume I of the History of the US Atomic Energy Commission*, 1962
Higham, R. *The Military Intellectuals in Britain 1918–1939*, New Brunswick 1966
Hirst, F. W. *Armaments, the Race and the Crisis*, London 1937
Hobart, F. W. A. *Pictorial History of the Machine Gun*, London 1971
Hoffman, A. J. S. *Great Britain and German Trade Rivalry 1875–1914*, Philadelphia 1933
Hogg, O. F. G. *The Royal Arsenal*, Oxford 1963
Holborn, H. *The Political Collapse of Europe*, New York 1951
Holland, T. *The Mineral Sanction as an aid to International Security*, Edinburgh 1935
Honze, E. L. *Arming the Luftwaffe. The Reich Air Ministry and the German Aircraft Industry 1919–1939*, Lincoln (Nebraska) and London 1976
Howard, M. *The Franco-Prussian War*, London 1961
  The Continental Commitment, London 1972
  (ed) *The Theory and Practice of War*, London 1965
Hughes, J. M. *To the Maginot Line*, Cambridge, Mass 1971
Huntington, S. P. 'Arms Races, Prerequisites and Results' in *Public Policy*, Cambridge, Mass 1958
Hyde, H. M. *British Air Policy between the Wars*, London 1976

Ibbeken, R. *Das aussenpolitische Problem; Staat und Wirtschaft in der deutschen Reichspolitik 1880–1914*, Schleswig 1928
Inter-Parliamentary Union. *What would be the character of a new War?*, London 1931

Jack, D. T. *Studies in Economic Warfare*, London 1940
Jeanneney, J-N. *François de Wendel en Republique. L'Argent et le Pouvoir, 1914–1940*, Paris 1976
Jenkins, E. H. *A History of the French Navy*, London 1973
Jewkes, J., Sawers, D. and Stillerman, R. *The Sources of Invention* (2nd edition) London 1969
Joffre, J. *Memoirs*, London 1932
Joinville, Le Prince de *Essais sur la Marine Francaise*, Brussels 1852
Jones, H. A. *The War in the Air*, Volumes II-V, *Appendices*, Oxford 1928-1937 (see also Raleigh, W.)
Jones, R. V. *Most Secret War*, London 1978

Katzenbach, E. L. 'The Modernisation of War 1880–1919' in Kreuzberg, M. and Pursell, C. W. (ed) *Technology in Western Civilisation*, Oxford 1967 Vol II
Keibel, R. 'Aus hundert Jahren deutscher Eisen-und Stahlindustrie'; *Schmollers Jahrbuch*, Volume 38, No 2, Munich/Leipzig 1915

Kennedy, J. R. *Modern War and Defence Reconstruction*, London 1936
Kennedy, P. M. 'The Development of German Operational Plans against England 1896–1914' in *English Historical Review*, 1974
Kessel, E. (ed) *Alfred Schlieffen, Briefe*, Göttingen 1972
Kieft, D. O. *Belgium's Return to Neutrality*, Oxford 1972
Kindleberger, C. *Economic Response*, Cambridge, Mass 1978
King, J. C. *Generals and Politicians*, Berkeley and Los Angeles 1951
   Foch versus Clemenceau, Cambridge, Mass 1960
Kingston-McCloughry, E. J. *The Direction of War*, London 1955
Kitchen, M. *The German Officer Corps 1890–1914*, Oxford 1968
Klass, G. von, *Krupps, the Story of an Industrial Empire*, London 1954
Knorr, K. and Morgenstern, O. *Political Conjecture in Military Planning*, Princeton 1968
Komarnicki, W. *La definition de l'agresseur dans le droit international modern*, Paris 1949
Kovacs, A. 'French military legislation in the Third Republic' in *Military Affairs*, Spring 1949
Kotzsch, L. *The Concept of War in Contemporary History and International Law*, Geneva 1956
Krache, E. 'Motives behind the Maginot Line' in *Military Affairs*, Summer 1944
Kuhl, H. von *Der deutsche Generalstab in Vorbereitung und Durchführung des Weltkrieges*, (2nd Edition) Berlin 1920

Langer, W. L. *The Franco-Russian Alliance*, Cambridge, Mass 1929
Larmour, P. J. *The French Radical Party in the 1930s*, Stanford 1964
Launay, L. *La Sarre et les marchands de canons*, Vaucresson 1934
   and Sennec, J. *Les Relations internationales des Industires de Guerre*, Paris 1932
Layriz, O. *Mechanical Traction in War for Road Transport*, London 1900
League of Nations: *Reports of the Temporary Mixed Commission on Armaments:* A 81, 1921: A 31, 1922: A 35, 1923: A 16, 1924 IX.
   Conference for the Control of the International Trade in Arms, C758 M258 1924 X
Lefevre, A. *Les Chemins de fer et la Politique*, Paris 1951
Lefranc, G. 'La construction des Chemins de fer et l'opinion publique vers 1830' in *Revue d'histoire moderne*, July–August 1930
Lehmann, F. 'The Costs of National Defense' in Speier, H. and Kohler, A. (ed) *War in Our Time*, New York 1939
Levine, A. L. *Industrial Retardation in Britain 1880–1914*, London 1967
Levy-Leboyer, M. *Les Banques Européènes et l'Industrialisation dans la premiere moitié du XIX siecle*, Paris 1964
Lewinsohn, R. *Zaharoff*, Paris 1929
   The Profits of War, London 1936
Liddell-Hart, B. *Reputations*, London 1928
   The Real War, London 1930
   Europe in Arms, London 1937
   Memoirs, London 1965
Loria, A. *The Economic Causes of War*, Chicago 1918
Lotz, W. *Die Deutsche Staatsfinanzwirtschaft im Kriege*, Stuttgart 1927
Lovell, B. *Blackett* (Royal Society Biographical Memoir Series), London 1975

Lumby, E. W. R. (ed) *Policy and Operations in the Mediterranean, 1912-1914*
Lumet, G. *Les Moteurs d'Aviation*, Paris 1910

Macleod, R. M. and Andrews, E. Kay, 'Scientific advice in the war at sea 1915-1917' in *Journal of Contemporary History*, Vol 6, No 2 1971
MacIsaac, D. *Strategic Bombing in World War Two*, New York and London 1976
Mackay, R. F. *Fisher of Kilverstone*, Oxford 1973
McKay, D. C. 'The Pre-war development of Briey Iron Ores' in McKay, D. C. (ed) *Essays in the History of Modern Europe*, New York 1936
McKear, F. R. *The Ingenious Mr Bessemer*, London 1966
McKenna, S. *Reginald McKenna*, London 1948
Macmillan, N. *Sefton Brancker*, London 1935
Macksey, K. *Armoured Crusader*, London 1967
Mallory, K. and Ottar, A. *Walls of War*, London 1979
Marcé, V. de *Les Budgéts militaires allemands et français et l'égalite des droits*, Paris 1935
Matthias, W. *Die staatliche Organisation der Kriegswirtschaft*, Berlin 1937
Mendelssohn-Bartholdy, A. *The War and German Society*, New Haven and London 1937
Menne, B. *Krupp: Deutschlands Kanonenkönig*, Zurich 1937
Messenger, C. *The Art of Blitzkrieg*, London 1976
Messimy, A. *Mes Souvenirs*, Paris 1937
Middlemas, K. *Politics in Industrial Society*, London 1979
Miller, J. K. *Belgian Foreign Policy between Two Wars, 1919-1940*, New York 1951
Milman, R. *British Foreign Policy and the Coming of the Franco-Prussian War*, Oxford 1965
Milward, A. S. *War, Economy and Society*, London 1977
Mises, L. von. *Nation, Staat und Wirtschaft*, Vienna 1919
Moltke, H. von. *Erinnerungen, Briefe, Dokumente*, Berlin 1922
Morazé, C. *The Triumph of the Middle Classes*, London 1970
Morris, J. *The German Air Raids on Great Britain 1914-1918*, London n.d.
Moulton, J. L. 'Defence Planning: the Uncertainty Factor' in *Long Range Planning*, June 1971
Muller, K. H. *Die wirtschaftliche Bedeutung der Bagdadbahn*, Munich 1917
Muller-Brandenburg, H. *Von Schlieffen bis Ludendorff*, Leipzig 1924.
Mumford, P. S. *Humanity, Air Power and War*, London 1936

Nef, J. U. *War and Human Progress*, Cambridge, Mass 1950
Neumann, R. *Zaharoff, the Armaments King*, London 1935
Newbold, J. T. W. *How Europe Armed for War*, London 1916
Railways 1825-1925, London 1925
Democracy, Debts and Disarmament, London 1933
Nickerson, H. *Can We Limit War?* London 1933
The Armed Horde, London 1940
Noel-Baker, P. *The Private Manufacture of Armaments*, London 1937

Oncken, H. *Politik und Kriegführung*, Munich 1928
Die Rheinpolitik Kaiser Napoleon's III, Stuttgart 1926

Orvik, N. *The Decline of Neutrality*, Oslo 1953

Perris, G. H. *The War Traders*, London 1914
Philipp, L. *Die Beeinflussung der Standortswahl durch kriegswirtschaftliche Momente*, Basel/Chur 1951
Pickles, D. M. *The Uneasy Entente*, Oxford 1966
Pirelli, A. *Economia e Guerra*, Milan n.d.
Pogge von Strandmann, H. 'Domestic origins of Germany's Colonial Expansion under Bismarck' in *Past and Present* No 42 1969
Poirier, J. *Les Bombardements de Paris 1914–1918*, Paris 1930
Porch, R. D. *Army and Revolution, France 1815–1848*, London and Boston 1974
Possony, S. *Tomorrow's War: Its Planning, Management and Cost*, London 1938
Post, G. *Civil-military fabric of Weimar Germany*, New Jersey 1973
Pottinger, E. A. *Napoleon III and the German Crisis*, Cambridge, Mass 1966
Pratt, E. A. *The Rise of Railways in War and Conquest 1833–1914*, London 1915
  British Railways in the Great War, London 1921
Preston, A. (ed) *General Staffs and Diplomacy before the Second World War*, London 1978
Pretelat, General *Le Destin Tragique de la Ligne Maginot*, Paris 1950
Price, A. *Instruments of Darkness*, London 1977
Primrose, H. *British Aviation; the Great War and British Aviation 1915–1919*, London 1969

Questor, E. H. *Deterrence before Hiroshima*, New York 1966

Raleigh, W. *The War in the Air*, Volume 1, Oxford 1922 (see also Jones, H. A.)
Rappard, W. E. *The Common Menace of Economic and Military Armaments*, London 1936
Rasin, A. *The Financial Policy of Czechoslovakia*, Oxford 1923
Reader, W. J. *Architect of Air Power*, London 1968 (see also Wilson, C. H.)
Reid, R. W. *Tongues of Conscience, War and the Scientist's Dilemma*, London 1969
Reiners, L. *The Lamps went out in Europe*, New York 1955
Renouvin, P. 'Les Relations franco-allemandes de 1871 a 1914' in Sarkissan, A. O. (ed) *Studies in Diplomatic History and Historiography in Honour of G. P. Gooch*, London 1974
Richardson, H. W. *Economic Recovery in Britain*, London 1967
Richardson, J. H. *Economic Disarmament*, London 1931
Riesch, E. *Der Begriff 'Militärhaftflugzeug' im Luftrecht*, Berlin/Bonn 1934
Ritter, G. *The Schlieffen Plan, Critique of a Myth*, London 1958
Robertson, F. L. *The Evolution of Naval Armament*, London 1921
Romain, C. *Les responsabilités de l' artillerie française en 1870*, Paris 1913
Ropp, T. *War in the Modern World*, Durham, North Carolina 1959
Rosinski, H. *The German Army*, New York 1940
Roskill, S. *Hankey, Man of Secrets*, London 1970–1974
  Naval Policy between the Wars, London 1968
Rota, E. *Questioni di Storia Contemporanea*, Milan 1953
Rothenstein, R. L. *Alliances and Small Powers*, New York 1968
Rowe, V. *The Great Wall of France*, New York 1959

Sanders, L. von *Fünf Jahre Türkei*, Berlin 1920

Sankey, C. F. P. 'The Campaign of the Future' in *Royal Engineers Journal*, January 1907

Scherer, F. M. 'Invention and Innovation in the Watt-Boulton Steam Engine Venture' in Kreuzberg, M. and Davenport W. H. (ed) *Technology and Culture*, New York 1972

Scheussler, W. *Weltmachtstreben und Flottenbau*, Witten-Ruhr 1956

Schmolke, G. von *Zwanzig Jahre Deutsche Politik 1897–1917*, Munich/Leipzig 1920

Schnapper, B. *Le Remplacement militaire en France*, Paris 1968

Schnerb, R. *Rouher et le Second Empire*, Clermont-Ferrand 1949

Scott, J. D. *Vickers*, London 1962

Sale, M. T. 'The Construction of Military Railways during the Russo-Turkish War of 1877–78' in *Journal of the Royal United Services Institution*, Vol 24, 1880, p. 104

Shaw, G. C. *Supply in Modern War*, London 1938

Sherwood, J. M. *Georges Mandel and the Third Republic*, Stanford 1970

Shey, R. P. *British Rearmament in the 1930s*, New Jersey 1977

Silberner, E. *The Problem of War in Nineteenth Century Economic Thought*, New Jersey 1946

Silberstein, G. *The Troubled Alliance*, Lexington, Kentucky 1970

Smyth, H. D. *Atomic Energy for Military Purposes*, New Jersey 1946

Snow, C. P. *Science and Government*, Oxford 1961

Somerset, Duke of and Grey, Sir F. W. *The Naval Expenditure from 1860–1866 and its Results*, London 1867

Spaight, J. M. *The Beginnings of Organised Air Power*, London 1927

Speier, H. and Kähler, A. (ed) *War in our Time*, New York 1939

Spengler, J. J. *France faces Depopulation*, Durham, North Carolina 1938

Spillmann, G. J. *Napoleon III: prophete méconnu*, Paris 1972

Staley, E. *Raw Materials in Peace and War*, New York 1937

Stehlin, P. *Temoinage pour l' Histoire*, Paris 1964

Steinberg, J. *Yesterday's Deterrent*, London 1965

  'The Copenhagen Complex' in *Journal of Contemporary History*, Vol 1, No 3 1966

Stone, J. *Aggression and World Order*, London 1958

Stone, N. *The Eastern Front, 1914–1917*, London 1975

Sturzo, L. *The International Community and the Right to War*, London 1929

Tajani, A. *La Nostra Marina Militare*, Rome 1900

Tedder, A. *With Prejudice*, London 1966

Thomas, G. *Geschichte der deutschen Wehr-und Rüstungswirtschaft 1918–1943/5*, Boppard am Rhein 1966

Tint, H. *The Decline of French Patriotism*, London 1964

Tirpitz, A. von *Erinnerungen*, Leipzig 1920

Tolles, M. D. *A History of French Subsidies to Civil Aviation*, Northampton, Mass 1933

Towle, P. 'The European Balance of Power in 1914' in *The Army Quarterly*, April 1974, Vol 104, No 3

Travers, B. 'A sitting on a Gate', London 1978

Trebilcock, C. *The Vickers Brothers, Armaments and Enterprise 1854–1914*, London 1977

Treue, W. *Der Krimkrieg und die Entstehung der modernen Flotte*, Göttingen 1954 and Frede, G. *Wirtschaft und Politik 1933–1945*, Hanover, n.d.

Trochu, L. J. *L'Armée francaise en 1867*, Paris 1867

Tuchman, B. *August 1914*, London 1962

Turner, L. C. F. 'The Russian Mobilisation in 1914' in *Journal of Contemporary History*, Vol 3, No 1 1968

Vagts, A. *Defense and Diplomacy. The Soldier and the Conduct of Foreign Relations*, New York 1956

A History of Militarism (revised edition) New York 1959

Vecchi, A. V. *Storia Generale della Marina Militare*, Livorno 1895

Völker, K-H. *Die Entwicklung der militärischen Luftfahrt in Deutschland, 1920–1933*, Stuttgart 1962

Waddington, C. H. *OR in World War 2: Operational Research against the U-boat*, London 1973

Wallach, J. L. *Kriegstheorien. Ihre Entwicklung im 19. und 20. Jahrhundert*, Frankfurt a/M 1972

Waller, W. (ed) *War in the Twentieth Century*, New York 1940

Wallin, F. W. 'French Naval Conversion and the Second Empire's Intervention in Industry' in Cox, F. J. and others, *Studies in Modern European History in Honour of Franklin Charles Palm*, New York 1956

Ward, D. and Dempster, D. *The Narrow Margin*, London 1961

Watt, D. C. *Too Serious a Business*, London 1975

Webster, C. and Frankland, N. *The Strategic Air Offensive against Germany, 1939–1945*, London 1961

Wehberg, H. *Limitation des armements relève des projets émis pour la solution du problème*, Brussels 1914

Weinwik, H. 'Left Wing opposition to naval armaments in Britain before 1914', in *Journal of Contemporary History*, Vol 6, No 4, 1971

Werner, M. *The Military Strength of the Powers*, London 1939

Wicksell, J. G. K. 'Hinauf mit den Bankraten!', in *Archiv für Wissenschaft und Sozialpolitik*, No 41, 1915–16, p. 745–757

Williamson, S. R. *The Politics of Grand Strategy*, Cambridge, Mass 1969

Wilson, C. H. and Reader, W. J. *Men and Machines*, London 1958

Winter, J. M. (ed) *War and Economic Development*, Cambridge 1975

Woodward, E. L. *War and Peace in Europe*, London 1931

Great Britain and the German Navy, London 1935

Wright, G. *Raymond Poincaré and the French Presidency*, Stanford 1942

Wright, Q. *A Study of War*, Chicago 1942

Young, R. S. 'The Strategic Dream: French Air Doctrine 1919–1939' in *Journal of Contemporary History*, October 1974

Zeiger, K. *Kalkulation und Preisbildung bei Rüstungsaufträgen*, Hamburg 1944

Select Bibliography

Zuckerman, S. *Scientists and War*, London 1966
  From Apes to Warlords 1904–1946, London 1978
Zurlinden, I. S. *Der Weltkrieg und die Schweizer*, Zurich 1917

Official Reports

UK:

Panmure Commission; *Report on the Manufacture of Iron and Brass Ordnance in Various Continental States*, London 1856
  Report of the Committee appointed to inquire into the conditions under which contracts are invited for the building or repairing of ships, including their engines, for Her Majesty's Navy, and into the mode in which the repair and refits of ships are effected in Her Majesty's Dockyards, (C 4219) London, 1884

USA:

US Congress, House of Representatives, 38th Congress; *Dockyards and Ironworks of Great Britain and France*, report by Chief Engineer King, Washington, DC December 1864
  US Commerce Department, *Industrial Education in Germany*, Special Consular Reports Series, Volume 33 1905

Germany:

Reichsarchiv; *Kriegsrüstung und Kriegswirtschaft*; Berlin, 1930

272

Index

Index